OCR ②
A2 Psychology
Key Studies Companion

Moira Donald with Louise Ellerby-Jones

HODDER EDUCATION
AN HACHETTE UK COMPANY

Picture credits

The author and publishers would like to thank the following for permission to reproduce material in this book:

Figure 9.1 © Rastislav Turek – Fotolia; Figure 10.1 © 2005 Lori Carpenter – Fotolia; Figure 11.1 © NAN – Fotolia

Every effort has been made to obtain necessary permission with reference to copyright material. The publishers apologise if inadvertently any sources remain unacknowledged and will be glad to make the necessary arrangements at the earliest opportunity.

Orders: please contact Bookpoint Ltd, 130 Milton Park, Abingdon, Oxon OX14 4SB. Telephone: (44) 01235 827720. Fax: (44) 01235 400454. Lines are open from 9.00 – 5.00, Monday to Saturday, with a 24 hour message answering service. You can also order through our website www.hoddereducation.co.uk

If you have any comments to make about this, or any of our other titles, please send them to educationenquiries@hodder.co.uk

British Library Cataloguing in Publication Data
A catalogue record for this title is available from the British Library

ISBN: 978 1 444 12344 9

First published 2011
Impression number   10 9 8 7 6 5 4 3 2 1
Year   2015, 2014, 2013, 2012, 2011

Copyright © 2011 Moira Donald and Louise Ellerby-Jones

Hachette UK's policy is to use papers that are natural, renewable and recyclable products and made from wood grown in sustainable forests. The logging and manufacturing processes are expected to conform to the environmental regulations of the country of origin.

Cover photo © Image Source / Getty Images
Illustrations by Barking Dog Art
Typeset by Servis Filmsetting Ltd, Stockport, Cheshire
Printed in Spain for Hodder Education, An Hachette UK Company, 338 Euston Road, London NW1 3BH

Contents

Introduction

This book has been written for students following the OCR A2 Psychology course. It is designed to support the *Psychology A2 for OCR: Applied Options* textbook, by giving extra depth on the Key Studies discussed in that book. It will help to ensure that you are fully prepared for the Options in Applied Psychology paper and on course to reach for those top marks.

The OCR A2 exams

The OCR A2 level assessment is formed of two exams:

Options in Applied Psychology

This will be a 2-hour written paper accounting for 100 marks (50 per cent of the total A2 marks). It is formed of four options: forensic psychology, health and clinical psychology, psychology of sport and exercise and psychology of education. You will be required to answer two questions from two of these options.

Approaches and Research Methods in Psychology

This will be a 1½-hour written paper accounting for 80 marks (50 per cent of the total A2 marks). It is formed of two sections, in section A you will be required to answer all the questions. In section B you will answer one question from a choice of two.

There are three assessment objectives:

AO1, Knowledge and understanding: candidates should be able to:
- recognise, recall and show understanding of scientific knowledge
- select, organise and communicate relevant information in a variety of forms, including extended prose.

AO2, Application of knowledge and understanding: candidates should be able to:
- analyse and evaluate scientific knowledge when presenting arguments and ideas
- apply scientific knowledge to unfamiliar situations including those related to issues
- assess the validity, reliability and credibility of scientific information
- bring together scientific knowledge from different areas of the subject and apply them.

AO3, Science in practice: candidates should be able to:
- demonstrate ethical, safe and skilful practical techniques selecting appropriate qualitative and quantitative methods
- know how to make, record and communicate reliable and valid observations and measurements with appropriate precision and accuracy, through using primary and secondary sources
- analyse, interpret, explain and evaluate the methodology, results and impact of their own and others' experimental and investigative activities in a variety of ways.

Walkthrough

Each Key Study in this book is presented in a uniform way, designed to make it as easy as possible for you to digest the information.

If you are also using the *Psychology A2 for OCR: Applied Options* textbook you might notice that not every section of the textbook has a corresponding Key Study in this book. This may be because the section refers to something other than a study, for example, a theory or a newspaper article. For a list of sections which do not have Key Studies in this book please see page x.

As well as key term definitions and synoptic links throughout, there are a number of consistent features that appear throughout the book to help you make the most of your learning:

Stretch and challenge

When you are confident with the material, this feature will help you enhance and extend your knowledge.

Evaluation

Evaluation is central to part (b) G543 examination questions. Each Key Study contains an Evaluation box with potential evaluation material that has been pinpointed as relevant to the Key Study. However, there are always more evaluative points that can be made and you should not feel limited to those made here.

Food for thought

Questions and points for discussion that will help you engage more deeply and think about the material.

Research methods

Outlining some of the key research methods you will need to know about for the exam.

Acknowledgements

I would like to thank Paul Fannon for his guidance on definitions of statistical terms, Libby Ahluwalia for her encouragement, Judith Silver for her invaluable guidance, students and colleagues at Stephen Perse and my family – Andrew, Imogen, Alec and Elsie Siantonas for their patience.

Study summaries not included in this study guide

Some of the areas covered in the textbook *Psychology A2 for OCR* do not have Key Studies linked to them. Below is a list of the areas that do not have a relating Key Study:

2.3.3 False confessions is an account of the cases of John Duffy and Rachel Nickel based on newspaper reports.

3.3.1 Stages and influences on decision making, Hastie *et al.* (1983), is a review article rather than an empirical study.

5.3.2 Measures of non-adherence. See the summary of Key Study 5.1.1 Health Belief Model: Becker *et al.* (1978), 'Compliance with a medical regimen for asthma: a test of the Health Belief Model', *Public Health Reports,* 93 (3), which used a combination of self-report and physiological measures to investigate compliance to a medical regimen for asthma.

6.2.1 Physiological measures of stress. See Key Study 6.1.3 Lack of control: James H. Geer and Eileen Maisel (1972), 'Evaluating the effects of the prediction–control confound', *Journal of Personality and Social Psychology* 23 (3), 314–319.

6.2.2 Self-report as a measure of stress. See Key Study 6.1.2 Hassles: Kerry Chamberlain and Sheryl Zika (1990), 'The minor events approach to stress: support for the use of daily hassles', *British Journal of Psychology* 81 (4), 469–481.

6.2.3 Combined approach to measuring stress. See Key Study 6.1.1 Work: Gunn Johansson and Gunnar Aronsson (1984), 'Stress reactions in computerized administrative work', *Journal of Occupational Behaviour* 21 (5), 159–181.

7.1.2 Definition of dysfunctional behaviour is based on a textbook (Rosenhan and Seligman, New York, 1984) rather than an empirical study, therefore no study summary is included in this study guide.

8.1.1 Psychotic disorders. This section refers to the characteristics of an anxiety disorder rather than an empirical study.

8.1.2 Anxiety disorders. This section refers to the characteristics of a psychotic disorder rather than an empirical study.

8.1.3 Affective disorders. This section refers to the characteristics of an affective disorder rather than an empirical study.

8.3.2 and 8.3.3 Treatments for an affective disorder – depression. See Key Studies 7.3.1, 7.3.2 and 7.3.3.

9.1.1, 9.1.2 and 9.1.3 Sport and the individual: Key Studies 9.1.1 Personality measures, 9.1.2 Theories of personality, 9.1.3 Relevance to sport: see *Psychology A2 for OCR* textbook for discussion of these.

9.2.1 Instinct theories is a theory rather than a Key Study.

10.1.1 and 10.1.3 Arousal: Key study 10.1.1 Theories of arousal (Raglin, 1992) is a review article, 10.1.3 Factors affecting arousal (Oxendine, 1980) is a discussion paper rather than an empirical study.

11.1.1 Theories of group cohesion is a theory rather than a Key Study.

11.2.1, 11.2.2 and 11.2.3 Audience effects: Key Studies 11.2.1 Theories, 11.2.2 Studies, 11.2.3 Home advantage: the studies featured in the textbook are theories and review articles rather than empirical studies.

11.3.1 Trait and type theories are theories rather than empirical studies.

11.3.3 Coaching (Turman, 2003) Most of the extra material not already summarised in the textbook consists of detailed excerpts from the qualitative interviews.

12.2.2 Benefits of exercise and mental health is a review article, not an empirical study.

12.3.2 Body image in sport is a review article rather than an empirical study.

12.3.3 Drug abuse in sport is a review article rather than an empirical study.

13.1.1, 13.1.2 and 13.1.3 Theories of knowledge acquisition: Key Studies 13.1.1 Stage theories, 13.1.2 Social construction theories, 13.1.3 Behaviourist models, focus on theory rather than empirical research.

13.2.1, 13.2.2 and 13.2.3 Personal approaches to learning: Key Studies 13.2.1 Variations on learning strategies, 13.2.2 Differences in cognitive styles, 13.2.3 Theories of multiple intelligences, focus on theory rather than empirical research.

14.1.1, 14.1.2 and 14.1.3 Theories of motivation: Key Studies 14.1.1 Intrinsic/extrinsic motivation, 14.1.2 The humanist theory of motivation, 14.1.3 Cognitive attribution theory, are theories rather than emprical studies.

14.2.1 and 14.2.3 Encouraging educational engagement: Key Studies 14.2.1 The importance of play and 14.2.3 The implications of ability grouping, are theories rather than emprical studies.

14.3.1 and 14.3.3 Student beliefs and expectations: Key Studies 14.3.1 Social roles and academic success, 14.3.3 Developing positive self-esteem, can be linked to the humanist theories (the main points of Key Study 14.3.3 are summarised in the textbook).

15.1.1 Developmental stages such as industry/inferiority: this is a theory rather than an empirical study.

15.2.1 Importance related to empathy and moral development.

15.2.3 Anti-bullying strategies: this is the report of a large-scale intervention rather than an empirical study.

15.3.3 Types and demands of questions used by teachers for primary and secondary school pupils: this is a report on teaching methods in science nationally and not an empirical study.

16.1.1 and 16.1.2 Dealing with additional needs: Key Studies 16.1.1 Individual support, 16.1.2 Provision for gifted and talented students, are both reviews/recommendations rather than empirical studies.

16.2.1, 16.2.2 and 16.2.3 Enabling minority ethnic groups. Key Studies 16.2.1 Engagement and achievement of ethnic groups, 16.2.2 Culture and grouping, 16.2.3 Role models and positive support.

16.3.1 and 16.3.3 Enabling genders: Key Studies 16.3.2 Differences in brain structure, 16.3.3 Strategies for enabling the learning of boys and girls.

H. Juby and D. P. Farrington (2001), 'Disentangling the link between disrupted families and delinquency', *British Journal of Criminology*, 41 (1), 22–40

Approach: Social/developmental

Aim: To compare delinquency rates among boys living in permanently disrupted families at age 15 with delinquency rates among those living in intact families

Hypothesis: That delinquency is more common among boys from permanently disrupted families (broken homes) compared to boys from intact families

Method: Prospective longitudinal survey

> **Research methods**
>
> **Longitudinal versus snapshot**
>
> The Cambridge Study is a prospective, longitudinal survey of boys born in South London in the 1950s. It is called the Cambridge study despite the fact that the participants lived in London because the research team is based at the University of Cambridge. It is **longitudinal** in design because data was collected over a long period – since the 1960s. It is **prospective** because the data was originally collected when the boys were aged 8–9 before it was known how the lives of the boys would turn out. Since then data has been collected at regular periods enabling researchers to monitor how the lives of the participants were shaped by their early experiences.
>
> > The key study discussed in 1.1.3 – the Peterborough Youth Study is by contrast a **snapshot** or **cross-sectional** study. It examined the offending behaviour of all the Year 10 students in state schools in Peterborough at one particular time.

Type of sample: Representative population

Participants: 411 boys from 6 state schools in South London aged 8-9 at the start of the study in 1961.

Procedure: Data were collected on the parents of the boys and the boys themselves. The data included juvenile convictions, juvenile self-reported delinquency and adult convictions. The participants were interviewed and tested at age 8, 10, 14 at school, at age 16, 18 and 21 in a research office, and at age 25, 32 and 46 in their homes. The tests in schools measured individual characteristics such as intelligence and personality. Interviews with the participants' parents were carried out annually from age 8 to age 14–15 by a psychiatric social worker. Parents (mainly mothers) reported on family income, parenting practices and family situation (for example, parental separation). Teachers also completed questionnaires when the boys were age 8, 10, 12 and 14 providing data on topics such as truancy, aggressive behaviour and school behaviour. Searches were carried out in the Criminal Record Office for data on criminal offences excluding minor offences such as traffic infractions.

Results: Juby and Farrington found that:

- Delinquency rates were higher among 75 boys who were living in permanently disrupted families on their fifteenth birthday compared to those boys living in intact families. Twenty-nine per cent of those from disrupted families were convicted as juveniles as opposed to 18 per cent of boys from intact families (odds ratio = 1.9).

> **Research methods**
>
> **Odds ratio**
>
> What is an odds ratio?
>
> Odds are the number of times an event occurs/ number of times it does not occur. It is a measure similar to probability.
>
> To find the odds ratio you divide the odds of one group by the odds of the other group
>
> An odds ratio greater than 2 is considered significant.

- Delinquency rates were similar in disrupted families to those in intact high-conflict families (OR 1.0 to 1.4).
- Boys who lost their mothers were more likely to be delinquent than boys who lost their fathers. Odds ratio for juvenile convictions for those who lost mothers was 3.7.
- Disruptions caused by parental disharmony (broken homes) were more damaging than disruptions caused by parental death.

- Boys from disrupted families who continued living with their mothers had similar delinquency rates to boys from intact harmonious families.

Discussion: Juby and Farrington concluded from their evidence that the multiple stressors involved in separation explain the link between disrupted families and delinquency. They concluded that disrupted families in general are associated with relatively high delinquency rates but they argued that analysis of the relationship should not be simplistic. Some kinds of disrupted families are criminogenic (likely to lead to crime) but so are some kinds of intact families (those with high parental conflict). Equally some kinds of disrupted families – in particular where the mother is a stable figure – are no more criminogenic than intact harmonious families.

Evaluation

Prospective studies

Prospective longitudinal studies allow hypotheses to be tested even though they do not use the experimental method. This is because the researchers make predictions then test those predictions by studying long term outcomes.

Research methods

Sampling methods

The OCR specification focuses on four types of sampling method: random sampling, stratified sampling, self-selecting and opportunity. However, researchers sometimes use mixed approaches or approaches that do not fall clearly into one of those categories. The term 'representative population' has been used here to refer to a method which should more properly be called 'purposive sampling'. This is when researchers seek out participants who share the characteristics of their target population, excluding others that do not. They hope to capture in this way a representative sample of that population but it cannot claim to be representative in the true statistical sense. For example, if all the young offenders in one institution participate in a study the sample cannot claim to be representative of all young offenders in that country. However, it is a practical approach that will provide meaningful insights into the attitudes of the target group.

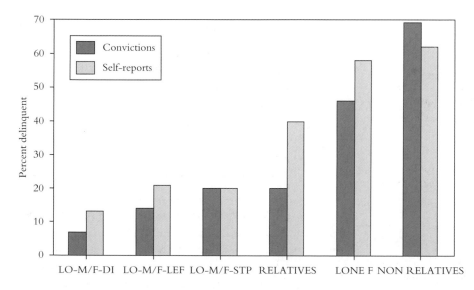

Key
LO-M/F-DI: Lone mother after father's death
LO-M/F-LEF; Lone mother after father left
LO-M/F-STP: Lone mother with stepfather
RELATIVES: Living with relatives
LONE F: Lone father
NON RELATIVES: Living with non-relatives, e.g. foster family

Figure 1.1 Graph to show percentage of delinquents in differently composed households
Source: H. Juby and D.P. Farrington (2001), 'Disentangling the link between disrupted families and delinquency', *British Journal of Criminology*, 41(1):22–40. Reproduced with permission of Oxford University Press.

1.1 Turning to crime: Upbringing
Key Study: 1.1.2 Learning from others
Ronald A. Akers, Marvin D. Krohn, Lonn Lanza-Kaduce and Marcia Radosevich (1979), 'Social Learning and deviant behaviour: a specific test of a general theory', *American Sociological Review*, 44, 636–55

Approach: Behaviourist

Aim: To test social learning theory of deviant behaviour with survey data on adolescent drinking and drug behaviour

Method: Self-report

Design: Cross-sectional (snapshot) survey

Type of sample: Sample of representative population

Participants: Approximately 2500 male and female adolescents attending grades 7–12 (age 13–18) in three midwestern states in the USA.

Procedure: Parental permission was obtained for the administration of a questionnaire about abstinence from/use of alcohol and marijuana to the participants. A subsample of respondents was selected for a follow-up interview to check reliability of responses. Dependent variables were abstinence-use of alcohol measured by a 6-point frequency-of-use scale: 1 = never; 6 = nearly every day. Abuse was measured by asking the respondents to check whether or not they had experienced problems on more than one occasion such as 'having an accident', 'not being able to remember later' what they had done. Influenced by Bandura's (1971) Social Learning Theory (SLT) and Sutherland's Differential Association theory, the experimenters selected five concepts as predictor variables: imitation; differential associations; definitions; differential social reinforcement and differential non-social reinforcement.

- *Imitation index:* Total of admired models (parents; friends; other adults) whom the respondent reported having observed using the substance (alcohol/drug).
- *Definitions:* Three aspects of definitions were examined – neutralising definitions, for example, denial/excuse; law-abiding/violating definitions; respondents' own approval/disapproval of use.
- *Differential association:* Three aspects of differential associations were examined:
  1) Respondents' perception of approving/disapproving attitudes towards them by
     a) adults whose opinion they valued
     b) other teenagers whose opinion they valued.
  2) Differential peer association – a scale of three items measuring how many of respondents' friends use the substance.
- *Differential reinforcement – social:* This assessed encouragement, praise, reward and punishment from parents/friends over use/abstinence.
- *Differential reinforcement – social/non-social:* This analysed positive and negative outcomes of use/abstinence including social reinforcers and non-social reinforcers such as a good high or a bad high or feeling good or bad afterwards.

The data collected were analysed using multiple regression techniques.

Research methods
Multiple regression

The purpose of multiple regression is to learn more about the relationship between several predictor variables and a dependent (criterion) variable. Multiple regression procedures are widely used in research to try to answer the general question 'what is the best predictor of . . .?' The general computational problem that needs to be solved in multiple regression analysis is to fit a straight line to a number of points. In the simplest case – one dependent and one independent variable – one can visualise this as a scatterplot with a line of regression. In the multivariate case, when there is more than one independent variable, the regression line cannot be visualised in two dimensional space, but can be still be computed. In analysing factors in school achievement, for example, one could have a number of predictor variables, for example IQ, motivation and self esteem. It is possible to construct a linear equation containing all those variables.

Results: The results of the regression analyses show strong support for the social learning theory of adolescent alcohol and drug behaviour. When all the independent variables are incorporated into the equation, the model explains 55 per cent of the variance in drinking behaviour and 68 per cent of the variance in marijuana behaviour.

Research methods

Explaining proportion of variance

Variance is a measure of the amount of variation within the values of a variable. If a model explains 55 per cent of the variance then (in rough terms) if you know the independent data for someone then you can predict the outcome and you will be right 55 per cent of the time.

Food for thought

Can you think of factors that might explain why young people use/don't use drink/drugs other than those investigated in this study?

SLT appears to explain more fully drug-taking than drinking among young people (68 per cent of the variance compared to 55 per cent of the variance explained).

Can you think of any reasons why this might be the case?

The factors selected for analysis together have strong explanatory power regarding young people's drinking- and drug-taking habits, although they do not completely explain differences between individuals. The least predictive variable was *imitation*, although it was still significantly related to the dependent variable in the expected direction. The most effective predictive variable set was found to be *differential association* and within that the specific factor of differential peer association was the single most important variable.

Discussion: It is perhaps surprising that imitation comes so low in the list of explanatory factors, as the concept of imitative learning was originally at the heart of SLT. However SLT is in fact broader than just the concept of imitative learning and the researchers concluded that their findings supported SLT. Moreover the results support Sutherland's 1941 theory that both differential association and definitions of acceptable/unacceptable behaviour are key to an understanding of why young people develop deviant behaviours. The fact the peer group influence is so high is not surprising, as previous research has shown this. Friends are important in part because we observe and imitate their behaviour, but more importantly because they provide social reinforcement for our behaviour and provide norms by which we define particular behaviours as acceptable/unacceptable.

Evaluation

Self-report

Research based on self-report is sometimes seen as **unreliable** because there is no objective data collected. We cannot know whether respondents are telling the truth or whether their answers are affected by **social desireability** factors. In this study however, the sample size is very large (2500) and generally the larger the sample size the more **reliable** the conclusions drawn from the data.

1.1 Turning to crime: Upbringing

Key Study: 1.1.3 Poverty and disadvantaged neighbourhoods

Per-Olof H Wikström (2003), 'Individual Risk, Life-Style Risk, and Adolescent Offending. Findings from the Peterborough Youth Study', *Report of the Work of the Institute of Criminology*, pp. 1–5

Approach: Social
Aim: To analyse the relationship between individual factors, life-style risk and adolescent offending
Method: Self-report
Design: Cross-sectional (snapshot) survey

Research methods

Cross-sectional (snapshot) study

A cross-sectional study is like a snapshot of what is occurring at what point in time, usually across a large population. This is a completely different methodology from the longitudinal approach of the Cambridge Study in which researchers followed family crime patterns through generations. A major benefit of a cross-sectional study is that it gives an instant picture of a problem rather than having to wait years for the research to bear fruit.

Type of sample: Representative sample population
Participants: Approximately 2000 male and female pupils in Year 10 (aged 14–15) in 13 state schools in Peterborough, Cambridgeshire.
Procedure: Questionnaires were distributed to nearly 2000 boys and girls with a return rate of 93 per cent. The questionnaire responses were analysed and a random subset of approximately 20 per cent of respondents were selected for participation in a more in-depth interview study and were asked to participate in a space- and time-budget analysis.

Research methods

Random sampling

A sample can be described as random when all participants in a population have had an equal chance of being picked. Although this process can be undertaken by putting the names of all possible participants in a hat and then drawing out a number without looking at the names, there are also more sophisticated methods that can be used. Wikström used a computer programme to ensure random generation of a predetermined percentage of all those who had completed the questionnaire.

continued...

In this case the randomly selected subset should be representative of the larger sample.

However, the original sample of 2000 was not randomly selected from the whole population.

Research methods

Space- and time-budget analysis

This is a method that can be used to investigate how and where people spend their time over a period. It is like keeping a diary but one that is structured by time categories. For example participants may be given a diary that looks like a school timetable, divided into categories such as: before school; during morning school; during lunch break; before bedtime. Each person fills in where they were and what they were doing during these time periods. The data can then be analysed alongside questionnaire data. The results should highlight issues such as whether there is a link between pupils who spend every evening out of the home and the number of minor offences they admit to committing.

All data will have been recorded anonymously but it is possible to use a system of computer linkage to combine data from different sources.

Results: The findings suggested that there are three main types of adolescent offenders:

- *Situationally limited offenders*: These are well-adjusted youths who may occasionally offend if they live a risky lifestyle but are unlikely to turn to a life of crime
- *Lifestyle-dependent offenders:* These are youths who are neither individually well adjusted nor individually poorly adjusted. Whether they become involved in offending depends largely on whether their lifestyle frequently brings them into situations of risk. For this group peer influence may be a major reason for offending.

Propensity-induced offenders: This group is small and consists of youths who are poorly adjusted and likely to have a high level of overall offending, regardless of lifestyle risk (in practice very few of them have a low-risk lifestyle).

Major findings

● **Offending of a less serious nature is a widespread experience in adolescence**

Committing common crimes like acts of aggression or shoplifting is a common experience in adolescence: 38 per cent reported having committed such offences. Serious offending was rarer however with 7 per cent having committed serious theft.

● **High frequency adolescent offenders are versatile in their offending and normally this includes committing more serious crimes**

The most serious crimes were committed by high-frequency offenders. Longitudinal research has also shown that persistent offenders often proceed from minor acts of crime to more serious crimes.

● **The strongest predictors of offending are youths' social situations, dispositions, individual routines and lifestyle**

● **The effect of gender on adolescent offending behaviour is modest**

Adolescent males offend more overall than adolescent females but most of the modest gender variance can be accounted for by the fact that females have strong protective factors (for example a stronger sense of shame) and fewer females have high-risk lifestyles.

● **Family structural characteristics have a modest impact on adolescent offending**

Social class and ethnic background do not have a strong direct influence on adolescent offending but they have an important effect on youths' individual risk-protective scores. Disadvantaged circumstances convey high risk factors but adolescent crime is not particularly a lower-class phenomenon.

● **There is no evidence for a social class or neighbourhood disadvantaged-based adolescent subculture of anti-social values**

The overwhelming majority of youths have strong pro-social values (for example they do not believe that it is right to commit crime) and are not likely to offend. Those who frequently offend are more like to mix with peers who also offend.

● **Youths' individual routines and related lifestyle risks are strong predictors of offending**

Youths with a high degree of peer-centred time use and a low degree of family-centred time use tended to be more involved in offending than others. The more activities were peer-centred, the more time was spent with delinquent peers, in public high-risk environments, and involving use of alcohol/drugs.

The study concluded that implications for crime prevention differed for the three groups of offenders. Situationally-oriented prevention approaches might work well for lifestyle-dependent offenders but would be unlikely to work for propensity-induced offenders. For the latter group, fundamental questions such as family history or substance abuse might need to be addressed. As far as lifestyle-dependent offenders were concerned, the researchers suggested that families and schools might help prevent such young people from turning to crime by, for example, ensuring better supervision of free time at home and school.

Evaluation

Cross-sectional studies

Although data can be collected more quickly when using a cross-sectional approach than a longitudinal one, a disadvantage is that the researcher only gains insight in to the respondents at one point in time. The students in this study were all in year 10.

Do you think we can **generalise** the results to other age groups? A longitudinal study wold enable the researcher to discover whether the findings are **reliable** (consistent) over time.

1.2 Turning to crime: Cognition
Key Study: 1.2.1 Criminal thinking patterns

Emma J. Palmer and Clive R. Hollin (2004), 'The use of the Psychological Inventory of Criminal Thinking Styles with English young offenders', *Legal and Criminological Psychology*, 9, 253–63

Approach: Cognitive

Aim: To test the effectiveness of the Psychological Inventory of Criminal Thinking Styles (PICTS) with a sample of imprisoned young offenders

Method: Self-report

Design: Cross-sectional (snapshot) survey

Type of sample: Representative sample population

Participants: 515 male young offenders (18–22 years) serving custodial sentences in six young offender institutions in England.

Procedure: A research team of psychologists trained in administration of the Psychological Inventory of Criminal Thinking Styles (PICTS) collected data by means of individual interviews from the young offenders who had a variety of convictions from driving offences to burglary and violent offences.

Measure: The PICTS was developed by Walters (1995) to measure the thinking styles proposed to be associated with a criminal lifestyle. Previous research had shown the scale to have good levels of reliability and validity with adult offenders. The scale comprised the following eight thinking styles measured using a four-point Likert scale:

- *Mollification:* High scores reflect a tendency to externalise blame and make excuses for actions
- *Cutoff:* High scores indicate low frustration tolerance
- *Entitlement:* High scores indicate an attitude towards believing one is entitled to things and an inability to distinguish between wants and needs
- *Power orientation:* High scores denote a need for control and authority over others
- *Sentimentality:* High scores indicate an unrealistic belief in self as a 'good person' despite criminal actions
- *Superoptimism:* High scores indicate an unrealistic belief that one can avoid the negative consequences of criminal behaviour
- *Cognitive indolence:* High scores reflect poor critical reasoning and tendency to seek easy answers (cognitive short cuts)
- *Discontinuity:* High scores denote inconsistency in thinking and behaviour

Results: The aim of the study was to test the reliability of the PICTS measure rather than to test the participants' thinking style. No significant correlations between number of previous convictions and scores on the PICTS were found. These results were in contrast to previous research on adults that showed that indices of previous offending behaviour were highly related to scores on the PICTS scales. Factor analysis was performed and two factors were extracted that together accounted for approximately 63 per cent of the variance. The first factor (50 per cent of the variance) contained five scales: cutoff, power orientation, superoptimism, cognitive indolence and discontinuity; and the second factor (13 per cent) was composed of scores on mollification, entitlement and sentimentality, reflecting offenders' justifications for offending. Research on adult offenders had in contrast found that the eight PICTS scales loaded on to one factor. A series of t-tests showed significant differences between adults and young offenders on four of the PICTS scales: cutoff, superoptimism, cognitive indolence and discontinuity. On all these scales young offenders scored significantly higher than adult offenders.

Research methods
Factor analysis

Factor analysis is a statistical method used to analyse large quantities of data. It is used to describe variability among observed variables in terms of a potentially lower number of unobserved variables called **factors**. In other words, it is possible, for example, that two or three observed variables together represent another, underlying variable, and factor analysis searches for these possible combinations. The information gained about the interdependencies between observed variables can be used later to reduce the set of variables in a dataset.

Discussion: The results of the study offer mixed findings with respect to the usefulness and reliability of the PICTS measure among young offenders in England. The scale was found to be less reliable than it had been when used on adult offenders. The fact that correlations were low between indices of criminal history and PICTS scores may reflect the fact that there was less variation between young people's criminal histories. Results suggest that young and adult offenders may have different attitudes towards their criminal activity. The researchers suggest that as the young offenders studies were serving a prison sentence it is likely that the majority were persistent offenders so their attitudes might be more fixed than in older offenders who would have been at a variety of stages in their criminal career.

Evaluation
Reliability and usefulness

The fact that the researchers decided that the PICTS scale was not as **reliable** a measure for testing criminal thinking patterns in young offenders as in adults does not mean that this key study itself is unreliable. The methods used to obtain and analyse data were rigorous, the sample large and the PICTS measure has been shown to reliably indicate criminal thinking patterns in other studies. It is likely therefore that this study has in fact found a reliable difference in thinking patterns between young offenders serving custodial sentences and adult offenders in prison. As the researchers have proposed, this may in part be explained by the fact that there was less variation between the young offenders in terms of their crime history, or it may reflect the fact that to have been given custodial sentences at such a young age the youths must already be persistent offenders. The most **useful** finding from this study is the evidence it provides that persistent young offenders are even more likely to score high on some measures of criminal thinking than adult offenders. This may help explain the high reoffending rate in young people who have been in prison and shows that rehabilitation work is particularly needed by this group. Another useful finding is that whereas one factor emerged when adult data was analysed (indicating that adult offenders share all eight of the thinking styles), two factors emerged from the responses of participants in this study. This suggests that there are two identifiable factors that may underlie different types of young offender. Most of the variance was explained by one factor related to feelings of being in control (cutoff, power orientation, superoptimism, cognitive indolence and discontinuity) but some of the variance was explained by a factor related to inability/unwillingness to take responsibility for one's actions (mollification, entitlement and sentimentality).

1.2 Turning to crime: Cognition

Key Study: 1.2.2 Moral development and crime

Chien-An Chen and Dennis Howitt (2007), 'Different crime types and moral reasoning development in young offenders compared with non-offender controls on', *Psychology, Crime and Law*, 13 (4), 405–16

Approach: Cognitive/developmental

Aim: To examine moral reasoning development among young offenders

Method: Self-report

Design: Cross-sectional (snapshot) survey

Type of sample: Representative sample population of young male offenders; representative sample population of normal controls

Participants: 330 male adolescent offenders (age range 12–18) in Juvenile Correctional Institutions in Taiwan and 114 non-offenders from one Junior High School and two Senior High School classes.

Procedure: All offender participants completed a questionnaire about their criminal history and as a result of information they provided, they were classified according to offence type: violent; theft; drug related. Both offender and non-offender participants responded to a short form of the Sociomoral Reflection Measure (SRM-SF).

Measure: Although the SRM-SF is based on Kohlberg's theory of moral development, it does not use dilemma-based moral situations as Kohlberg did. The SRM-SF consists of five moral values:

- *Contract and truth:* The importance of keeping promises to friends; promises to people who are hardly known and the importance of telling the truth
- *Affiliation:* Whether attachments to people make a difference in moral decision making
- *Life:* The importance of saving the life of a stranger and the importance of saving someone's life even if that person does not want to live
- *Property and law:* Moral judgements about ownership
- *Legal justice:* Distinguishing between legal and moral justice

Results: While age correlated with moral reasoning development in the control group, there was no correlation between age and moral reasoning score in the combined offender groups or any of the individual offence type groups. Moral reasoning development of the control group was significantly higher in the control group than any of the offender groups. There were also differences in moral reasoning development between the different offender groups with the drug group having higher moral reasoning than the other groups, although these differences were not significant.

Moral reasoning cognitive–developmental delay models were only of limited usefulness in differentiating offender types but were good at differentiating offenders from non-offenders. Multiple regression techniques were used in order to assess which of the moral development variables differentiated the three offender groups. Only one of the five moral values (life) distinguished between offender groups. The offender and control groups differed in terms of relative developmental level for the five moral values. Both offender groups and controls tended to show lowest development of moral reasoning with regard to 'property and law' and 'legal justice'. 'Life' was the least developed moral value for the control group and second least for the violent offenders, while it was the most developed moral value for the theft group and the second most developed value for the drug group. The moral values of 'contract and truth' and 'affiliation' tended to be among the most highly developed moral values of all four groups.

> For explanation of multiple regression, see Key Study 1.1.2

Discussion: The findings of this study confirmed previous findings that moral cognitive-developmental stage is less advanced in offender groups than non-offender controls; and that less mature moral development is a risk factor for juvenile offending. The lower correlations between age and moral reasoning development for the offender groups suggest that normal age-related developmental processes are different in offender groups. Drug offenders had the highest overall moral reasoning development of the three offender groups but this was not significant when age was controlled. It was found that those with developmentally more advanced reasoning were less likely to be involved in criminal violence. There was some evidence to suggest that the moral value of 'contract' was relatively highly developed in all groups including the offender groups. The researchers suggest that this particular moral value encourages commitment to other people, making the individual more vulnerable to social pressures, and that 'differential association' theory may help explain this finding.

> For 'differential association' theory, see Key Study 1.1.2

Evaluation

Usefulness

This study is **useful** because it tests a psychological measure developed in the United States in a different cultural context – young offenders and controls in Taiwan. This enables researchers to generalise findings from studies using the SRM-SF. Moral reasoning cognitive-developmental delay models were found to be only of limited usefulness in differentiating offender types but were good at differentiating offenders from non-offenders.

This is an example of research that is **not ethnocentric** because it allows cross-cultural comparisons to be made.

1.2 Turning to crime: Cognition
Key Study: 1.2.3 Social cognition

Gisli H. Gudjonsson and Jon Fridrik Sigurdsson (2007), 'Motivation for offending and personality. A study among young offenders on probation', *Personality and Individual Differences*, 42, 1243–53

Approach: Cognitive/individual differences

Aim: To examine the relationship between motivation for offending and personality, anger problems and attitudes towards offending

Method: Self-report

Design: Cross-sectional (snapshot) survey

Type of sample: Representative sample population

Participants: 128 male youths, age range 15–21, from Reykjavík, Iceland, who had been given a conditional discharge after a guilty plea. Most of the offences were property offences followed by car crimes, assault and criminal damage.

Procedure: Participants had pleaded guilty to an offence and were required to attend regular supervision sessions with a probation officer during their period of discharge. Each participant was asked during a visit to their probation officer whether they would be willing participate in a study into offending and personality. Several psychological scales were administered: the Offending Motivation Questionnaire (OMQ); the Gudjonsson Compliance Scale; the Eysenck Personality Questionnaire (EPQ) and Eysenck Impulsivity Scale (EIS); the Novaco Anger Scale and the Blame Attribution Inventory.

Measures:

- *The Offending Motivation Questionnaire (OMQ) (Gudjonsson and Sigurdsson, 2004):* A 22-item questionnaire that measures the motivation behind offending which comprises four main factors:
  1. Compliance: Items relating to the offence being committed in order to please a peer or because the person felt pressured into it (example, 'Gave in to pressure from peer(s)').
  2. Excitement: Items indicating that the main motive for the offence was fun or excitement (example, 'Did it for excitement').
  3. Provocation: Items involving taking revenge, losing control, and self-defence (example, 'To take revenge on somebody').
  4. Financial: Items reflecting a financial or a monetary need as the explanation for the offence (example, 'In hope of financial gain').

- *The Gudjonsson Compliance Scale (Gudjonsson, 1997):* a scale comprising two factors: eagerness to please; conflict avoidance. This is a 20-item scale rated with true or false that measures the tendency of the person to go along uncritically with requests made by others in order to avoid conflict. The higher the score, the more compliant the individual is.

- *The Eysenck Personality Questionnaire (Eysenck and Eysenck, 1975):* A much tested personality questionnaire that measures three main 'super-factor' personality dimensions (psychoticism, extraversion, neuroticism).

> See *Psychology A2 for OCR* textbook Section 1.1, p.4 for more on the Eysenck Personality Questionnaire

- *The Eysenck Impulsivity, Venturesomeness and Empathy Scale (Eysenck and Eysenck, 1991):* This is a 54-item questionnaire which was included because it has been argued that primary personality traits (for example impulsivity, need for stimulation or sensation seeking) may be better predictors of delinquency than the three super-factors.

- *The Novaco Anger Scale (Novaco, 1994):* This two-part scale measures anger reactions. Part A contains items divided into three domains: cognitive, arousal and behavioural. Part B consists of items providing an index of anger intensity in potentially anger provoking situations.

- *The Blame Attribution Inventory:* This is a 42-item inventory, with a true-false format, which measures how offenders attribute blame for a specific criminal act. It comprises three subscales: External Attribution (that is blaming the offence on provocation and society), Mental Element Attribution (that is blaming the offence on mental factors, such as poor self-control), and Guilt Feeling (that is the extent to which the offender expresses regret and feelings of remorse for the offence).

Results: The first finding was that out of 120 cases, 103 respondents (86 per cent) said that they had committed the offence in the company of others, Gudjonsson and Sigurdsson concluded that motivation for offending therefore must take into consideration peer group influence and pressure.

Food for thought

How does this finding relate to the findings of Akers *et al.* (Key study 1.1.2) and the Peterborough Study (Key study 1.1.3)?

The second finding was that the highest mean scores on the OMQ were for the excitement and financial motives. In addition, 38 per cent of the participants claimed that they did not think about the consequences of what they were doing and 36 per cent were very confident that they would get away with the offence.

Food for thought

How does this finding relate to the 'superoptimism' variable in the Psychological Inventory of Criminal Thinking Styles (Key study 1.2.1)?

Gudjonsson and Sigurdsson present the argument that there are individual differences in offending motivation factors and that these are related to personality variables. It was hypothesised that different types of motivation for the offence (compliance, provocation, excitement and financial) would be predicted by different psychological measures. It was found that neither Extraversion (EPQ) nor Empathy (EIQ) correlated with any of the OMQ factors. The Gudjonsson Compliance scale correlated significantly with the compliance motive, but not with any other OMQ factors. Psychoticism (EPQ) correlated significantly with the excitement and provocation motives. The Novaco Anger Scales correlated significantly with the excitement, provocation and financial factors. External attribution of blame (Gudjonsson Blame Attribution Inventory) correlated with the compliance motive and there was a significant negative correlation between guilt (Gudjonsson Blame Attribution Inventory) and the excitement motive.

Discussion: The study shows that a compliant disposition is significantly related to participants'

claims that they were pressured into crime, or that they had been trying to impress peers by committing the offence. It also shows that perceived peer pressure can encourage youngsters to offend (for example, being unable to resist offending when pressured to do so by peers). Excitement was found to be the single most important motive for youth offending. The excitement motive had the strongest overall relationship with the other psychological measures. This study also demonstrates the importance of anger in relation to offending motivation. It was an important predictor in three out of the four OMQ factors (excitement, provocation, and financial). This fits with Agnew's (1985) strain theory which proposes that adolescents are pressured into delinquency by strong negative reactions, such as anger, that arise from adverse life events and frustration.

Evaluation

Sample issues

The homogeneity of the sample (young men who had committed relatively minor offences) is both a strength and weakness. The strength is that there are likely to be fewer confounding variables associated with age, gender, substance abuse and repeated offending. The disadvantage is that the influences of different types of offences could not be ascertained and possible gender differences could not be investigated.

Confounding variables: **These are invisible variables that may affect findings thus reducing reliability**

1.3 Turning to crime: Biology
Key Study: 1.3.1 Brain dysfunction

Adrian Raine, Monte Buchsbaum and Lori LaCasse (1997), 'Brain abnormalities in murderers indicated by Positron Emission Tomography', *Biological Psychiatry*, 42 (6), 495–508

Approach: Biological

Aim: To identify areas of brain dysfunction in individuals charged with murder but found not guilty by reason of insanity.

Hypothesis: That violent individuals have relatively localised brain dysfunction in specific regions of the brain linked to violence (for example, prefrontal cortex), but that no dysfunction is expected in other brain areas not implicated in violence (for example, cerebellum)

Method: Quasi experiment

Design: Matched pairs

Type of sample: The experimental group was an opportunity sample; the control group were volunteers (self-selecting)

Participants: 41 murderers (39 males; 2 females), mean age 34 who had all been charged with murder or manslaughter, who all pleaded not guilty by reason of insanity/incompetence and who were referred to the University of California for confirmation of their diminished capacity. Six were diagnosed schizophrenics. The control group were volunteers matched on age and sex, including six schizophrenics.

Procedure: The participants were given an injection of a 'tracer' (fluorodeoxyglucose) while engaged in a continuous performance task which aims to activate specific areas of the brain. Half an hour after the injection, a PET scan was conducted. Ten slices (images) of the brain were taken. Multivariate analyses of variance (MANOVA) were conducted in order to compare the PET scans of the 'murderers' with those of the controls.

Research methods
Positron Emission Tomography

Positron Emission Tomography (PET) is a brain scanning method in which a short-lived radioactive tracer isotope is injected into the blood stream. The tracer is chemically incorporated into a biologically active molecule (usually fluorodeoxyglucose – FDG).

continued...

After a waiting period while the active molecule becomes concentrated in tissues of interest, the participant is placed in the imaging scanner. As the radioisotope undergoes positron emission decay, it emits a positron (positively charged). After travelling a few millimetres the positron encounters an electron (negatively charged). Both are destroyed, producing photons which create a burst of light in the scanning device. PET neuroimaging is based on an assumption that areas of high radioactivity are associated with brain activity. What is actually measured indirectly is the flow of blood to different parts of the brain, which is generally believed to be correlated with brain activity.

Research methods
Analysis of Variance

Analysis of Variance (ANOVA) provides a statistical test of whether or not the means of several groups are equal or different.

Multivariate analysis of variance (MANOVA) is used in cases where there are two or more dependent variables.

Results: It was found that murderers pleading not guilty by reason of insanity are characterised by:

- Reduced glucose metabolism in bilateral prefrontal cortex, the posterior parietal cortex (bilateral superior gyrus and left angular gyrus), and the corpus callosum
- Abnormal asymmetries of activity (left hemisphere less activation than right) in the amygdala, thalamus, and medial temporal gyrus including the hippocampus
- No difference in the caudate, putamen, globus pallidus or midbrain

Discussion: The study provides preliminary evidence that 'murderers' have different brain functioning from normal controls (supporting the hypothesis that prefrontal cortex is implicated in brain dysfunction in violent criminals).

Interpreting data from PET/fMRI scans: **Did you notice that the findings show reduced activity in murderers in brain areas that have been hypothesised to be implicated in aggression? This goes counter to expectation as we might assume that you would find increased activity in regions linked to aggression. We know that the prefrontal area is involved in planning and regulation of emotions so this finding may be explained by the fact that in this group, self-control (regulation) is problematic but it is hard to predict the direction of difference in brain activation. For example, if you give people mathematics problems to solve, more able participants will show less brain activity in the right hemisphere – the hemisphere that we associate with numbers. This may be because able mathematicians' brains work more efficiently than those of non-mathematicians but at this stage much is still conjecture in terms of interpretation of brain scans. Raine *et al.* used two-tailed hypotheses in their study. That is to say that they predicted differences between 'murderers' and normal controls in particular regions, but they did not try to predict the direction of those differences.**

Research methods

Correlation versus causation

Although this study is a quasi experiment (IV being the difference between murderers and normal controls), the data PET scanning produces are correlational. That is although differences are observed between the two groups, it is not possible to say that these differences cause violent behaviour – it is possible that violent behaviour causes brain differences! You cannot conclude from this study that criminals are born with different brains because it is possible that their brains have been affected by their experiences, including the experience of committing a very violent act.

Evaluation

Reductionism and determinism

Studies in the biological approach are often criticised for reductionism and determinism.

Reductionism is when complex factors are broken down into simpler components. In psychology, reductionist sometimes appears to be used as a term of criticism as though it is always misguided to reduce things to a simpler level but this is not always the case. However most psychologists would argue that human behaviour is usually too complex to be reduced to one explanatory factor.

Determinism is the doctrine that behaviour is shaped by internal or external forces over which we have no control rather than an individual's **free will** to act according to their own wishes.

Key study 1.3.1 is not reductionist or determinist as the authors stress that their findings do not support the view that violence is determined by biology alone as other factors such as social and **situational** ones may also play a role in predisposing an individual to commit an act of violence.

1.3 Turning to crime: Biology
Key Study: 1.3.2 Genes and serotonin
Avshalom Caspi *et al.* (2002), 'Role of genotype in the cycle of violence in maltreated children', *Science*, 297, 5582, 851–4

Approach: Biological

Aim: To investigate the role of genotype in antisocial behaviour exhibited by individuals who had been maltreated in childhood

Hypothesis: That the Monoamine Oxidase A (MAOA) genotype can moderate the influence of childhood maltreatment on neural systems implicated in antisocial behaviour

Method: Correlation

Design: Longitudinal study

Type of sample: Representative population sample

Participants: 1037 individuals (52 per cent male) – participants in the Dunedin Multidisciplinary Health and Development Study begun in 1972.

Procedure: A polymorphism of the MAOA gene was tested in the birth cohort of 1037 children who were the subjects of the Dunedin Multidisciplinary Health and Development Study and who had been assessed periodically since birth to the age of 30. Between the ages of 3 and 11 years, 8 per cent of the children in the study experienced 'severe' maltreatment while 28 per cent experienced 'probable' maltreatment. Data was also available on:

- Diagnosis of adolescent conduct disorder
- Diagnosis of personality disposition towards violence
- Symptoms of antisocial personality disorder
- Convictions for violent crimes

Regression analysis was conducted to examine gene–environment interactions by predicting/testing scores on an antisocial index comprising the four measures of antisocial behaviour listed above.

> **Conduct disorder:** Children with childhood-onset conduct disorder are usually male They frequently display physical aggression and usually have disturbed peer relationships. Adolescent-onset type is defined by the absence of conduct disorder prior to age 10. Compared to individuals with the childhood-onset type, they are less likely to display aggressive behaviours. These individuals tend to have more normal peer relationships, and are less likely to have persistent conduct disorders or to develop adult antisocial personality disorder.

> **Antisocial personality disorder:** Antisocial personality disorder is characterised by a pervasive pattern of disregard for, and violation of, the rights of others that begins in childhood or early adolescence and continues into adulthood. To be diagnosed with antisocial personality disorder, an individual must be 18 years of age or over and must have a documented history of a conduct disorder diagnosed before the age of 15.

Findings: A significant main effect was found of maltreatment but not of MAOA genotype. A test of interaction between MAOA and maltreatment was significant. The effect of childhood maltreatment on antisocial behaviour was significantly weaker among males with high MAOA activity than among males with low MAOA activity. Eighty-five per cent of males having low activity MAOA and who had been severely maltreated in childhood developed some form of antisocial behaviour. Although individuals having the combination of low-activity MOAO genotype and maltreatment were only 12 per cent of the male birth cohort, they accounted for 44 per cent of the cohort's violent convictions.

> **Research methods**
>
> **Reporting statistical findings**
>
> A **main effect** is the effect of an independent variable on a dependent variable averaging across the levels of any other independent variables.
>
> An **interaction** may arise when considering the relationship among three or more variables, and describes a situation in which the simultaneous influence of two variables on a third is not additive (that is, has a higher effect than simply adding the effects of both together). The interaction between an explanatory variable and an environmental variable suggests that the effect of the explanatory variable has been moderated or modified by the environmental variable.

continued...

In this study the effect of low MAOA on its own does not explain a significant amount of the variance, whereas childhood maltreatment does. However the conclusion should not be drawn from this that MOAO is not a factor in antisocial behaviour. When the 'childhood' maltreatment' and 'low MAOA' factors are combined, they have a higher explanatory value of antisocial behaviour than 'childhood maltreatment' alone or than both factors added together. This shows that one variable is moderated by the other.

Discussion: These findings provide evidence that a functional polymorphism in the MAOA gene moderates the impact of early childhood maltreatment on the development of antisocial behaviour in males.

Evaluation

Ethics

Cohort studies like the Dunedin one are very **useful** because they collect a large amount of data relating to a wide range of health issues and involving a high number of participants. They do however, raise **ethical** issues as the participants (or in this case their parents) have probably given blanket consent for research without being informed of the details of the projects for which their data will be used.

The same cohort was reported on by Caspi *et al.* (2003) in a study on depression. See Key Study 8.2.2.

1.3 Turning to crime: Biology
Key Study: 1.3.3 Gender

Margo Wilson and Martin Daly (1985), 'Competitiveness, Risk Taking and Violence: The Young Male Syndrome', *Ethology and Sociobiology*, 6, 59–73

Approach: Biological

Aim: To examine gender and age patterns in crime of violence

Method: Analysis of data from police records

Design: Cross-sectional (snapshot)

Type of sample: Opportunity sample

Participants: No participants as such – data analysis in homicide cases

Procedure: This study reviewed homicidal conflicts in Detroit in 1972, analysing age and sex of perpetrators and victims

Results: The study found that homicide was overwhelmingly a male affair. Victim and offender populations were almost identical: unemployed, unmarried young men were greatly overrepresented.

It was found that most homicides concern status competition (showing off, jealously, retaliation). Wilson and Daly also argued that other sorts of risk-taking such as daredevilry and gambling were overwhelmingly masculine pursuits facilitated by the presence of peers pursuing the same goals.

Discussion: Wilson and Daly place their findings firmly in the evolutionary framework. They argue that dangerous, confrontational conflict is not unique to humans but is widespread in the animal kingdom. The evolutionary theory is that different selective pressures produce distinct male and female behavioural strategies; the more intense the competition for females among males, the more males are inclined to risky tactics, increasing male

Table 1.1 Homicidal conflict in Detroit

Type of homicide case	Male–male	Male–female	Total homicides by males	Female–male	Female–female	Total homicides by females
Social conflict	195	61	256	67	16	83
Crime specific	148	13	161	7	0	7
Type unknown	5	0	5	0	0	0
All closed cases	348	74	422	74	16	90

Source: adapted from Wilson and Daly (1985)

Table 1.2 Social conflict homicides where offender and victim were not related

Type of conflict	Male–male	Male–female	Total male crimes	Female–male	Female–female	Total female crimes
Jealousy	20	5	25	6	3	9
Business	10	1	11	2	0	2
Showing off	26	0	26	2	1	3
Retaliation	75	9	84	6	5	11
Intervention in family quarrels	5	0	5	0	0	0
Miscellaneous	2	0	2	1	1	2
Unknown	26	4	30	1	1	2
Total	164	19	183	18	11	29

Source: adapted from Wilson and Daly (1985)

mortality. The ratio of male to female offenders was higher for crime-specific homicides (that is, homicides that occurred during another criminal act, for example burglary) in Detroit than social conflict offences. Very few offenders or victims of these crimes were women. Most of the handful of such crimes committed by women were committed in self-defence during the perpetration of a criminal act by another person (male). Wilson and Daly make a strong case for the evolutionary explanation for gendered crime patterns.

Evaluation

Reliability

Findings from any study are only as **reliable** as the data collected. This is based on police records of homicides. The researcher has subsequently categorised the data into different types of crimes.

Do you think that the full facts will have been known in every case?

2.1 Making a case: Interviewing witnesses
Key Study: 2.1.1 Recognising faces

Vicki Bruce, Hayley Ness, Peter J.B. Hancock, Craig Newman and Jenny Rarity (2002), 'Four heads are better than one: combining face composites yields improvements in face likeness', *Journal of Applied Psychology*, 87 (5), 894–902 (Experiment 2)

Approach: Cognitive

Aim: To investigate whether better likenesses of a suspect might be produced if multiple witness composites of the same remembered person are generated and combined

Hypothesis: That combined composites will be found to be more similar to a target than individual composites

Method: Laboratory experiment

Design: Independent measures

Type of sample: There were four stages to Experiment 2: in Stages 1, 2 and 4, paid volunteers were used, Stage 3 used an opportunity sample

Participants:

- *Stage 1*: 16 paid volunteers aged 18–40, all university staff from Edinburgh
- *Stage 2*: 20 paid volunteers aged 17–60, shop employees
- *Stage 3*: 32 senior students and staff from the psychology department at the University of Stirling
- *Stage 4*: 64 volunteers aged 17–60, Open University students

Procedure:

Stage 1: Generation of composites

Participants (16 volunteer university staff) were shown a 30-second video of a target woman (four target women – all members of the staff from the psychology department at the University of Stirling) who was unfamiliar to the participants. The participants were asked to recall the target's appearance so that the experimenter could build a full face composite. Four of the composites of each of four targets were combined.

Stage 2: Likeness ratings

Participants (20 paid volunteer workers from a supermarket) were shown five different full-face composites of each target including individual composites and the 4-morph versions alongside photographs of the target women and asked to rate them for likeness to the photograph on a scale from 1 (low) to 10 (high).

Results of Stage 2

The 4-morphs were given higher likeness ratings than the average of the individual composites, significantly so for two of the four targets.

Stage 3: Identification task

Participants from the psychology department at the University of Stirling were asked to identify the composites. Each participant was shown one best composite, one worst composite, one 4-morph composite or a set of all four individual composites and asked to identify them. Eight participants attempted to identify each woman in each condition. After this procedure, at the debriefing stage, participants were asked if they were familiar with all four targets and only the data from those who were familiar with all four targets were retained.

Results of Stage 3

Recognition rates overall were relatively low and did not differ significantly among the four conditions. The highest rate was found for the condition where all four composites were shown (38 per cent correct, no false positives), followed by the 4-morph (28 per cent correct, 6 per cent false positives); the best individual composite (22 per cent correct, no false positives), with the worst composite yielding the lowest rate (16 per cent correct, 6 per cent false positives). The false positives were two errors made, both wrongly identifying a woman professor from the department who was not in the target set.

Stage 4: Identification from line-ups

Participants were shown the same four conditions (4-morph, best, worst and all four individual composites) against an array of female faces of similar general appearance. On half of the arrays no target image was present – making eight different conditions in all. Participants were asked to decide to compare the composite with the array and to decide if the target person was there, and if so which one it was.

Results of Stage 4

The 4-morph condition yielded the most correct responses from both target-present and target-absent arrays and generated the fewest false choices.

Table 2.1 Percentage of responses to different composite types

Composite array type	4-morph		All four		Best		Worst	
	Present	Absent	Present	Absent	Present	Absent	Present	Absent
Correct	41	41	28	13	34	19	28	28
Total Incorrect	59	59	72	87	65	81	72	72
Not picked	22		9		15		9	
False choice	37	59	63	87	50	81	63	72

Source: adapted from Bruce et al. (2002)

Treating participant-target combinations as independent, the four conditions of the experiment did not differ significantly when all four conditions were compared using chi-squared analysis. However a comparison between the 4-morph condition and the other three conditions combined was significant, $p < 0.05$.

Research methods

Chi-squared analysis

In some types of experiment we wish to record how many individuals fall into a particular category, such as blue eyes or brown eyes, and whether the number in each category fits the expected value, or null hypothesis. The null hypothesis in this case would be that there would be no significant difference in the number of correct responses in each category.

Discussion: It was found that better likenesses are obtained when facial images from multiple witnesses are combined. Combined composites (that is 4-morphs) were at least as good as the best individual composite. Given that there is no way of knowing whether an individual witness will produce a good composite, the use of multiple witnesses and composites is advisable. The researchers acknowledged that the production of composites by more than a single witness to the same crime is currently forbidden by the police code of conduct but they argue that as long as proper procedures are maintained (for example, no discussion between witnesses), it should be possible to bring in the use of composites in future.

Evaluation

Usefulness

This study shows that previous methods of trying to produce likenesses of offenders on the basis of individual feature recognition were not very **reliable**. Combinations of several recalled faces give an overall impression that is more recognisable than individual composites. The software that these researchers developed as a consequence of this research (Evofit) was further developed for use by the police and has proved helpful in identifying offenders.

2.1 Making a case: Interviewing witnesses
Key Study: 2.1.2 Factors influencing identification
Elizabeth F. Loftus, Geoffrey R. Loftus and Jane Messo (1987), 'Some facts about "weapon focus"', *Law and Human Behavior*, 11 (1), 55–62

Approach: Cognitive

Aim: To investigate the effect of the presence of a weapon on witness recall

Hypothesis: That recall will be better in the non–weapon condition than the weapon condition

Experiment 1

Method: Laboratory experiment

Design: Independent measures

Type of sample: There were two experiments; participants were a mixture of paid volunteers and an opportunity sample

Participants: Participants were 36 students, age 18–31; half were paid volunteers and half were psychology students who participated for college credits

Procedure: Participants watched a series of 35 mm slides. There were two series of slides, both of which showed a queue of customers in a fast food restaurant. In the control condition the second person in the queue hands the cashier a check (dollar bill) and the cashier gives the customer change. In the experimental condition the slides are all identical except that the second person (person B) pulls a gun on the cashier and then she hands him money. In Experiment 1 eye movement data of participants was recorded. Participants were told that they would see two series of slides and they would be tested on the second series only. They were told to view the first series normally while their eye movements were recorded. During a 15-minute interval the subjects watched a second series of slides and were told to write a detailed description of the slides. Participants were then asked to respond to a questionnaire. Seven of twenty multi-choice items pertained to person B, for example 'What colour was person B's coat?' Other items pertained to miscellaneous details about the event. Participants were also given a line-up test in which 12 photos were presented in a random pattern and they had to attempt to identify person B and also give a confidence rating of their identification on a scale from 1 to 6, with 1 representing guessing and 6 representing 'very sure'.

Results of Experiment 1

Participants in the weapon condition were slightly, but not significantly, less accurate than controls on the 20-item questionnaire. Weapon participants were correct on 46 per cent of the items, while controls were correct on 50 per cent of the items. On the seven questions relating to person B, weapon participants were correct on 46 per cent of the items while control participants were correct on 51 per cent of the items. In the 12-person photo line up, seven of the control participants chose the correct person, but only two weapons participants did so. A test of statistical significance was not performed as so few participants were correct in the weapon condition. Eye movement data showed that participants made more fixations on the gun than on the cheque and the difference was significant, $p < 0.01$.

Experiment 2

Method: Laboratory experiment

Design: Independent measures

Type of sample: Opportunity samples

Participants: Participants were 80 psychology students

Procedure: Materials and procedure were the same as in Experiment 1 with the exceptions that eye movements were not recorded and the participants only responded to the seven-item multiple choice questions pertaining to person B rather than the 20-item questionnaire. Participants were given the 12-person line up test as in Experiment 1.

Results of Experiment 2

Participants in the weapon condition were significantly less accurate in responding to the questionnaire than controls ($p < 0.05$). Weapon participants were correct on 56 per cent of the items while control participants were correct on 67 per cent of the items. On the 12-person line up test, participants in the weapon condition were again significantly less accurate than controls ($p < 0.05$). Participants in the weapon condition were correct only 15 per cent of the time, while control participants were correct 35 per cent of the time.

Discussion: Loftus *et al.* argued that their results supported the concept of weapon focus. They also argued that in a real life crime, this fixation on a weapon would be intensified. However real life research does not support the suggestion that memory is affected negatively by high emotional arousal. The researchers accepted that the same effect might have been obtained by production of any unusual object (for example, a banana) rather than being a necessary consequence of the presence of a weapon specifically.

Evaluation

Ecological validity

Although this study was **useful** in establishing the possible effect of a weapon on participant recall of details of the person holding the weapon, the study lacks **ecological validity** so must be treated with caution. Also not all the findings showed a significant difference between the weapon condition and the control condition. Replication as well as alternative methods with higher ecological validity are required in order to confirm whether Loftus's preliminary results can be **generalised**.

2.1 Making a case: Interviewing witnesses

Key Study: 2.1.3 The cognitive interview

R. Edward Geiselman and Ronald P. Fisher (1985), 'Memory enhancement in the police interview: cognitive retrieval mnemonics versus hypnosis', *Journal of Applied Psychology*, 70 (2), 401–12

Approach: Cognitive

Aim: To compare the effectiveness of three interview procedures for optimising eyewitness memory performance

Method: Laboratory experiment

Design: Independent measures

Type of sample: Self-selecting and opportunity samples

Participants: Interviewer participants were volunteers recruited through an advertisement in a forensic hypnosis journal, policemen and from various law-related professions. Interviewee participants were 89 undergraduate students: 55 males, 34 females. Interviewers were randomly assigned to one of three interview conditions: cognitive, hypnosis and standard.

Procedure: The interviewee participants viewed police training films of simulated violent crimes and were questioned individually in interactive interviews forty-eight hours later by experienced law-enforcement personnel.

Standard interview:

Interviewers were told to follow standard procedures with the restriction that each 'witness' was to be asked to describe in their own words what they remembered before any questions were asked.

Hypnosis interview:

The 'witnesses' were again asked to describe the film in their own words prior to any hypnosis induction. The interviewer was then to perform a hypnosis induction, and then to follow their normal techniques.

Cognitive interview:

In this condition the interviewers were to describe four general memory retrieval techniques to the interviewees before beginning the interview. Otherwise the format was the same as for the standard interview. The techniques were:

a) Reinstate the context: try to reinstate in your mind the context surrounding the incident
b) Report everything: report everything, however trivial
c) Recall the events in different orders: try to remember things in reverse order or starting from the most striking thing
d) Change perspectives: try to recall the incident from different perspectives

All the interviews were tape-recorded, transcribed and scored according to quantities of data correctly recalled. Analysis of variance was performed to ensure that there were no significant differences between scorers.

Results: Both the cognitive and hypnosis procedures elicited a significantly greater number of correct items of information from participants than did the standard interview. This result was most pronounced for crime scenarios in which the density of events was high.

Discussion: The observed memory enhancement was interpreted in terms of the memory guidance techniques common to both the cognitive and hypnosis interviews

Evaluation

Generalisability

As with the Loftus experiment, the **generalisability** of these findings is limited by **low ecological validity** as the interviewees watched film clips of simulated crimes. However Geiselman also conducted a field study comparing detectives trained in CI techniques with untrained detectives conducting interviews with real witnesses. The results of the follow-up study confirmed the results of this key study.

2.2 Making a case: Interviewing suspects
Key Study: 2.2.1 Detecting lies
Albert Vrij and Samantha Mann (2001), 'Telling and detecting lies in a high-stake situation: the case of a convicted murderer', *Applied Cognitive Psychology*, 15, 187–203

Approach: Cognitive/individual differences

Aim: To investigate the behaviour of a suspect telling lies during police interviews and to assess police accuracy in detecting lies and truthful statements while observing videoclips of the interviews

Hypothesis: That individual differences would be found among observers with those who hold popular stereotypical views on deceptive behaviour proving less effective in judging lies

Method: Preparatory coding study followed by laboratory experiment

Design: Repeated measures

Type of sample: Volunteer (self-selecting) sample

Participants: In Study 1 the interviewee was a convicted criminal interviewed before conviction by two experienced police officers and the videotapes were analysed and observed by the experimenters and independent observers. In Study 2 the participants were 65 (59 male, 6 female) police officers from various police stations in West Sussex. Mean age of participants was 30 (range, 22–52 years) and mean length of service was 6 years (range, 1–29 years).

Procedure:

Study 1:

A case was used in which a suspect who was later convicted of a murder was videotaped during several hours of interview. The police had good reason to believe they had the right man from the beginning because they had eyewitness descriptions from several witnesses and the man arrested showed a clear resemblance to the sketch that had been compiled. Two experienced police officers interviewed the suspect with his lawyer present and the interviews were videotaped. The suspect consistently denied involvement in the murder but gradually what came out in the interviews convinced the police of the suspect's guilt. After a couple of weeks the police had substantial material evidence of the man's guilt (a hair from the victim and fibres of the cloth in which the dead body had been wrapped were found in the suspect's car). After being faced with this evidence, the man eventually confessed and was later convicted for murder. Even once he made his confession, however, the suspect continued to lie about various details. The videotapes were subsequently analysed and six fragments were isolated (three known to be truthful and three known to be deceptive). Two fragments were taken from the interviews before the suspect confessed and four from the interviews after he confessed and analysed for selected excerpts where the evidence was available to indicate whether the interviewee was lying or telling the truth. The interview fragments were then coded for twelve behaviours by two observers who did not know whether the interviewee was telling the truth. The behaviours included gaze aversion, smiling, head movements, speech rate, length of pauses, speech disturbances, and so on. Correlations showed evidence of strong consistency between the two coders.

Results of Study 1

During the pre-confession interview the murderer showed more gaze aversion, had longer pauses, spoke more slowly and had more speech disturbances than when he was telling the truth. In the confession interview while lying he showed less gaze aversion, had longer pauses, spoke more slowly and made slightly more speech disturbances. He also made fewer movements with hands and fingers during the confession interview. The behavioural pattern shown by the murderer provides some evidence that when he was lying he had to think hard and when telling the truth he tried to control his behaviour. The difference in gaze aversion during the two stages of interview was attributed by the researchers to different styles of interview.

Study 2:

The selected videotape fragments were shown to the participants (65 serving police officers) who were asked after each fragment to respond to four questions: 'Is he lying?' (yes or no) then on a 7-point Likert scale ranging from 1 – definitely not to 7 – definitely, the following questions: Is he tense? Is he controlling his behaviour? Is he having to think hard? After responding, participants were asked each time to write down what behavioural cues had prompted them to make their decision. There were two independent variables in this experiment:

whether the murderer was lying or not, and whether the clips were taken from the interviews before or during his confession.

Results of Study 2

The overall accuracy rate of the police officers was 64 per cent which was significantly above the level of chance ($p < 0.01$) and was slightly higher than usually found in deception studies. However, mean scores on truth/lying separately revealed that participants were better at detecting truths (70 per cent) than lies (57 per cent). Accuracy rate in detecting lies was not above chance. Another finding was that individual differences in performance were large. Eleven officers out of 65 performed very badly (making only one or two correct judgements) while six officers correctly judged all six fragments. It was found that those who were poor at judging relied more on stereotypical behaviours, for example eye gaze and fidgeting than those who were good at judging who used more subtle clues such as speech rate.

Discussion: The researchers stated that no other study had examined lying/truth telling in such a realistic high-stakes situation. They found that the man was more nervous when he was lying than when he was telling the truth but in general he did not exhibit nervous behaviours, contradicting the widespread belief among professionals that liars behave nervously. The suspect had been previously interviewed by the police and may have realised that showing stereotypical deceptive behaviour such as fidgeting and gaze aversion would raise suspicion, so he probably tried to control his behaviour and avoid unnecessary movements. The researchers concluded that while little is yet known about what makes someone a good lie detector, avoiding stereotypical beliefs in detecting lies may be a useful first step towards improving police effectiveness.

Evaluation

Ecological validity

The researchers claim that this study is higher in **ecological validity** than previous studies examining deception under laboratory conditions. Why is this the case?

Generalisability

The researchers admitted that a limitation of this study is that it involved assessing deceptive behaviour in only one individual. It may be that this individual's behaviour in a high-stakes situation may not be typical. He might be a gifted liar, or alternatively a poor liar. Therefore while the study has ecological validity, this does not mean that we can **generalise** from it. More studies are needed to test the findings of the present study.

Key Study: 2.2.2 Interrogation techniques

Pär Anders Granhag and Leif A. Strömwall (2001), 'Deception detection based on repeated interrogations', *Legal and Criminological Psychology*, 6, 85–101

Approach: Cognitive

Aim: To investigate the effect of multiple interrogations on deception detection and also to test the finding that interrogators in face-to-face situations are more likely to believe suspects than non-involved observers

Hypothesis 1: That there would be no differences in detection accuracy between observers watching one interrogation and those watching three interrogations with the same suspect

Hypothesis 2: (a) That overall detection accuracy would be modest and (b) accuracy in detecting truth-tellers would be significantly higher than accuracy in detecting liars

Hypothesis 3: That interrogators (interacting face to face with suspects) would show a more pronounced truth bias than observers

Hypothesis 4: (a) That confidence in judgements concerning truth/lying would be weakly related to accuracy; (b) that it would be higher for statements regarded as truthful than deceptive and (c) that it would be higher when judging truth-telling participants than lying participants

Method: Laboratory experiment

Design: Independent groups

Stage 1

Type of sample: Paid volunteer sample

Participants: 51 undergraduate students from Göteborg University (Sweden); 24 psychology students (10 male, 14 female) acted as witnesses, 3 participants acted as interviewers for Interrogation 1 only, and 24 students from various departments (10 male, 14 female) acted as interrogators in Interrogations 2 and 3.

Procedure: A staged event was performed by semi-professional actors. The scenario was a robbery scene written by the experimenters. After watching the live event the witnesses were divided into two groups. The truth-tellers were told to recapitulate what had happened as accurately as possible. The liars were guided by the experimenters to distort what had happened to make it appear as if the victim was to blame and to construct a believable story around what had happened.

Interrogation 1:

Each witness was videotaped as he/she gave free recall to one of three interviewers. The interviewers prompted the witnesses and listened to their statements. The interviewers were blind as to whether the witness was telling the truth. The witnesses afterwards rated the degree of truth of their statement on a scale of 1–10, 1 = completely untrue; 10 = completely true.

Interrogation 2:

Four days after the event the witnesses returned and 24 interrogators were paired randomly with the witnesses. The interrogators were given instructions and the interrogations were videotaped. The interrogators again allowed free recall and then asked a series of directed questions. After the interrogation the witnesses rated the truth of their accounts.

Interrogation 3:

A week later all witnesses and interrogators returned. Each interrogator watched the first two interrogations conducted with his/her witness then received instructions on how to conduct the third interrogation. The interrogators told the suspects that different witnesses had provided reports that were inconsistent with their statements. The witnesses were again asked to provide free recall followed by more specific questions. The interrogation was videotaped and the witness asked to rate the truth of their statement.

After the third interrogation each interrogator was asked if they thought the witness had been telling the truth or not, and were asked how confident they were in their judgement. They were also asked to assess the degree of truth of each of the witness's three statements.

Stage 2

Type of sample: Volunteer sample

Participants: 144 undergraduate students (92 female, 52 male) from various departments of Göteborg University

Procedure: The 24 videotaped testimonies from Stage 1 were used in Stage 2. The 144 participants (observers) were divided into two experimental conditions. In the single condition they watched three interrogations with one witness and made one set of ratings. In the repeat condition the observers watched the first interrogation and made one set of ratings, then watched the two remaining interrogations and made a second set of ratings.

Results: For every interrogation session the truth-tellers rated the degree of truth significantly higher than liars.

Hypothesis 1 was supported – no difference was found between observers watching one interrogation and observers watching three interrogations. The only judges who performed slightly better than chance were the observers in the repeat condition. The overall deception detection accuracy was not better than chance, lending support to hypothesis 2a. For both interrogators and observers in the single condition, accuracy was significantly higher for truthful statements than deceptive statements, confirming hypothesis 2b. In the interrogator condition, 77 per cent judged the witness to be a truth-teller as compared to 62.5 per cent in the single condition and 47 per cent in the repeat condition. These results confirm hypothesis 3, that interrogators are more prone to truth bias than observers. The accuracy–confidence correlation was weak, supporting hypothesis 4a. Judges making truth judgements were not more confident than judges making lie judgements, therefore hypothesis 4b was not confirmed. Mean confidence when judging truth-telling witnesses was not significantly higher than when judging lying witnesses so hypothesis 4c was not confirmed. Of the total 72 observers in the repeat condition, 14 changed their veracity (truthfulness) judgement: 12 moved from an incorrect to a correct judgement.

Discussion: If a police officer has doubts about whether a suspect is telling the truth, normal procedure is to conduct a further interrogation. The findings suggest that further interrogation alone is not likely to change accuracy of truth-telling judgements. The evidence from this study suggests that this is only a useful procedure if it is accompanied by repeated assessments of truth-telling. The researchers recommend that interrogations are videotaped and at least one other person makes an independent assessment based on the videotape.

Evaluation

Ecological validity and reliability

This study has lower **ecological validity** than Key study 2.2.1, Vrij and Mann, 2001. Nevertheless it is a well constructed and well **controlled** study that offers valuable insights into interrogation techniques and how they might be improved. The study was based on a large sample and significant differences were found that supported several of the study hypotheses. The findings may be considered **reliable** and the study **valid** within certain limitations. This is a good example of reliable data supporting valid conclusions regarding detection of deception amongst undergraduates in a low-stakes situation. This is what the study sought to measure and therefore it has validity. Whether the results would be replicated in a study involving trained police officers is another question. However the evidence appears to be supported by the findings from Vrij and Mann in terms of the low success rate of trained interrogators in detecting lies. These two studies together provide strong evidence that the police would do well to examine and amend interrogation techniques.

2.2

2.2 Making a case: Interviewing suspects
Key Study: 2.2.3 False confessions
Gisli H. Gudjonsson, Jon Fridrik Sigurdsson, Bryndis Bjork Asgeirsdottir and Inga Dora Sigfusdottir (2006), 'Custodial interrogation, false confession and individual differences: A national study among Icelandic youth', *Personality and Individual Differences*, 41, 49–59

Approach: Individual differences

Aim: The aims of this study were two-fold: firstly, to ascertain a national base rate of custodial interrogation, confession, denial and false confession among Icelandic youth and secondly to investigate psychological and criminological factors associated with false confession.

Hypothesis: That those with frequent interrogation experience would be particularly likely to report false confessions and that the reporting of false confession during interrogation would be associated with disturbed mental state, poor self-esteem, negative attitudes towards school and involvement in delinquency.

Method: Self-report

Design: Cross-sectional (snapshot)

Type of sample: Representative sample population

Participants: The participants were 10 472 students in further education in Iceland (80 per cent of total). The students were from all 38 further education colleges in Iceland. There were 5129 males and 5305 females (38 participants did not state their gender); average age was 18 (range 16–24).

Procedure: As part of a large national study into the background, behaviour, and mental health of adolescents, each pupil was asked four questions relevant to the aims of this study. They were asked to rate on a five-point frequency scale in relation to each question (never, once, twice, three–five times, six or more times) in response to the question 'How often (if at all) have you experienced the following during your life?':

- Been interrogated by police at a police station about a suspected offence
- Confessed during an interrogation to an offence that you did commit
- Confessed during interrogation to an offence that you did not commit.
- Denied during interrogation an offence that you had committed

Participants were also asked to respond to several psychological measures in order to discriminate between participants who reported having made a false confession, and those who did not. These were an anxiety and depression scale; an anger scale; a self-esteem scale; a measure of parental support; an attitude towards school measure and an involvement of self and friends in delinquency measure.

Results: Of the total sample of 10 192 participants who responded to the question about whether they had been interviewed by the police, 1896 (18.6 per cent) reported that they had been questioned at a police station as suspects. There was a significant difference between males and females, 28 per cent of the males and 10 per cent of the females reported having been questioned. Most of those who had been questioned had only been interrogated once (55 per cent), while 22 per cent had been interrogated twice, 14 per cent had been interrogated three–five times and 8 per cent had been interrogated six or more times.

Table 2.2 Rates of confessions, denials and false confessions (participants interrogated once)

	Total		Male		Female	
	N	per cent	N	per cent	N	per cent
True confessions	484	46	302	46	182	47
False confessions	35	3	24	4	11	3
True denials*	350†	33	191	29	156	40
False denials	183	18	140	21	43	11

*True denials were only calculated for those participants who reported being interrogated once only, otherwise more than one outcome would have to have been calculated
† Three respondents who reported true denials were of unspecified gender
Source: adapted from Gudjonsson *et al.* (2006)

Table 2.3 Rates of confessions, denials and false confessions (participants interrogated more than once)

	Total		Male		Female	
	N	per cent	N	per cent	N	per cent
True confessions	514	62	438	63	76	57
False confessions	102	12	85	12	17	13
False denials	457	55	398	57	59	43

Source: adapted from Gudjonsson et al. (2006)

Table 2.4 Rates of confessions, denials and false confessions (all interrogations)

	Total		Male		Female	
	N	per cent	N	per cent	N	per cent
True confessions	998	53	740	55	258	49
False confessions	137	7	109	8	28	5
False denials	640	34	538	40	102	19

Source: adapted from Gudjonsson et al. (2006)

A small minority of those interrogated claimed to have made false confessions to the police (7 per cent). The false confession rate was highest among those interrogated more than once (12 per cent) and lowest among those interrogated only once (3 per cent). These findings suggest that some people who are frequently interrogated by the police are at a high risk of making false confessions. There were significant differences between those who reported having made false confessions and those who did not on all the psychological measures, but those factors that contributed most to discriminating between the two groups were delinquency (self); delinquency (friends) and depression.

Discussion: Gudjonsson et al. concluded that the fact that false confession was more common amongst those who had been interrogated frequently by the police suggests that for these youths lying to the police may be part of their antisocial life style, whether that means making a false denial or a false confession. They also concluded from the results of the psychological measures that personality and individual differences are important in discriminating between false confessors, as well as lifestyle factors (rate of delinquency of self and friend).

Evaluation

Sample

The sample is an unusually **representative** cross-section of the 16–18 year olds across the whole of one country (80 per cent of those at further education college). However as the school leaving age in Iceland is 15, pupils who did not stay on to college were not in the sample, and it is likely that they might have more involvement with the police, so the figures may be an underestimate of police interrogation and false confession rates for all young persons in Iceland.

Self–report

The findings are dependent on self-report and could not be corroborated so they rely on participants having replied in an honest manner to the questions.

Quantitative data collection

The only data collected were quantitative – responses on a Likert scale to the four key questions (and psychological measure responses). There were no questions allowing participants to provide further detail about the nature or severity of the offences which they had falsely confessed to, nor any opportunity for the participants to discuss why they had made false confessions.

2.3 Making a case: Offender profiling
Key Study: 2.3.1 Top-down typology
David V Canter, Laurence J Alison, Emily Alison and Natalia Wentink (2004), 'The organized/disorganized typology of serial murder. Myth or model?', *Psychology, Public Policy and the Law*, 10 (3), 393–420

Approach: Individual differences

Aim: To investigate the organised/disorganised classification of serial killers in offender profiling

Hypothesis: That features characteristic of organised crime scenes will form a distinctly different and coherent pattern from those of disorganised crime scenes

Method: Analysis of different type of crime scenes for co-occurrence of reported criteria using the psychometric procedure of multidimensional scaling

Type of sample: Retrospective data analysis

Participants: 100 cases (serial crimes committed in the United States) from the Missen Corpus of Serial Killer archive

Procedure: Material was collected from accounts of serial killers and their crimes published in US newspapers, magazines, trial transcripts and case histories. A content analysis of the case report material enabled 39 criteria to be identified that corresponded to those crime scene characteristics outlined in Douglas *et al.* (1992), *Crime Classification Manual* as either an organised or disorganised offence. Behaviours were coded dichotomously (present = 1, behaviour not present/presence not known = 0) across the offences. One hundred crimes were selected, one from each of the series of one hundred convicted serial killers

Research methods
Content analysis
Content analysis is a methodology in the social sciences for studying the content of communication. It can be used to analyse content as recorded in a variety of modes such as recorded transcripts of interviews, books, documents and websites. It is done by coming up with a set of categories (such as 'body left exposed') and deciding for each case whether this was true.

Results: The five most frequently occurring variables identified for each of the two categories are shown in Table 2.5.

The remaining variables which occurred at lower frequencies were mostly characteristic of crime scenes designated as disorganised. A direct test of the organised/disorganised dichotomy is the co-occurrence of various aspects of the crime that indicate that the crime falls into this subgroup. This was examined by considering the proportion of all occurrences of any pair of actions that are co-occurrences of those actions together. The authors explained that there is no model available for calculating statistical significance in the case of features of serial killings but that Jaccard's coefficient provides an acceptable alternative. This deems it a significant level of co-occurrence when actions occur together in two of every three cases.

Table 2.5 Highest frequency variables from the Missen Corpus reflecting organised or disorganised crime scenes (according to Douglas *et al.*, 1992)

Organised		Disorganised	
Variable	**%**	**Variable**	**%**
Victim alive during sex acts	91	Vaginal rape	74
Body positioned	75	Overkill	70
Murder weapon missing	67	Multiple sex acts	66
Multiple crime scene	61	Beaten	61
Body concealed	58	Body left in isolated spot	54

Note: Frequency across the sample of 100 cases

Applying Jaccard's coefficient revealed that only three sets of same-category variables reached the designated level (67 per cent co-occurrence). Two sets of variables co-occurred in the organised category: sexual activity with a live victim happened in 75 per cent of cases in which a body was also positioned and in 70 per cent of cases where the body was concealed there were also multiple crime scenes. Only one set of variables co-occurred in the disorganised category: vaginal rape with multiple sex acts. However when the researchers analysed co-occurrence across the typologies, they found several co-occurrences across category with the highest being body being left in an isolated spot (disorganised) occurring in 74 per cent of the cases in which there are multiple crime scenes (organised). Other cross-category co-occurrences that reached the designated level were rape (organised) and victim alive during sex (disorganised) which co-occurred in 72 per cent of cases and body left in an isolated spot (disorganised) and body concealed (organised) which also co-occurred in 72 per cent of cases. (See Table 2.6.)

To ensure reliability of the finding that the dichotomous model does not best explain the typology of serial killing, further analysis was carried out using Smallest Space Analysis (SSA), a type of multi-dimensional scaling.

> **Research methods**
> **Smallest space analysis (SSA)**
> Smallest space analysis is away of visualising data that has proven of particular power in the examination of qualitative material derived from witness statements, police reports and crime scene information (Canter and Heritage, 1990).

Discussion: The SSA shows no clear division between organised and disorganised variables. The majority of organised variables are clustered in the central, high-frequencies region whereas the disorganised variables are spread around the plot. This suggests that what serial killings have in common is the features classified as organised and

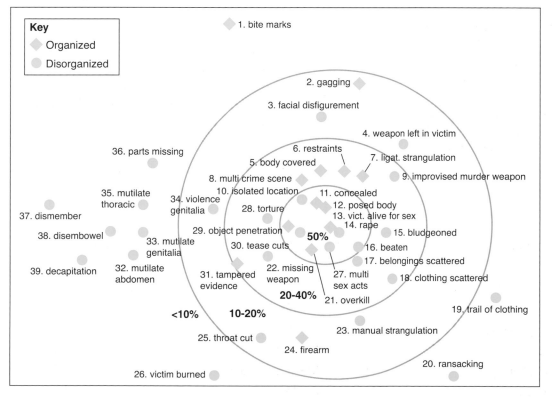

Figure 2.1 Spatial representation of organised/disorganised criteria
Source: D. Canter *et al.* (2004), 'The organized/disorganized typology of serial murder. Myth or model?', *Psychology, Public Policy and Law*, 10(3), 393–420.
Published by American Psychological Association and reproduced with permission.

Table 2.6 Relationships between frequently occurring organised and disorganised features across 100 serial killings

	Victim alive during sex	Body positioned	Weapon missing	Many crime scenes	Body concealed	Rape	Overkill	Multiple sex acts	Victim beaten	Left isolated
Victim alive during sex	–									
Body positioned	.71*	–								
Weapon missing	.61	.54	–							
Many crime scenes	.63	.62	.58	–						
Body concealed	.57	.58	.52	.70*	–					
Rape	.72*	.64	.48	.53	.50	–				
Overkill	.64	.59	.65	.46	.41	.53	–			
Multiple sex acts	.60	.60	.51	.53	.49	.69*	.49	–		
Victim beaten	.58	.49	.47	.39	.43	.48	.52	.44	–	
Left isolated	.54	.57	.51	.74*	.72*	.47	.43	.43	.35	–

Key: Organised features in green; disorganised features in black
*Designated significant
Source: D. Canter *et al.* (2004), 'The organized/disorganized typology of serial murder. Myth or model?', *Psychology, Public policy and Law*, 10(3), 393–420.
Published by American Psychological Association and reproduced with permission.

what distinguishes one serial killer's offences from another is the nature of the variables classified as disorganised. Canter *et al.* conclude that the hypothesis that serial murders fall into one or two types, either organised or disorganised, is not supported by the evidence of this study. Key study 2.3.1 is seen by the researchers as a first step towards submitting top-down offender profiling to systematic, scientific investigation.

Evaluation

Reliability

The researchers have used two well **controlled** and tested methods of data analysis that provide consistent results. The results of the Jaccard's coefficients test and the SSA independently support the null hypothesis that there is no clear distinction between variables associated with organised and disorganised crime scenes.

References:

J. E. Douglas, A. W. Burgess, A. G. Burgess and R. K. Ressler (1992), *Crime Classification Manual: a standard system for investigating and classifying violent crime*, New York: Simon and Schuster

D. Canter and R. Heritage (1990), 'A multivariate model of sexual offence behaviour: developments in offender profiling', *Journal of Forensic Psychiatry*, 1, 185–212

Key Study: 2.3.2 Bottom-up approaches

Brent Snook, David Canter and Craig Bennell, (2002), 'Predicting the home location of serial offenders: a preliminary comparison of the accuracy of human judges with a geographic profiling system', *Behavioral Sciences and the Law*, 20, 109–18

Approach: Cognitive

Aim: To investigate whether human judges could learn and apply heuristics from geographic profiling to identify likely home location of serial offenders

Hypothesis: That following two heuristics (distance-decay and circle hypothesis) participants would be able to improve predictions of likely home location of serial offenders

Method: Laboratory experiment

Design: Independent measures

Type of sample: Not stated

Participants: 42 students (undergraduate and postgraduate) studying a variety of different disciplines at the University of Liverpool who had no knowledge of geographic profiling techniques. The control group consisted of 21 students (10 males, 11 females), mean age 26 years (range 19–40) from a variety of nationalities and the experimental group consisted of 21 students (13 males and 8 females), mean age 28 years (range 21–61), from a variety of nationalities.

Procedure:

Phase 1

All participants from both groups were given ten different spatial displays. Each display represented as points on an otherwise blank sheet of paper the locations of five offences committed by an American serial murderer. The points were drawn from actual maps but adjusted to fit on to an A4 sheet of paper. These spatial displays were used because current geographical profiling systems like Dragnet do not take account of topography or land use. The heuristics and algorithms built into such systems are purely geometric. Participants in both conditions were asked to mark with an 'X' somewhere on each display where they thought the serial murderer was likely to be found. Participants were also given the opportunity to indicate the heuristics they had used to reach their conclusions.

Phase 2

The spatial displays were collected in. Participants in the control group were given the same displays again and asked to indicate a second time where

they thought the home location of each of the serial murderers was likely to be located and how they came to their conclusions. They were not given any feedback between the two phases which were just a few minutes apart. After Phase 1 participants in the experimental group were told that

1) The majority of offenders commit offences close to home.
2) The majority of offenders' homes can be located within a circle with its diameter defined by the distance between the offender's two furthermost crimes.

This is the essential information utilised by geographic profiling systems. The participants in the experimental group were then given the same displays and asked to go through the same procedure.

Results: There was virtually no change in the predictions made between phases by participants in the control group. There was no difference found between predictions made by the control group and the experimental group in Phase 1. There was a significant difference between predictions using Dragnet and predictions from both groups in Phase 1. Dragnet was more accurate than either group in that stage of the experiment. However the difference between predictions made by the control group and the experimental group in the second phase of the experiment was significant. The error distances for participants in the experimental group were not significantly different from the error distances produced by Dragnet. Thus participants who received a small amount of training on some basic geographic profiling techniques were on average as accurate as Dragnet. Although there was a general trend for the participants provided with heuristics to improve in their predictions, there were a number of spatial displays where there were no significant reductions in error distance after training. In the experimental group significant reductions in error distance were found between Phase 1 and Phase 2 but in half no such reduction was found. It was found that where there was no error reduction in the experimental group, this was because offenders were commuters and hence lived some distance away from their crime sites. Dragnet was also less accurate in predicting likely home location for these offenders. Where participants reported their heuristics in Phase 1, it was found that errors made were due to inappropriate heuristics such as participants guessing that a perpetrator would not have committed a crime close to his own home.

Discussion: This study shows that some of most frequently cited results in the research literature on offender spatial behaviour can be gained using people without special training so long as they are provided with appropriate heuristics. The power of heuristics appears to be that they focus the decision-making process of participants. Without this guidance participants reported using 'gut feelings', 'intuition' or 'experience' in their decision-making which may lead to variable and incorrect results. The study shows that there may be limited value in using specialised geographic profilers or computer-based packages as the study indicates that once basic processes underlying offenders' spatial behaviour are understood, untrained individuals may predict as successfully as trained individuals. In fact there may even be a risk that experienced criminal investigators may act with less objectivity and be misled by their experience.

Evaluation

Representativeness and generalisability

The researchers reported that the sample of cases was drawn at random from a larger database but that they could not be sure how **representative** the spatial displays were. However as they were random samples there is no reason to believe that they were unrepresentative. The researchers point out that the sample size of ten is quite small and might have been easily skewed by the number involving commuting offenders. The participants were of varied ages, both sexes and various nationalities. To this extent the results should be **generalisable**. However as the sample was all students, and mainly postgraduate students, it may be that the heuristics were learned and applied more easily than they might be by a more **representative** population.

3.1 Reaching a verdict: Persuading a jury
Key Study: 3.1.1 Order of testimony
Donald C. Pennington (1982), 'Witnesses and their testimony: Effects of ordering on juror verdicts', *Journal of Applied Social Psychology*, 12 (4), 318–33

Approach: Cognitive

Aim: To investigate the effects of order of witnesses and order of testimony in juror decision making

Hypothesis: That recency effects would be found with respect to witnesses and their testimony and their influence on jury decision making in a trial simulation involving traditional adversary protocol

Method: Laboratory experiment

Design: Independent measures

Type of sample: Not stated but presumably volunteer sample

Participants: Stage 1: 20 participants; Stage 2: 192 undergraduate students, 96 male, 96 female. All participants were eligible for jury service.

Procedure:

Stage 1

Scaling task

Twenty participants completed a scaling task in which they read the summarised transcript of a rape trial in the original order and classified the guilt/innocence of the two defendants, Bryce and Harrison, and also the guilt/innocence of each statement included in the testimony. Previous research indicated that most people believed Bryce to be innocent while verdicts concerning Harrison were more uncertain. The trial was transcribed from an audiotape originally lasting 2.5 hours which was summarised without changing the structure.

Stage 2

Forty-eight subjects were randomly assigned to one of four conditions (24 male, 24 female). The four conditions were: witness innocent; witness guilty; testimony innocent; testimony guilty. Witness order was varied by first determining the degree of guilt/innocence represented by each witness according to the scaling. All the prosecution witnesses fell into the guilty category and all the defence witnesses fell in to the innocent category, but within each category they were rated as indicating most guilt to least guilt or most innocence to least innocence. Testimony order manipulation was made by ordering the statements made by each witness from

strongest guilty to strongest innocence. Each participant received a booklet containing instructions, an account of the rape trial (identical apart from order of witness/testimony) and a questionnaire. Participants were instructed to read through the trial and answer the questionnaire. Participants were asked to make two kinds of judgements:

1) Whether they thought each of the two defendants was guilty of rape, attempted rape, or not guilty of either charge
2) To indicate on a 8-point scale how confident they were of their verdict where 1 = not confident at all and 8 = very confident

On average it took participants 45 minutes to read the summarised trial transcript and answer the questionnaire.

Results:

Verdicts

By far the greatest number of guilty verdicts on the charge of attempted rape was in the witness guilty-testimony guilty (WG-TG) condition. For Harrison the effect of ordering of witness and testimony did not affect the number of not guilty verdicts but the WG-TG condition produced greater numbers of guilty verdicts on the charge of rape and fewer numbers of guilty verdicts on the charge of attempted rape. For Bryce the number of guilty verdicts on the charge of rape did not differ significantly between conditions but the WG-TG condition produced a greater number of guilty verdicts for the charge of attempted rape and fewer not guilty verdicts than the other conditions.

Confidence levels

Both witness – guilty conditions (WG-TG and WG-TI) produced greater confidence in guilty verdicts and lowest confidence in not guilty verdicts.

Discussion: In contrast to the experimental hypothesis that recency effects would be found, in fact primacy effects were demonstrated. This is indicated by two findings with respect to verdicts;

Table 3.1 Effects of ordering

	Guilty of rape			
	WG–TG	WG–TI	WI–TG	WI–TI
Harrison	22	13	10	13
Bryce	4	4	3	5
	Guilty of attempted rape			
Harrison	14	22	23	21
Bryce	17	8	7	7
	Guilty of either rape or attempted rape			
Harrison	36	35	33	34
Bryce	21	12	10	12
	Not guilty			
Harrison	12	13	15	14
Bryce	27	36	38	36

Source: adapted from Pennington (1982)

the WG-TG condition produced the greatest number of guilty verdicts for Harrison on the charge of rape and the greatest number of guilty verdicts for Bryce when the charges of rape and attempted rape were combined. (See Table 3.1.)

Evaluation

Ecological validity

Pennington suggested that his findings of primacy effects reflected the fact that the study was designed to follow criminal courtroom protocol as much as possible. In other words he believed that the study has **high ecological validity**. Pennington highlighted two particular aspects of the study that may have led (in contrast to previous studies) to the finding of primacy effects:

1) The stimulus material was of considerable length and that perhaps this encourages primacy effects.

2) The type of case used – a rape trial – is emotive and may be more likely to give rise to strong feelings. Usually the victim of rape appears first in a rape trial, describing the incident and being cross-examined. This would lend their account a high degree of salience therefore facilitating recall.

continued...

Food for thought

Pennington has described how he attempted to recreate the protocol of the courtroom in his study. From this account of the procedure do you agree that the study has high **ecological validity?**

This key study is a **well-controlled** experiment involving a large number of participants within a framework that attempts to recreate accurately courtroom procedure. There seems little reason to doubt that it provides a **reliable** and **valid** test of the issue of effect of order of testimony on jury verdicts in the case reported. However, the results were not as expected as Pennington had hypothesised that he would find recency effects – that is that the last testimony heard would prove the most influential. Pennington argues that primacy effects may be more significant in cases where the testimony is highly vivid or emotionally laden (for example, a rape case) and in a lengthy trial (the participants read a relatively long trial account). Thus he suggests that his results may **not** be **generalisable** to other types of cases.

Elizabeth F. Loftus (1980), 'Impact of Expert Psychological Testimony on the unreliability of eyewitness identification', *Journal of Applied Psychology*, 65 (1), 9–15

Approach: Cognitive

Aim: To investigate the influence on jurors of expert testimony about eyewitness identification

Hypothesis 1

That expert psychological testimony might have a greater influence on jurors' attitudes to eyewitness testimony in violent crimes than non-violent crimes

Hypothesis 2

That jurors who are exposed to expert testimony about eyewitness testimony might pay more attention to eyewitness accounts

Method: Laboratory experiment

Design: Independent measures

Type of sample: Self-selecting sample

Participants: Experiment 1: 240 students at the University of Washington who volunteered to participate in return for course credits. Experiment 2: 120 students at the University of Washington who volunteered to participate in return for course credits. All participants were eligible for jury service.

Procedure:

Experiment 1

Two hundred and forty students were randomly assigned to four conditions. Half the participants read expert psychological testimony introduced by the defence, half did not. Within each of these conditions, half read a violent version of the crime while the other half read a non-violent version. The experiment took place in a laboratory. Participants took part in groups of 2–9. They were given a booklet containing instructions, a description of the crime, a summary of the trial and a questionnaire requesting a verdict. Expert testimony included information that people are less good at recognising members of another race (the testimony was from a white witness about a black assailant); and that other factors such as stress, the presence of a weapon and the fact that the witness had been drinking are factors known to interfere with accurate identification.

Results

The expert psychological testimony reduced the percentage of guilty verdicts from 58 per cent to 39 per cent. There were fewer guilty verdicts in the non-violent version than the violent one (41 per cent compared to 56 per cent). Expert testimony led to a 12 per cent reduction of guilty verdicts in the non-violent case as opposed to a 25 per cent reduction of guilty verdicts in the violent case.

Experiment 2

One hundred and twenty students participated in groups of six. In a laboratory they were told that the purpose of the study was to determine the nature of decision making in juries. They were given a booklet containing instructions, a description of the crime and a summary of the trial. Instead of reaching an individual verdict they were asked to deliberate for 30 minutes then asked for a group verdict. All participants read the violent version of the crime. Ten juries (composed of half of the participants) read the expert psychological testimony, ten did not. While each jury deliberated, observers with stopwatches listened in an adjoining room and with the use of stopwatches determined the amount of time spent discussing eyewitness testimony. After 30 minutes, if a verdict had not been reached deliberations were terminated.

Results

In the absence of expert testimony, seven juries voted to convict, two to acquit and one failed to reach a verdict. When expert testimony had been heard, the conviction rate was lower. Three voted to convict, four to acquit and three were unable to reach a verdict. The latter finding may be due to the fact that more time was spent discussing eyewitness testimony, in these groups. In the presence of expert testimony, the juries spent over 10 minutes on average discussing eyewitness testimony whereas in the absence of expert testimony, they spent an average of 7 minutes.

Discussion: Expert testimony on the subject of eyewitness identification influenced behaviour of jurors in two ways. It promoted discussion of the eyewitness evidence and appeared to increase doubts about the defendant's guilt. The aim of course of such testimony is to encourage jurors to be more cautious in basing verdicts on such evidence. However this raises the possibility not only that the innocent will go free but that the guilty will also! As Loftus points out, it is not the aim of the expert psychologist to reduce guilty verdicts but to ensure that jurors base decisions on the best possible understanding of the evidence in front of them. Clearly the word of an expert is influential, and, as Loftus accepts, if each side brings in their own expert, this may lead to a 'battle of the experts' and as a result issues may become further confused rather than clarified.

For a newspaper report on the potential effects of expert testimony see *Psychology A2 for OCR* textbook, p.57.

Evaluation

Validity

Loftus's study is a **well-controlled**, easily **replicable** experiment involving a large number of participants. The findings appear to be **reliable**. However there is one important difference with a real trial. If an expert witness appeared for the defence in a real trial, that witness would have had to have undergone cross-examination by prosecuting counsel. Also the prosecution may have presented their own expert witness who may have presented a different view of the reliability of eyewitness evidence. Thus although Loftus in this experiment has shown the persuasive nature of clear, one-sided expert testimony, she has not replicated fully real trial conditions and therefore not examined the effects of expert testimony once the expertise of the expert has been challenged. This gives the study **low ecological validity** and therefore might bring into question the overall **validity** of the study. However there are real life case studies that support Loftus's research and indicate that her results may be **generalisable** to the courtroom.

Key Study: 3.1.3 Inadmissible testimony

Kerri L. Pickel (1995), 'Inducing jurors to disregard inadmissible evidence: a legal explanation does not help', *Law and Human Behaviour*, 19 (4), 407–23

Approach: Cognitive

Aim: To investigate the influence on jurors of testimony ruled inadmissible by a judge

Hypothesis: That jurors will find it difficult to ignore evidence of a previous conviction even when instructed to do so by a judge

Method: Laboratory experiment

Design: Independent measures

Type of sample: Self-selecting sample

Participants: 236 psychology students from Ball State University who participated in partial fulfilment of a course requirement

Procedure: Participants were randomly allocated to one of eight conditions. They listened to an audiotape of a fictional theft trial and then completed a questionnaire asking them to make several decisions about the case. There were eight different versions of the audiotape. The first independent variable was admissibility of evidence. The witness statement was either ruled admissible by reason of reference to the defendant's credibility (i.e. not his character) or it was ruled inadmissible. There were two inadmissible conditions. In one, the defence attorney objected to the evidence and the judge sustained the objection and instructed the jury to ignore the evidence. In the other, there was the same sequence of events but the judge explained the legal basis for the ruling before telling the prosecution to continue. There was also a control condition in which the evidence of a previous conviction was not disclosed. A second independent variable was witness credibility – high or low. The two independent variables produced in combination eight different conditions altogether (for example, altogether evidence admissible/ witness credibility high). Participants were asked to provide a verdict; an estimate of the probability of the defendant's guilt; a rating on a 10-point scale of the extent to which the evidence of a prior conviction caused them to believe that the defendant was guilty; and a rating on a 7-point scale of the credibility of each witness.

Results: The percentage of guilty verdicts was highest in the admissible condition (64 per cent) and lowest in the control (42 per cent) and inadmissible without explanation conditions (43 per cent). However in the inadmissible with explanation condition, the percentage of guilty verdicts was 55 per cent. This showed that jurors were less able or willing to forget the critical evidence following the judge's legal explanation as to why they should do so. The credibility of the witness was also significant. More participants chose a guilty verdict when that witness's credibility was high rather than low. Probability estimates of defendant's guilt were affected by both independent variables. It was found that the defendant's credibility was not altered by admissibility condition which shows that participants did not use the critical evidence as an indication of honesty (therefore it can be inferred that they used it instead as evidence of 'bad character' which they had been instructed not to do).

Discussion: The results showed that most participants were willing to accept a judge's ruling that a particular piece of evidence they had heard should be disregarded. However when a legal explanation was provided they were unable to disregard the critical evidence completely. Pickel felt that the judge's explanation might draw attention to the critical evidence and make it harder for the jury to forget what they had heard.

Evaluation

Ecological validity

Although efforts were made to make the design of this study as realistic as possible, it suffers from the same drawbacks as other studies using mock trial evidence and mock jurors, that is, it lacks **ecological validity.** It may be that people make different decisions when taking part in a research study from those they would reach in a real court room situation when a defendant's freedom or even his life is contingent on their verdict.

3.2 Reaching a verdict: Witness appeal
Key Study: 3.2.1 Attractiveness of the defendant

Wilbur A. Castellow, Karl L. Wuensch, Charles H. Moore (1990), 'Effects of physical attractiveness of the plaintiff and defendant in a sexual harassment case', *Journal of Social Behavior and Personality*, 5 (6), 547–62

Approach: Cognitive

Aim: To investigate using a mock trial simulation the effects of physical attractiveness of the defendant and the plaintiff on jury decision-making

Hypothesis: That physical attractiveness would reduce the frequency of guilty verdicts/length of sentences recorded by participants

Method: Laboratory experiment

Design: Independent measures

Hypothesis 1 That an attractive defendant would be found guilty less frequently than an unattractive one

Hypothesis 2 That an attractive plaintiff would arouse a positive response, leading to a higher frequency of guilty verdicts

Hypothesis 3 That physical attractiveness of the plantiff/defendant would only have a significant effect on male participants

Type of sample: self-selecting

Participants: Undergraduates (71 male; 74 female) registered for psychology classes at the University of East Carolina who participated in return for course credits

Procedure: There were three independent variables: gender of participant; attractiveness of defendant and attractiveness of plaintiff. This produced four different conditions (male participant/attractive defendant/unattractive plaintiff; male participant/unattractive defendant/attractive plaintiff; female participant/attractive defendant/unattractive plaintiff; female participant/unattractive defendant/attractive plaintiff). Attractiveness of defendants and plaintiffs was established by asking other students (91 female; 58 male) to rate 120 male and female faces on a 9-point scale from very unattractive to very attractive. The lowest- and highest-scoring females and males were then selected for the four attractiveness conditions. Participants were asked to read a summary of a sexual harassment case that was constructed by the experimenters but based on two real life cases in which a male employer was accused of sexually harassing his female employee. In the final part of the summary, summations of both the plaintiff's and defendant's counsel were provided. The plaintiff's counsel argued that the defendant

was guilty as charged of sexual harassment and that the plaintiff should be awarded substantial damages, whereas the defendant's counsel argued that his client had been the subject of a vindictive woman's false accusations and should be found innocent of sexual harassment. The main dependent variable was response to the question 'Do you think that Mr R. is guilty of sexual harassment?' to which the response required was yes/no. Participants were also asked to rate both the defendant and the plaintiff on eleven 9-point bi-polar adjective scales, for example dull–exciting; warm–cold. The adjectives dealt with general personality characteristics and were based on previous research.

Results: The first two hypotheses were supported, that is attractiveness of the defendant and the plaintiff had a significant effect on mock juror verdicts. The third hypothesis was not upheld as physical attractiveness was seen to have an effect on the judgements of both male and female participants.

Table 3.2 Percentage of participants voting guilty

	Defendant	
	Attractive	**Unattractive**
Attractive plaintiff		
Female participants	70	84
Male participants	72	81
All	71	83
Unattractive plaintiff		
Female participants	56	76
Male participants	26	61
All	41	69

Source: adapted from Castellow *et al.* (1990)

Both male and female participants rated the attractive defendant higher on all eleven personality variables. Two effects of gender were found. Male participants rated the attractive plaintiff as more sincere than the unattractive plaintiff while female participants did not. Male participants rated the defendant as more calm and the plaintiff as less sincere and less warm than did female participants. Female participants rated the unattractive plaintiff more favourably than male participants. However this did not carry over to a higher frequency of guilty verdicts.

Discussion: The results show that in a sexual harassment case, jurors may be influenced by the physical attractiveness of both the defendant and the plaintiff. The fact that there was no effect of gender of participant on frequency of guilty verdicts shows that the 'halo effect' of attractiveness is a robust finding in terms of both male and female mock jurors. Even where the female participants may have identified with the female plaintiff (shown by their more favourable personality ratings with regard to the unattractive plaintiff), the attractiveness effect was sufficiently strong to overcome empathy bias.

Evaluation

Generalisability, sample issues and ecological validity

As the authors of this study indicate, their findings can only be **generalised** to cases in which jurors may assume (rightly or wrongly) that attractiveness may have played a part in the offence, for example sexual harassment or rape cases. Evidence from other studies indicates that where jurors do not see attractiveness of the defendant or plaintiff as a relevant issue, for example burglary, they may be able to disregard physical attractiveness in reaching a verdict. Also the participants were all undergraduate students at one university so the sample would not have been **representative** of the wider population.

In terms of **ecological validity**, the same criticisms can be made of this study as of most of the other key studies involving mock juries. The study lacks ecological validity because mock jurors read a transcript with a photograph attached rather than seeing for example a mock trial with actors playing the parts of the defendant and plaintiff. Also as the participants were aware that this was an experiment, they knew that nothing rested on their decision – this was not a 'high stakes' situation – and therefore we do not know whether the results can be generalised to a real life case.

3.2 Reaching a verdict: Witness appeal
Key Study: 3.2.2 Witness confidence

Jacqueline M. Wheatcroft, Graham F. Wagstaff and Mark R. Kebbels (2004), 'The influence of courtroom questioning style on actual and perceived eyewitness confidence and accuracy', *Legal and Criminological Psychology*, 9, 83–101

Approach: Cognitive

Aim: To investigate the effects of examination style on witness confidence and accuracy and the effects on jurors' perceptions of witness confidence and accuracy

Study 1

Method: Laboratory experiment

Design: Independent measures (between-subjects and within-subjects design)

> ### Stretch and Challenge
>
> At AS you will have met the main different types of experimental design (independent measures, repeated measures and matched pairs). However experimental design is actually more complex than this and an experiment may involve elements of both independent samples and repeated measures. 'Between-subjects' analyses can be made (comparing results of different groups of participants in different conditions) and 'within-subjects' analyses can be made (comparing the same participants' responses in different conditions).

Type of sample: Opportunity sample

Participants: Students and researchers at the University of Liverpool (60 participants; 12 male; 48 female)

Procedure: Participants were randomly assigned to one of three conditions; a 'lawyerese' condition; a 'lawyerese with negative feedback' condition and a control condition.

Participants watched a videotape of a simulated crime scene of an abduction and then responded to a series of questions to which they had to answer 'yes' or 'no' and also rate their confidence in the response they had given on a 9-point Likert scale ranging (where 1 = pure guess and 9 = absolutely certain). Some of the questions were rated 'easy', for example, 'Did two men carry out the attack?'. Some were rated 'moderately difficult' and others were rated difficult, for example, 'Would you say that this car had four doors?' In the control condition participants were asked straight questions, while in the

'lawyerese' condition, the questions were phrased so as to replicate cross-examinations in court. The questions became: 'Do you also remember that two men carried out the attack on the victim?' and 'Isn't it also right this car had four doors?' These phrases prompted more affirmative responses than in the control condition. In the 'lawyerese with negative feedback' condition the same procedure was followed but subtle negative feedback was applied to each 'no' answer in order to question the reliability of the response, for example 'Is it possible that you might be mistaken. . .?'

Results:

Witness accuracy

- There was no significant main effect on witness accuracy for questioning type on the 'easy' or 'moderate' items but there was a significant main effect for the 'difficult' items. The mean accuracy score for the 'lawyerese with negative feedback' condition on difficult items was significantly lower than in the control condition.

Accuracy-confidence correlations

- The only significant overall correlation was a between-subjects correlation between accuracy and confidence for witnesses in the 'lawyerese with negative feedback' condition.
- For 'difficult' questions there was a significant main effect for within-subjects confidence-accuracy correlations as the relationship for 'lawyerese' questioning was significantly poorer than in the other two conditions.

> ### Stretch and Challenge
> #### Main effects and interactions
>
> The **main effect** of an independent variable is the effect of that variable averaging over all levels of other variables in an experiment.
>
> Two independent variables **interact** if the effect of one of the variables differs depending on the level of the other variable

Discussion: Questioning style did not generally affect witnesses' recall accuracy. However mean accuracy score for the 'lawyerese with negative feedback' condition on difficult questions was significantly lower than in the control conditions, showing that this style of questioning led to witnesses doubting their recall. For difficult questions the 'lawyerese' questioning did not reduce accuracy but it lowered within-subjects confidence-accuracy correlations, showing that it led witnesses to be over-confident in the accuracy of their answers.

Study 2

Method: Laboratory experiment

Design: Independent measures (between-subjects and within-subjects design)

Type of sample: Opportunity sample

Participants: 60 students from the University of Liverpool (19 male, 41 female); none of whom had participated in the first study

Procedure: Participants were randomly assigned to the same three conditions as in the first study ('lawyerese'; 'lawyerese with negative feedback'; control). Participants in all conditions heard recordings of each of two witnesses (one good/one poor witness) in the condition allocated, then responded to the following questions: a) How accurate do you think the witness was? b) How confident do you think the witness was? Participants were asked to rate the witnesses on a 9-point Likert scale, ranging from 1 – extremely inaccurate/unconfident to 9 – extremely accurate/confident.

Results:

Main findings:

- A significant main effect was observed for good/poor witness with accuracy ratings higher for the good witness.
- The interaction between order of testimony and good/poor witness was significant. The good witness was rated significantly higher in accuracy than the poor witness when presented first, but no difference between good and poor witnesses was found when the poor witness was presented first.
- A significant interaction was found for questioning style x good/poor witness. Mean accuracy ratings were significantly higher in the control and 'lawyerese' conditions for the good

witness but not in the 'lawyerese with negative feedback' condition.

Discussion: Study 2 shows that mock jurors were able to discriminate between accurate and inaccurate witnesses in the control and 'lawyerese' conditions but not in the 'lawyerese with negative feedback' condition. This suggests that their discriminations were based primarily on differences in perceived confidence. Successful inferences about relative confidence and accuracy disappeared when the poor/less confident witness was interviewed first which may be a primacy effect.

Evaluation

Ecological validity

Various features of this study were unlike a real-life courtroom situation, hence lowering the **ecological validity** of the study potentially affecting the findings. The main accuracy findings related only to the category of 'difficult' items but in a real life situation, the effect might be more pronounced as the easy items in the simulation were probably much easier to remember than under courtroom conditions. Also in Study 2 jurors only had verbal report to go on, while in a real courtroom there would be many factors on which to base judgement of confidence (for example, body language; tone of voice). However these limitations suggest that the findings of this study may underestimate the effects of questioning style on witness accuracy and confidence and jurors' judgements.

Key Study: 3.2.3 Effect of shields and videotape on children giving evidence

David F. Ross *et al.* (1994), 'The impact of protective shields and videotape testimony on conviction rates in a simulated trial of child sexual abuse', *Law and Human Behavior*, 18 (5), 553–66

Approach: Cognitive

Experiment 1

Aim: To investigate using a mock trial simulation the effects of different modalities of child testimony (open court/protective shield/video recording) on jury verdicts

Hypothesis 1 That modality of child testimony will have an impact on verdicts returned by mock jurors

Hypothesis 2 That modality of child testimony will have an effect on credibility of the child witness

Method: Laboratory experiment

Design: Independent measures

Type of sample: Not stated (presumably self-selecting sample)

Participants: 300 US college students (150 male; 150 female) from an introductory psychology class. The majority were white middle class.

Procedure: Participants watched a videotape simulation of a sexual abuse trial in which a 10-year-old child testified in one of three different modalities:

1) In open court directly confronting the defendant randomly allocated.
2) In the court with a protective shield placed between the child and the defendant.
3) Outside the court on a video monitor.

The trial was based on actual court transcript and videotaped in a courtroom by a film company using professional actors and actresses. The case involved an accusation of sexual abuse by the girl against her father. The researcher did not provide information concerning the age of the actress who played the child witness. The child was the first to testify, followed by an expert witness for the prosecution, the child's mother, the defendant and an expert witness for the defence. The testimony was exactly the same in all three conditions except that in the video and shield conditions, the judge warned the jury that the use of those devices should not in any way be taken to imply that the defendant was guilty. After viewing the trial, the participants indicated whether the defendant was guilty or not guilty and rated the credibility of the child witness and the defendant on a 7-point Likert scale.

Results: The modality of the child's testimony did not have a significant effect on conviction rates

Table 3.3 Conviction rates by modality of child's testimony (Experiment 1)

	Open court	Shield	Testimony
Guilty	51 %	46 %	49 %
Not guilty	49 %	54 %	51 %

However gender of the juror had a significant impact; 59 per cent of female jurors returned a guilty verdict as compared to 39 per cent of the male jurors. Modality of testimony did not influence jurors' perceptions of the defendant's or the child witness's credibility. However there was again a main effect of sex, with female participants rating the child witness as more credible and the defendant as less credible than did male participants.

Experiment 2

Aim: To investigate using a mock trial simulation the effects of different modalities of child testimony (open court/protective shield/video recording) on jury verdicts when the trial was stopped immediately after the child witness testified

Hypothesis 1: That modality of child testimony will have an impact on verdicts returned by mock jurors if the trial is stopped immediately after the testimony

Hypothesis 2: That modality of child testimony will have an effect on credibility of the child witness if the trial is stopped immediately after the testimony

Method: Laboratory experiment

Design: Independent measures

Type of sample: Not stated (presumably self-selecting sample)

Participants: 300 US college students (150 male; 150 female) from an introductory psychology class. The majority were white middle class.

Procedure: Procedure was the same as in Experiment 1 apart from the fact that the trial was stopped in all conditions immediately after the child witness had given her testimony. Although participants did not hear the defendant's testimony, they were still asked to rate his credibility on the basis of the child witness's testimony. Participants were randomly assigned to five conditions: open court; shield with judge's warning; shield without judge's warning; videotape with judge's warning; and videotape without judge's warning.

Results: Preliminary analysis revealed no effect of judge's warning so for the rest of the analysis the data were collapsed across this variable. In contrast to Experiment 1, modality of the child's testimony had a significant impact on conviction rates. Participants in the open court condition were significantly more likely to convict the defendant than in either the shield or the videotape condition.

Table 3.4 Conviction rates by modality of child's testimony (Experiment 2)

	Open court	Shield	Testimony
Guilty	77 %	65 %	61 %
Not guilty	23 %	35 %	39 %

There was no effect of modality on perceived defendant credibility but there was again a significant main effect for sex of juror. As in Experiment 1, female participants rated the defendant as significantly less credible than did male participants. Neither modality nor sex of participant had a significant effect on perceived credibility of the child witness.

Discussion: The results of Experiment 2 indicate that mock jurors were less likely to convict the defendant when the child testified using a protective device – especially in the videotape condition, thus suggesting that the use of protective device may work on behalf of the defendant. This poses a legal dilemma as it raised the issue of how to ensure the psychological safety of the child witness without biasing the trial process against either party, with the more likely risk apparently being in the direction of reducing conviction rates of defendants. However the results of Experiment 1 show that the effects of shielding a child may be reduced once all the other testimony is taken into consideration.

Evaluation

Sample issues and ecological validity

The sample was a large one but it was composed entirely of students of mainly white middle-class background. This may reduce the **generalisability** of the results. Also, as the researchers state, the fact that the simulation was not live but that all three conditions were observed on videotape by mock jurors reduces the **ecological validity** of this study. However the researchers suggest that they would expect that a live simulation would increase the strength of the finding that jurors may be less likely to convict when a child gives evidence using a shield or video testimony.

3.3 Reaching a verdict

Key Study: 3.3.2 Majority influence

Solomon E. Asch (1955), 'Opinions and social pressure', *Scientific American*, November Issue, 2–8

Approach: Social

Aim: To investigate the extent to which social forces constrain people's opinions (social conformity)

Method: Laboratory experiment

Design: Independent measures

Type of sample: Not stated but presumably self-selecting sample

Participants: 123 students from three institutions of higher learning in the United States

Procedure: The experiment was run on 123 occasions. Each time the same procedure was followed. A group of 7–9 students were assembled in a classroom, all of whom were confederates apart from the one genuine naive participant. They were told they were taking part in an experiment on visual judgement. The students were first shown a white card with a single vertical black line. From a second card with three lines they were asked to choose the line that was the same length as the line on the first card. The students announced their answers one at a time, in the order in which they were seated. The last student was the real participant. The first two times this is done, all the confederates were instructed to give the correct answer. However on the third occasion the confederates had been instructed as to how to answer. Either they all gave the same wrong answer or most of them gave the same wrong answer with one or two giving the correct answer. This was repeated 18 times with each of the 123 participants and on 12 of the 18 trials the majority responded erroneously. In one series of trials the size of the opposition was varied from 1 to 13 persons. In another series the participant was given the support of a truthful partner. In another version of the experiment, one of the confederates was instructed to disagree with the majority but to also disagree with the naive participant by selecting a line that was different from that chosen by the majority but not the correct response.

Results: Asch reported that in ordinary trials participants matching lines will make mistakes less than 1 per cent of the time. He found across his trials that the minority participants swung to acceptance of the misleading majority's judgement in 37 per cent of the selections. There was a large range in individual differences in responses. At one extreme about one quarter of participants showed complete independence and never agreed with the erroneous judgements of the majority. At the other extreme, some individuals went with the majority nearly all the time. In the series in which the size of the opposition was varied, there was a clear effect of the manipulation. When a participant was confronted with just one individual who contradicted his/her answers, they continued to answer independently and correctly in nearly all trials. When the confederate group size was increased to two, minority participants accepted the wrong answer 14 per cent of the time. When the participant was faced with three confederates giving an erroneous answer, the participants' errors jumped to 32 per cent. However increasing the size of the majority beyond this did not have a significant effect on participants' responses. In the series where the participant was given a truthful partner, this had a significant effect on group dynamics. Participants answered incorrectly only one quarter as often in this condition. In the condition where a confederate was told to choose an alternative wrong answer, it was found that this encouraged independence and errors dropped to only 9 per cent.

Discussion: The findings showed how unwilling most people are to go against the verdict of the majority. There are two ways of interpreting Asch's results. Either 1) Participants lacked confidence in their own judgement and accepted the judgement of others despite the fact that everybody else's judgement clearly appeared incorrect or 2) They were not really swayed into believing that their judgement was wrong but nevertheless chose to go along with the erroneous verdict of others in order to fit in/avoid embarrassment, etc. In debriefing after the experiment, Asch found that many of the individuals suspected that the majority were 'sheep' following the first responder but despite this suspicion they could not bring themselves to show disagreement with the majority. All the participants who conformed underestimated the frequency with which they conformed.

Evaluation

Debates: Individual vs situational

This experiment highlights the fact that humans are social beings and that their behaviour is best understood in terms of social interactions. This lends support to **situational** explanations of behaviour. If asked as **individuals** the participants would have made the right call, but in a **situation** where other people around them were mainly or unanimously giving erroneous judgements, many participants conformed against their better judgement. This was true even of participants who continued to believe that their judgement was correct. On the other hand this experiment provides evidence for the importance of **individual differences**. Participants varied considerably in their reactions to the pressures towards conformity and a quarter proved themselves to be able to maintain consistent independence of thought.

3.3

3.3 Reaching a verdict
Key Study: 3.3.3 Minority influence
Russell D. Clark (1998), 'Minority influence: the role of the rate of majority defection and persuasive arguments', *European Journal of Social Psychology*, 28, 787–96

Approach: Social

Method: Laboratory experiment

Design: Independent measures

Type of sample: Not stated but either opportunity or self-selecting sample

Participants: 270 students from two US universities (150 male; 120 female)

Procedure: Participants were randomly allocated to different conditions. The experiment was a 2x2x5 **factorial design**. The factors were gender (x 2 – naturally occurring difference), high/low persuasiveness (x 2, random allocation) and no jury verdict/jury verdict, no change/jury verdict slow change/jury verdict moderate change/jury verdict fast change (x 5, random allocation).

Stretch and Challenge

Factorial experiments

What is a 2x2x5 factorial design experiment? This is the term used in statistics to describe an experiment, the design of which consists of two or more factors, each with a number of discrete levels and in which analysis can be run on all possible combinations of these levels across all the factors. Such an experiment allows studying the effect of each factor on the dependent variable, as well as the effects of interactions between factors on the dependent variable. In most factorial experiments each factor has only two levels, for example gender (male/ female). With two factors each at two levels, the experiment would have four conditions in all. Clark's experiment is unusual in having five levels of one factor. This could probably have been simplified into three factors which might have given clearer results (no jury verdict, unchanging jury verdict and moderately fast changing verdict).

Participants were asked to read an account of a real first degree murder case, in which a young man was accused of murdering his father. The account consisted of one page of factual information about the case in which the evidence against the defendant was summarised, followed by three pages summarising jury deliberations. There were ten different versions of the jury discussions. Half the

accounts presented arguments high in persuasion from a minority jury member who unequivocally refuted the evidence against the defendant. In the other half, the low-persuasion condition, the minority jury member consistently argued against the evidence without categorically refuting it. Each of these versions had the further level of jury verdict. In one fifth there was a no verdict given; in another fifth a verdict was given that remained unchanged during the deliberations; and in the other three conditions verdicts were given but they changed at different points during the deliberations (slow/ moderate/fast). In all the conditions (apart from no jury verdict) the jury's verdict was given at four different times: after the end of the summary of the evidence against the defendant and after the jury's summary discussion of each piece of evidence. In the no change condition the jury vote was given as 11 (guilty):1 (innocent) each time. In the slow change condition the vote went 11:1; 10:2; 6:6; 0:12. In the moderate change condition the vote went 11:1; 7:5; 3:9; 0:12. In the fast change condition the vote went 11:1; 4:8; 1:11; 0:12. Participants were asked to estimate guilt of the defendant on a 9-point scale where 1 = definitely innocent and 9 = definitely guilty at four different points during their reading of the summary.

Results: For each participant three difference scores were computed for the guilt measures. The first difference score was computed by subtracting the second guilt measure from the first; the second by subtracting the third guilt measure from the first; the third difference score was the fourth guilt measure subtracted from the first guilt measure. The larger the difference score, the greater the minority influence. It was found that participants were more influenced by the minority when it provided persuasive arguments by refuting the majority viewpoint than when the minority simply argued against guilt without refuting the evidence. More minority influence occurred when the minority obtained majority defectors than when the minority did not. It was further found that the rate of majority defection made a difference. Minority influence was not obtained with the initial acquisition of a single defector and the significant influence that occurred with the acquisition of four defectors was not further increased by the acquisition of additional defectors.

Discussion: Participants were clearly influenced by both the jurors' decisions and the persuasiveness of the minority's arguments. The failure to find any increase in minority influence when only one majority member defected to the minority is not consistent with other studies. Clark hypothesised that this inconsistency may be the outcome of the large group (12) as most previous research has been based on the influence of minorities on smaller groups. It may be that it takes more than one defector to threaten majority confidence in their position in a group of jury size. If this is the case, then it may well be that the historical use of 10:2 as the level at which a majority verdict may be obtained is based on sound psychology. If the minority has a good case, it should be possible for them to secure additional defections from the majority. If the majority were to move too easily to the minority position, it might cast doubt on the effectiveness of the jury system.

Evaluation

Individual vs situational

This study taken together with Key Study 3.3.2 provides useful support for the importance of **situational** influences on behaviour. If each individual were to remain an island, unaffected by the views of his/her fellow jury members/neighbours, and so on, the result would probably be anarchy. Majority rule, but with the majority open to persuasive arguments from the minority might seem to be a sensible way of both reaching jury decisions and running society generally.

4.1 After a guilty verdict: Imprisonment
Key Study: 4.1.1 Planned behaviours once freed from jail

David P. Farrington, John Ditchfield, Philip Howard and Darrick Joliffe (2002),
'Two intensive regimes for young offenders: a follow-up evaluation', *Home Office, Research, Development and Statistics Directorate, Research Findings* 163, 1–4

Approach: Behaviourist

Aim: To evaluate two intensive regimes for young offenders based on behaviourist methods

Method: Field experiment

Design: Independent measures

Type of sample: Opportunity sample

Participants: Young male offenders with approximately six months sentence left to serve who were suitable for open conditions and were screened and found able mentally and physically to cope with the intervention regime. Each intervention group was compared with a control group of young offenders with a similar profile who were not selected for any intervention but left to serve their sentence in custody. Total number of participants at Thorn Cross, n = 175 (control group, n = 127); total number in Colchester programme, n = 61 (control group, n = 97).

Procedure: Both regimes were physically demanding. Thorn Cross was based on a 16-hour day including basic classroom skills; vocational training; life and social skills training; and a community release work placement. The Colchester regime was based at a Military Corrective Training Centre and was run and staffed by Army personnel as well as prison personnel. It consisted of three stages, starting with a very strict routine of drilling and no access to television or telephone and gradually providing increased privileges.

A common core of psychological tests was used to assess the impact of the interventions on participants' attitudes and behaviour and an extra Attitude Survey was specially designed for the Colchester intervention.

Results:

- **Psychological evaluation:** tests on the Thorn Cross participants at the beginning and end of the intervention showed no significant differences between the experimental group and the control group in 'before and after' performance. There was little difference between the Colchester participants and their control group, with the exception that the Attitude Survey showed that the Colchester participants became less unhappy, felt more

physically fit and in better health than the controls and were more hopeful about the future.

- **Two-year reconviction rates:** the intervention groups and control groups were not sufficiently well matched for meaningful comparison therefore the findings are based on comparing actual rates of reoffending in each intervention group and control group with predicted rates.

Thorn Cross: percentage of offenders in both the experimental and control groups who were reconvicted was similar to the predicted percentage for both groups but the average time between release and reoffending was significantly longer for the intervention group. During the two-year follow-up period, young offenders in the Thorn Cross programme on average committed significantly fewer offences leading to reconvictions than control young offenders. Based on Home Office estimates, participants in the Thorn Cross intervention each cost society approximately £2500 less than control offenders (taking into account regime cost and cost of reconviction).

Table 4.1 Thorn Cross reconvictions

	Experimental group N = 175	Control group N = 127
Predicted conviction rate	66%	75%
Actual conviction rate	65%	76%
Average number of days between release and reoffending	228	177
Average number of offences during two-year period	3.5	5
Approximate average cost per young offender	£7500	£10 000

NB It is important to compare predicted and actual conviction rates within each group rather than actual conviction rates of each group.

Source: adapted from Farrington *et al.* (2002)

Colchester: Reconviction rates for both the experimental and control groups were lower than expected. Average time between release and reoffending was similar for both groups. During the two-year follow-up period, the Colchester participants committed fewer offences on average than those in the control group. However the average cost to society per person was very slightly higher for those in the experimental group than the control group, primarily because they committed more costly (violent) offences. After adjusting for the fact that the experimental group were of lower risk, the average extra cost amounted to £850.

Table 4.2 Colchester reconvictions

	Experimental group N = 61	Control group N = 97
Predicted conviction rate	51%	58%
Actual conviction rate	44%	53%
Average number of days between release and reoffending	226	219
Average number of offences during two-year period	1.5	2
Approximate average cost per young offender	£4650	£3800

NB It is important to compare predicted and actual conviction rates within each group rather than actual conviction rates of each group

Source: adapted from Farrington *et al.* (2002)

Discussion: The authors of this Key Study concluded that Thorn Cross was a success because of the longer mean period before reconviction in the experimental group than the control group and because the intervention saved money. The Colchester programme, which relied heavily on military drilling and physical training, did not in the researchers' assessment have a significant effect on reconviction rates and was expensive.

Evaluation

Matching issues and validity of findings

It is unfortunate that the experimenters were unable to match the participants more effectively. The fact that calculations were based on comparing expected (predicted) values and actual values for each group undermines the **validity** of the findings because it means that in part what is being tested is the way in which reoffending rates are estimated rather than the effects of the interventions alone. Thorn Cross was apparently a success because of the longer period before reconviction for the Thorn Cross participants as compared to their controls. However it is clear that these two groups were not well matched as the predicted and actual reconviction rates were both significantly lower for the experimental group than for the control group and this difference could explain the shorter period before reconviction in the experimental group. Also although the authors did not judge the Colchester intervention a success on the basis that both the control and experimental group reoffended at lower rates than expected, the difference between predicted and actual reconviction rate was greater for the experimental group and it is therefore not clear why this intervention was not regarded as a success other than for the reason that it was an expensive option. It is unfortunate that the interesting findings with regard to the Colchester Attitude Survey were not discussed further by the authors as this does seem to give clear self-report evidence for the effectiveness of the intervention.

Key Study: 4.1.2 Depression/suicide risk in jail

Emma J. Palmer and Rachael Connelly (2005), 'Depression, hopelessness and suicide ideation among vulnerable prisoners', *Criminal Behaviour and Mental Health*, 15 (3), 164–70

Approach: Individual differences

Aim: To compare depressive characteristics of prisoners who report previous self-harm with those who do not

Method: Self-report

Design: Independent measures

Type of sample: Opportunity sample

Participants: The researchers approached adult male prisoners in a Category B local prison in England who were new to custody and asked whether they would be willing to participate in the study. Over 100 prisoners gave their consent, of whom 24 were identified who reported previous self-harm. A group of 24 prisoners was drawn from the remaining volunteers. This group was matched on mean age, ethnic origin, penal status (on remand or convicted, offence type, whether they had previously been in custody and number of previous custodial sentences. Statistical analyses revealed no significant differences between the groups on any of the variables.

Measures:

Beck Hopelessness Scale (Beck, 1978)

This was developed to assess extent of negative expectancies about the immediate and long-term future. It is composed of 20 items scored either 1 (hopelessness) or 0 (non-hopelessness). A score higher than 14 indicates severe hopelessness.

Beck Depression Inventory II (Beck, 1996)

This was developed to assess level of depressive symptoms. It is composed of 21 items (each rated on a 4-point scale from 0 (not depressive) to 3 (3 = depressive) and is scored by summing the ratings (maximum = 63). Severe depression is indicated by a score greater than 28.

Beck Scale for Suicide Ideation (Beck, 1991)

This was developed to assess suicide intent and ideation (thoughts). The first five items serve as a screen for suicide ideation. If a participant scores on these items, they are then required to respond to the following 14 items which refer to specific information about the respondent's plans and attitudes. At the end of the questionnaire are two questions referring to actual suicide attempts. Responses to the first 19 items are summed and the higher the score, the greater the suicidal risk.

Table 4.3 Mean scores of prisoners with and without self-harm history on the self-report measures

Scale	Vulnerable prisoners N = 24	Control group N = 24
Beck Hopelessness Scale	10	6
Beck Depression Inventory II	27	15
Beck Suicidal Ideation Inventory	6	1

Source: adapted from Palmer and Connelly (2005)

Results: Mean scores of the group with self-harm history were higher on all measures than the control group. One-way analyses of variance were conducted which showed that the difference between groups was significant on each scale.

Discussion: The results clearly showed that the prisoners with a previous history of self-harm were significantly more vulnerable than controls. This suggests that such prisoners should be identified and monitored during their period of imprisonment.

Evaluation

Individual/situational

Assessments were conducted on arrival and it may be that the results reflect the fact that the initial period of imprisonment is the most stressful period and that individuals who have conducted self-harm and/or exhibited suicidal behaviours may be particularly unable to cope with this initial stress. If this is the case the results may reflect an interaction between state and trait hopelessness/depressed mood. This means that it is not possible to distinguish between **individual** and **situational** factors on the basis of this research. As the authors suggest, future research should be conducted after a period in which the prisoners have settled. Of course the whole situation of imprisonment must contribute to feelings of depression but this effect may be exacerbated during the initial phase of confinement.

Key Study: 4.1.3 The prison situation and roles

Craig Haney, Curtis Banks and Philip Zimbardo (1973), 'A study of prisoners and guards in a simulated prison', *Naval Research Reviews*, 30 (9)

Approach: Social

Aim: To investigate the dispositional (situational) explanation of the behaviour of guards and prisoners in a simulated prison environment

Method: Field experiment

Design: Independent measures

Type of sample: Self-selecting sample

Participants: 22 well-adjusted male students selected from 75 volunteers who had undergone a series of psychological tests to establish physical and mental stability

Procedure: Prisoners were randomly allocated to guard and prisoner conditions, having agreed to play whatever role was allocated them for up to two weeks. The prisoners were kept in a simulated prison.

Prisoners remained in the prison throughout the study. Guards worked three-man eight-hour shifts, going about their normal lives for the remainder of the time.

The guards were told that they could maintain a reasonable degree of order and should deal appropriately with any situation that arose. They mistakenly believed that the focus of the study was prisoner behaviour. Guards dressed in military style clothing and had whistles, police night sticks and reflective sunglasses. At the beginning of the study the prisoners were 'arrested' at their home, taken for fingerprinting and stripped and humiliated. Prisoners wore emasculating loose-fitting muslin smocks with numbers front and back, no underwear and a light chain and lock on one ankle. Guards only referred to prisoners by number to further dehumanise them.

Results: Guards and prisoners developed increasingly negative attitudes towards each other and themselves.

Guards were not allowed to use physical abuse but they often expressed aggression verbally.

Five prisoners had to leave early due to extreme depression, crying, rage and acute anxiety.

Individual differences were found among both guards and prisoners. Some guards behaved quite passively whereas others went beyond the rules in terms of harassment and cruelty. Some prisoners became sick while others coped by being obedient.

The experiment was ended after only six days because of concern for the participants' well-being.

Discussion: The experiment was remarkably effective if unethical. Most of the guards appeared to enjoy the experience of power and the more aggressive guards were unchallenged. The prisoners displayed a range of responses ranging from disbelief to going on hunger strike. In the end the model prisoner behaviour was one of passivity and flattened mood.

The prisoners lost their sense of individuality. Unpredictable behaviour by guards led the prisoners to accept whatever they were told to do. Feelings of learned helplessness developed.

Depending on guards for their needs, emasculated prisoners and developed the sense of learned helplessness. The authors concluded that destructive and abnormal social relationships between prisoners and guards were created by the situation rather than being the outcome of individual traits of aggression or passivity.

Behaviourist perspective: Learned helplessness: Seligman developed the idea of learned helplessness with dogs. He found that once a dog was not rewarded for a behaviour and once this was repeated several times, the animal gave up on the behaviour. He learned that his behaviour would not be rewarded and therefore that it was not in his power to affect his fate. Seligman applied his theory to humans. He argued that it explained apparently strange aspects of human behaviour such as battered women staying with their husbands.

Evaluation

Ecological validity: individual versus situational

The study appears to have created a believable prison environment and that **ecological validity** was high is shown by the results which indicate that the role play worked extremely effectively.

The researchers felt that their experiment supported the theory that people's behaviour is created by the **situation** they find themselves in rather more than by inborn personality differences. Do you agree?

Key Study: 4.2.1 Probation

George Mair and Chris May (1997), 'Offenders on Probation', *Home Office Research Study 167*

Approach: Cognitive

Aim: To investigate the views of offenders on their experience of probation

Method: Self-report

Design: Cross-sectional (snapshot)

Type of sample: Random sample

Participants: Researchers used random sampling methods (using the Home Office's Probation Index) to contact 3299 offenders on probation in 22/55 probation areas in England and Wales. Of these, 1986 were successfully contacted and a final total of 1213 were interviewed by researchers. Eight percent of those contacted refused to participate. As Table 4.4 shows, participants were mainly male, young and unemployed. Nearly half of respondents reported taking drugs over the past year and around 80 per cent of respondents admitted a previous conviction.

Table 4.4 Sample characteristics

	Males % of sample	Females % of sample
Probation	71	17
Combination orders	11	2
Total	82%* (n = 983)	19%* (n = 213)

*weighted percentages

Table 4.5 Participant characteristics

	% of sample males	% of sample females	% of sample
Age 16–24	43	45	44
Age 25+	57	55	56
Employed	23	12	21
Other (e.g. unemployed, sick)	77	88	79
Previous conviction	87	64	82
Respondents admitting to have taken cannabis during past year	45	29	42

Procedure: Participants were asked whether they would be willing to participate in the study when they next attended a scheduled meeting at their local probation office. They were interviewed individually by a researcher who asked a series of questions in an interview that lasted on average just under an hour. Questions were designed to gain information about the respondents' backgrounds, their offending history and their experiences while serving the probation sentence. Questions were either closed questions, multiple choice or had Likert scale responses.

Results: As noted above, many questions focused on discovering information about the offender; his/her background; socio-economic situation; health; previous criminal history; and drug and alcohol history. The aim of the study however was not so much to find out about people on probation (although this is important background information) as to assess the effectiveness of the probation system and offenders' attitudes towards it. The study found that of those who responded, 47 per cent felt that their probation order was extremely useful; 62 per cent felt that the probation officer would help them to sort out problems; 45 per cent felt that being on probation was helping them keep out of trouble and 37 per cent felt that their probation experience would stop them reoffending altogether.

Table 4.6 Good points about probation

	Male %	Female %	All %
Current probation order was very useful	46	52	47
Having someone independent to talk to	53	61	54
Getting practical help and advice	32	37	33
Being helped to keep out of trouble	20	14	19
Only a minor restriction on liberty	16	9	15
To help understand offending behaviour	9	6	8

Table 4.7 Attitudes to probation officers

	Strongly agree
Probation officer will help sort out my problems	62
Probation officer is there to for me to talk to	66
Being on probation helps to keep me out of trouble with the law	45
Being on probation will help me to stop offending altogether	37

Discussion: The majority of those who participated expressed positive opinions about their experience of probation and their treatment by probation officers. However these results must be considered in the light of the fact that the majority of offenders selected randomly for participation were either not contactable, unwilling to respond or simply failed to turn up to their appointment. Given the likely reasons for lack of response, it is reasonable to infer that many of those who were not interviewed would probably have been less positive in their assessment of probation. Although 37 per cent of respondents said that the probation sentence would stop them reoffending, the proportion of the original sample can be calculated at only 14 per cent. Of course, it is not known what the response to this question might have been had the other randomly selected participants been in a position to respond but it is unlikely to have been as positive given the reasons for which they were unable to participate or refused to do so.

Evaluation
Sampling method

Q. When is a random sample not a random sample?

A. When it is self-selecting.

This study attempted to use a random sampling technique. However in order for the conclusions drawn to be **valid**, there has to be a reasonably high fit between those randomly sampled and those who respond. In this case it would seem more correct to describe the sample as a self-selecting or volunteer sample in the light of the fact that nearly two-thirds of those randomly selected did not in the end participate. This level of attrition would not matter as much if it was reasonable to suppose that response was random. In this case, however, where lack of response was allied for example to reconviction or failing to attend a probation interview, it is likely that the self-selecting group that responded held different attitudes towards the probation experience than those who did not participate.

Source: all tables adapted from Mair and May (1997)

Key Study: 4.2.2 Restorative justice

Lawrence J. Sherman and Heather Strang (2007), *Restorative Justice: the Evidence*, The Smith Institute

This study was a review of restorative justice programmes in the UK and internationally. Research was conducted through internet and database searches. It does not fit the typical study format but the main findings are outlined below:

The authors found that restorative justice:

- substantially reduced repeat offending for some, but not all, offenders
- reduced crime victims' post-traumatic stress symptoms
- provided both victims and offenders with more satisfaction with justice than traditional criminal justice
- reduced crime victims' desire for violent revenge against their offenders
- reduced recidivism (reoffending rates) more than prison for adults and as well as prison for youth offenders

The authors based these conclusions mainly on two forms of restorative justice:

1) Face-to-face meetings among all parties connected to a crime, including victims and their families and offenders.
2) Court-ordered financial restitution.

Violent crimes

Six rigorous field tests found that restorative justice reduced recidivism after adult or youth violence. Three of these were randomised controlled trials conducted with different populations (youth under 30 in Canberra, Australia, females under 18 in Northumbria, UK and youths under the age of 14 in Indianapolis, USA). The results of these studies were generally supported by data from other studies on adult males in West Yorkshire and West Midlands (UK) and violent families in Canada.

Research methods

Randomised controlled trials

Randomised controlled trials are a type of scientific experiment used frequently in medical research but also in criminological research. Participants are randomly allocated to different experimental conditions, or between an experimental condition and the control condition (for example placebo-controlled trials). The aim of an RCT is to eliminate selection bias while allowing a full range of outcomes.

Property crimes

Five tests of restorative justice have found reductions in recidivism in cases of property crime. Four of these were randomised controlled trials undertaken with young offenders in Northumbria (UK) and three US states. However in Canberra (Australia) a study found that arrest rates increased among a small sample of Aboriginal offenders treated in a restorative justice programme rather than a criminal justice programme.

Victim benefits

Two randomised controlled trials in London found that restorative justice reduced post-traumatic stress in victims. Four randomised controlled trials found that restorative justice reduced the desire for violent revenge in victims and that victims preferred it over traditional criminal justice.

Restorative justice versus prison

One randomised controlled trial in Idaho, US (court-ordered restitution) found that recidivism rates were no worse among youth offenders in the restorative justice programme than among those given short prison sentences. In Canada adults diverted from prison to restorative justice had lower reconviction rates than a matched sample of inmates.

Discussion

The authors of this study drew positive conclusions from their research and state their hope that restorative justice programmes might be rolled out across the UK. They concluded that:

- Crime victims who receive restorative justice do better, on average, than victims who do not, across a wide range of outcomes, including post-traumatic stress.

- Offenders who receive restorative justice in many cases commit fewer repeat crimes than offenders who do not.

- In no test using a large sample was it found that restorative justice led to an increase in repeat offending in comparison to traditional criminal justice.

- Restorative justice reduces repeat offending more consistently with violent crimes than with less serious crimes.

- Restorative justice can do as well as, or better than, short prison sentences, as measured by repeat offending.

Evaluation

Review method

As this study is not an empirical one (the researchers reviewed the results of studies carried out by themselves and others) it is difficult to evaluate the findings. The review appears to have been conducted with rigour and the authors were successful in ensuring an internationally varied range of studies. Sample size was generally large, ranging from 14 to over 400, with a mean sample size of 138 for studies of violent crimes and 181 for studies involving property crime. Also the reviewers assessed the methodology used in the studies and described the tests conducted as 'reasonably unbiased'. However the conclusions reached in any review study are necessarily limited by the **validity** and **reliability** of the individual empirical studies selected.

Key Study: 4.2.3 Looking 'deathworthy'

Jennifer L Eberhardt, Paul G. Davies, Valerie J. Purdie-Vaughns and Sheri L. Johnson (2006), 'Looking Deathworthy: Perceived Stereotypicality of Black Defendants Predicts Capital-Sentencing Outcomes', *Psychological Science*, 17 (5), 383–6

Approach: Cognitive

Aim: To investigate the effects of stereotypically black facial appearance on sentencing for crimes of murder involving black and white victims

Method: Laboratory experiment

Experiment 1

Design: Independent measures

Stage 1: Ratings for stereotypicality

Raters

41 undergraduates (26 White, 4 Asian and 2 other ethnicities) from Stanford University who were naïve to the aim of the experiment participated in the rating stage

Procedure

The experimenters searched a database containing more than 600 death-eligible cases from Philadelphia during a 20 year period from 1979–1999 projected on a screen. They found 44 cases in which black defendants were convicted of murdering white victims and obtained photographs of the defendants.

The black and white photographs of defendants' faces were projected on screen to the raters. Raters were divided into two groups and the photographs were shown in different random orders in order to control for order effects.

Raters were asked to record stereotypicality ratings using a scale from 1 (not at all stereotypical) to 11 (extremely stereotypical).

Stage 2: Data analysis

The experimenters conducted an analysis of covariance using stereotypicality as the independent variable (low/high) and percentage of death sentences imposed as the dependent variable. Six non-race related factors known to influence sentences were also included as covariates in the analysis:

1. Aggravating circumstances (e.g. prior conviction; characteristics of the crime, e.g. torture)
2. Mitigating circumstances (e.g. emotional state; lack of prior conviction)
3. Severity of the murder (rated by other raters once the cases were purged of race-related information)
4. Defendant's socio-economic status
5. Victim's socio-economic status
6. Defendant's attractiveness

Results: It was found that defendants who were rated as more stereotypically black were more likely to have received the death sentence than those perceived as less stereotypically black (approximately 25 per cent), even controlling for the effects of the other variables ($p < 0.05$). Nearly 60 per cent of those rated as of high stereotypicality were condemned to death compared to approximately 25 per cent of those related as low in stereotypical features. The data were also analysed for order effects and effects of rater's race but no significant effects were found.

Experiment 2

Design: Independent measures

Stage 1: Ratings for stereotypicality

Raters

18 raters (12 White, 6 Asian) who were naïve to the aim of the experiment participated in the rating stage

Procedure

The procedure was the same as for Experiment 1 other than that as there was a much higher number of cases of black defendants convicted of murdering black victims (308), the experimenters selected randomly 118 cases. As fewer defendants were sentenced to death than were not, different proportions were randomly selected from each subset in order to achieve a near 50/50 distribution. As in Experiment 1, raters were asked to record stereotypicality ratings using a scale from 1 (not at all stereotypical) to 11 (extremely stereotypical).

Stage 2: Data analysis

Data were analysed according to the same criteria and also data from both experiments were combined and analysed for interaction effects

Results: Data from Study 2 did not show an effect of stereotypicality on sentencing of defendants for murdering black victims. Death sentences were distributed evenly among black defendants of low and high stereotypicality. The combined data revealed a significant interaction effect of victim's race and defendant's stereotypicality ($p > 0.05$).

Discussion: The authors suggest that racial characteristics may be more salient when a crime has an interracial character. Where cases involve a stereotypically black defendant and a white victim, the chance of the defendant receiving the death penalty may be more than doubled.

Evaluation

Reliability/test-retest

This is an interesting and potentially disturbing study. However caution should be exercised with regard to the results and conclusions drawn by the authors. One way of checking the **reliability** of results is test/retest. This means that you basically run the experiment again to see whether you get the same results. In a way this is what the experimenters did but they changed one variable – the race of the victim. The result did not support the original hypothesis, that stereotypical black features would predict a higher percentage of death sentences for the defendants in the study. One way of dealing with this is to alter the original hypothesis to one that in interrace crimes only, the stereotypicality of black features will predict a higher rate of death sentence. Another way of approaching the issue would be to consider whether there are any other factors that distinguish the two experiments, and whether these might have affected the results. The sample size was much larger in the second experiment and the number of raters was smaller. If these factors could equally explain the different result, then this casts doubt on the first set of results and suggests that a replication of both experiments should be carried out using as large a sample size and number of raters as possible.

4.3 After a guilty verdict: Treatment programmes

Key Study: 4.3.1 Cognitive skills programmes

Caroline Friendship, Linda Blud, Matthew Erikson, Rosie Travers (2002), 'Evaluation of Cognitive Behavioural Treatment for Prisoners', *Home Office Research Study 161*

Approach: Cognitive

Aim: To analyse the effects of a cognitive behavioural treatment programme on reconviction rates

Method: Retrospective quasi-experiment

Design: Independent measures

Type of sample: Representative sample

Participants: Treatment group: 670 adult male offenders serving a custodial sentence of at least two years who voluntarily participated in one of two Cognitive Skills programmes run by Her Majesty's Prison Service between 1992 and 1996, of whom 10 per cent dropped out. Comparison group: 1801 adult male offenders serving at least two years' custodial sentence who had not participated in a treatment programme. There were six matching variables employed:

1. Current offence
2. Sentence length
3. Age at discharge
4. Year of discharge
5. Number of previous convictions
6. Probability of reconviction

Procedure: Treatment consisted of two multi-modal programmes including cognitive behavioural components. In one programme (Reasoning and Rehabilitation – R&R) participants received 36 2-hour sessions and in the other (Enhanced Thinking Skills – ETS) they received 20 2-hour sessions of treatment. Sessions focused on:

- Self-control (thinking before acting)
- Inter-personal problem-solving skills
- Social perspective-taking
- Critical reasoning skills
- Cognitive style
- Understanding the values that govern behaviour

As the two programmes shared common features, the groups were combined for the purposes of reconviction rate calculation although the different programmes were also analysed separately.

Results: Reoffending probabilities were calculated using the Offender Group Reconviction Scale. The treatment and comparison group samples were divided into quartiles to create four risk levels (low, medium-low, medium-high and high). Observed two-year reconviction rates were compared with expected rates.

Logistic regression analysis (a form of multiple regression, see p.4) was carried out to assess the respective influence of treatment and other variables related to reconviction. The dependent variable was reconviction within two years of discharge from prison and the independent variables were those which had been demonstrated to be related to reconviction. These variables were:

- Age at first conviction
- Age at sentence
- Age at discharge
- Number of previous appearances in court (at sentence)
- Sentence length
- Nature of offence
- Treatment type (R&R or ETS)
- Risk score
- Ethnicity

Factors that explained variance in reconviction patterns were found to be treatment, risk score, sentence length and ethnicity. Both treatment programmes resulted in a significant reduction in the probability of reconviction ($p < 0.001$). Being of Asian ethnicity was also associated with reduced

Table 4.8 Two-year observed reconviction rates for treatment and comparison group samples by level of risk

Risk category	Treatment group reconvictions		Comparison group reconvictions		Percentage points reduction
	No	%	No	%	
Low	5	5	46	8	3
Medium-low	26	18	126	32	14
Medium-high	72	43	229	11	11
High	189	75	319	5	5

Source: Friendship *et al.* (2002)

chances of reconviction and this is in keeping with the low representation of Asian offenders in the prison population in the UK.

Discussion: This study supports the value of cognitive behavioural treatment programmes for offenders. The positive results in terms of lowering recidivism would also suggest that such programmes are cost–effective. The authors suggest that the design of this study could be improved upon by adopting a randomised controlled experimental design but they accept that such a study would entail both ethical and practical implications. If prisoners were denied treatment because they were allocated to the control group this could affect their chance of early release. Instead they suggest that a future study could be prospective rather than retrospective as this would enable researchers to match on a wider range of variables and collect data such as motivational factors for both groups.

Evaluation

Retrospective quasi-experimental method

The authors of this study have obligingly suggested some methodological limitations in the approach they have taken, that is a retrospective quasi-experiment. Nevertheless within its own terms it is a well-executed study involving large sample sizes matched on a range of variables and performing multiple regression that successfully identifies four factors that contribute to variance in reoffending rates. As the authors propose, replication of this study, or even better, modification to a prospective design would enable the **reliability** of these findings to be tested.

4.3 After a guilty verdict: Treatment programmes

Key Study: 4.3.2 Anger management

Jane L. Ireland (2004), 'Anger management therapy with young male offenders: an evaluation', *Aggressive Behaviour*, 30, 174–85

Approach: Cognitive

Aim: To analyse the effects of an anger management programme on the behaviour and attitudes of young male offenders

Hypothesis: That prisoners completing the interventions would show significantly reduced observed and self-reported anger after treatment

Method: Retrospective quasi-experiment

Design: Independent measures

Type of sample: Opportunity sample

Participants: The experimental group was composed of 50 young male offenders who had completed an anger management course. The control group was a group of 37 young male offenders who had been assessed as suitable for such a course but had not been treated on a programme. It was not possible either to match participants or to randomly allocate participants to the two conditions. However the groups were reasonably similar on age and offence characteristics (see Table 4.9 below).

Procedure: All participants were assessed two weeks prior to start of the course for the experimental group and were reassessed eight weeks after the end of the course, while the control group remained on a waiting list for the intervention. All members of both groups were interviewed by a psychologist who used cognitive behavioural techniques. Offenders were asked about their feelings of anger and whether they were ready to take a course in anger management. They were also assessed for aggressive behaviour by prison staff using the Wing Behaviour Checklist. The anger management programme followed was the Wakefield Prison Anger Management Course, widely followed in the UK in the 1990s. This programme is based on cognitive behavioural techniques. The course consisted of twelve one-hour sessions over a three-day period. The sessions addressed the question of what triggers anger; the consequences of temper loss, and the importance of behaviour, thoughts and feelings. Participants were asked to complete anger diaries, contribute to group discussions, take part in role-play and other group exercises and to complete 'homework'.

Results: Prior to pre-/post-analysis the groups were compared on age, offence type, self-report anger measure and Wing checklist and there were found to be no significant differences between the groups. Pre-/post analysis showed a significant reduction in the treatment group in both self-report anger feelings and in guard observation of angry/aggressive behaviours (see Table 4.10).

There was a significant difference found on the Wing Behavioural Checklist in number of angry behaviours in the experimental group observed by prison officers but not in the control group ($p < 0.01$). There was a significant difference found in the number of self-reported angry behaviours reported by offenders in the experimental group but not the control group ($p < 0.01$). In the experimental group, 92 per cent of offenders showed improvement on at least one of the measures and 48 per cent showed improvement on both. Thirty-five per cent showed improvement on the Anger Management Assessment alone and 17 per cent showed improvement solely on the Wing Behaviour Checklist. However 8 per cent showed no improvement or even deterioration on both measures.

Discussion: This study appears to show the effectiveness of a brief intervention addressing anger among young male offenders. Results supported the

Table 4.9 Comparison of characteristics of treatment group and control group

	Treatment group, $n = 50$	Control group, $n = 37$
Mean age	19	18
% imprisoned for violent offences	62	68
% imprisoned for acquisitive offences (e.g. theft)	30	24
% imprisoned for drug-related offences	4	5
% imprisoned for other offences	4	3

Source: adapted from Ireland (2004)

Table 4.10 Mean pre- and post-intervention scores on the Anger Management Assessment questionnaire and the Wing Behavioural Checklist (rounded to nearest whole number)

	Anger Management Assessment Questionnaire		Wing Behavioural Checklist	
	Point 1* mean (sd) (Max = 58)	Point 2** mean (sd)	Point 1* mean (sd) (Max = 106)	Point 2** mean (sd)
Experimental group (n = 50)	13 (10)	9 (8)	43 (23)	27 (2.7)
Control group (n = 37)	12 (10)	10 (8)	40 (22)	37 (26)

*Pre-intervention for experimental group
** Post-intervention for experimental group
Source: adapted from Ireland (2004)

hypothesis that prisoners completing the intervention would show decreased observed and self-reported anger. However the researchers admitted that it would be important too to follow up on the finding that a minority of young offenders showed no improvement or deterioration following treatment. They also accepted that the study was limited to an examination of short–term effects and that research into the longer–term impact of anger management training including possible effect on reoffending should also be studied.

Evaluation

Interpreting statistics

Tests of significance run by the experimenters showed significant post-intervention improvements in reducing angry feelings and behaviours in young offenders. However the results may not be **valid**. The reason for this is that in the case of the self-report measure, those who have participated in an anger management intervention may have been strongly affected by **demand characteristics** and **social desirability** factors in responding on the second occasion. The result of the Wing Behaviour Checklist may appear at first sight to offer a more objective measure of reduced anger. However it is unlikely that the guards providing the checklist responses will have been unaware of whether a particular offender had been involved in the treatment programme. Their responses may therefore also have been affected by **demand characteristics** and social desirability factors – in other words they may have been willing the treatment to have

continued...

been successful and for this reason subconsciously adopted a less critical interpretation of observed behaviours of those who had completed the intervention. A more **reliable** result might have been achieved if outside observers who were naïve as to which prisoners had been involved in the treatment had completed the checklist.

Do you have any suggestions as to why the behaviour of a minority of the offenders deteriorated?

One possible explanation is that the transparency of the self-report measure may have shaped responses in two directions. Most of the offenders who had undergone the intervention may have wanted to show they had learned something but a small minority may have seen it as an opportunity for a type of protest vote. Alternatively it could be argued that as this group had low mean scores the first time round on both measures, there was really no way to go but up!

Key Study: 4.3.3 Ear acupuncture treatment

Arthur Margolin *et al.* (2002), 'Acupuncture for the Treatment of Cocaine Addiction. A randomized controlled trial', *Journal of the American Medical Association*, 287(1) 55–62

Approach: Biological

Aim: To investigate the effectiveness of ear acupuncture as a treatment for cocaine addiction

Hypothesis 1 That in comparison to those in the two control conditions, patients in the acupuncture condition would be more likely to provide negative urine screens during the study and at follow-up

Hypothesis 2 That those in the acupuncture treatment condition would be more likely to complete treatment than those in the control conditions

Method: Randomised, controlled, single-blind clinical trial

Design: Independent measures

Type of sample: Opportunity sample

Participants: 620 cocaine-dependent adult patients (mean age, 39 years; 69 per cent male from various US states. Four hundred and twelve used cocaine only; 208 used both opiates and cocaine and were receiving methadone treatment (a prescription drug used to aid individuals trying to kick cocaine addiction).

Procedure: Patients were randomly allocated to receive ear acupuncture (n = 222), a needle-insertion control group (n = 203), or a relaxation control condition (n = 195); treatments were offered five times per week for eight weeks. Financial incentives were provided for attendance and drug counselling was also offered to all patients. In the ear acupuncture treatment, needles were inserted into the ears bilaterally at four points in or near the concha (centre of the external ear, see Figure 4.1) commonly used in addiction treatment and thought to have beneficial properties.

In the needle insertion control condition, four needles of the same type and size as those used in acupuncture treatment were inserted into the helix of the ears (the external skin fold) bilaterally at three regions not commonly used for addiction treatment. In the relaxation control condition, participants viewed videos depicting relaxation strategies and containing relaxing visual imagery and soft music. Outcome measures were retention in treatment, use of cocaine during treatment and at three- and six-month follow-up screening tests. Urine samples were collected three times a week and cocaine use was reported (self-report) and at a structured interview at the end of the trial, the Addiction Severity Index was administered to all patients. All assessments were carried out by staff blind to patients' treatment assignment.

Results:

- Checks were made on attendance at assigned treatment and there was no significant difference in attendance between groups.
- Overall attendance at drug counselling sessions was poor with 50 per cent across all conditions reporting that they attended less than one counselling session per week.
- There was no significant difference found in reported credibility of treatment which indicates that patients in the needle insertion condition were not aware that they were in a control condition.
- Relaxation-control patients reported significantly more relaxation effects following their treatment than patients in either the acupuncture or needle-control condition.
- Methadone-maintained cocaine users were significantly more likely to complete treatment than primary cocaine users ($p < 0.001$) but there was no significant difference in treatment completion across randomised conditions.
- Cocaine use declined across all conditions during treatment but there was no significant difference between acupuncture and the control

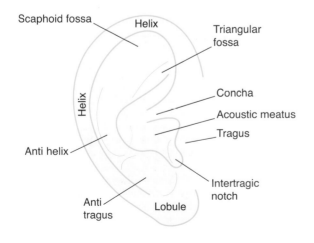

Figure 4.1 The ear

conditions in treatment effectiveness as determined by positive results from urine tested for cocaine during treatment.

- There were no significant differences on self-reported use of, or craving for, cocaine across conditions.
- There were no significant differences in percentage of patients using cocaine at time of either the three-month or six-month follow-up.
- Severity of drug, alcohol and psychiatric problems decreased significantly across all conditions during treatment and improvements were maintained at follow-up.

Discussion: The data did not support the experimental hypotheses. Acupuncture treatment did not prove more effective than either of the control conditions in reducing cocaine use or enabling completion of treatment. However all the conditions resulted in reduced cocaine use despite the fact that patients did not attend many counselling sessions. The authors acknowledged that these results were out of line with other research studies that found acupuncture treatment to be more effective than control conditions. Methodological differences between the current study and previous research were discussed and the conclusion the authors came to was that the large sample size in the current study might indicate greater reliability of findings than in previous studies. They therefore suggested that further research should be done on the effectiveness of ear acupuncture treatment but that at this point they could not support previous conclusions with regard to superior efficacy of this treatment as compared to no clinical treatment but regular monitoring of addicted patients.

Evaluation

Randomised controlled trials

The two preceding key studies were, as mentioned, somewhat limited by methodological issues. In **Key Study 4.3.1** the experimenters were unable to run randomised controlled trials but had to rely instead on retrospective data analysis, and in **Key Study 4.3.2** random allocation to conditions was not possible and assessment was carried out by observers (guards) who were not blind as to treatment condition. The findings of **Key Study 4.3.3** however really underline the importance of following a **well-controlled** procedure with **random** allocation to experimental and control conditions and with those assessing effectiveness remaining blind to treatment condition. Taken together with large sample size, these features suggest the data provided by this study are **reliable** and that the conclusion drawn by the researcher that acupuncture does not provide effective treatment is a **valid** one until and unless future research supports the experimental hypothesis that it does. However one limitation of this study in terms of its use in forensic psychology is that it was not based on a prison population. It would be **useful** if researchers could apply the method used in this study with a sample of convicted addicts.

Marshall H. Becker, Susan M. Radius, Irwin M. Rosenstock, Robert H. Drachman, Kenneth C. Schuberth and Katherine C. Teets (1978), 'Compliance with a medical regimen for asthma: a test of the Health Belief Model', *Public Health Reports* , 93 (3)

Approach: Cognitive

Aim: To test the ability of the Health Belief Model (HBM) to explain mothers' differential compliance with a drug regimen prescribed for their asthmatic children

Method: Self-report/clinical tests/correlation

Type of sample: Opportunity sample

Participants: 111 mothers (mean age 31; mean age of child 8; 94 per cent black) from a low-income clinical population who brought their children to a paediatric emergency facility for treatment of acute asthma episodes agreed to participate in the study

Procedure: Mothers who brought their children to a paediatric emergency facility at John Hopkins University, Baltimore between October 1976 and February 1977 were interviewed about their health motivations and attitudes and about various aspects of asthma and its consequences. Each mother was asked to recall her handling of the child's current asthma attack, including whether the most recently prescribed asthma medication had been administered. Compliance was checked by a covert blood sample being taken and tested for presence of theophylline, a substance present in all of the drugs prescribed for asthma by doctors of the children involved. However the conditions of the emergency facility made it difficult for the blood sample to be taken each time so the compliance check was available in 70 per cent of cases only.

Results: Two measures of compliance were constructed. Compliance 1 has three levels: absence of theophylline or mother's statement that she did not give the drug, or both; no test available but mother states that she gave the drug; presence of theophylline in the blood. Compliance 2 has two levels: laboratory confirmation of the presence or absence of theophylline.

Samples were positive for 53/80 children (compliance rate of 66 per cent of those tested). Associations between each compliance measure and mothers' general health motivations were as follows:

- Perception of the overall severity of the child's asthma was the best predictor of compliance.
- Highest level of statistical significance was found on the question of whether the mother gives asthma medicine even when the child feels well.
- Perceptions of the child as being in poor health and susceptible to health problems and whether the child's asthma interfered with the child's normal functioning were good predictors of adherence.
- Mother's stated level of concern about her child with asthma was correlated with compliance only when asked whether she had greater concern for the child with asthma than her other children.
- Compliance was correlated with possession of a thermometer.
- Mothers who complied were significantly more likely to feel in control of the situations generally.
- Mothers who complied were more likely to feel that most illnesses are preventable.

All the above associations present support for the relationships hypothesised by the HBM to exist between measures of general health motivations, susceptibility, severity and mothers' adherence to prescribed medication regime.

One interesting finding that appeared to conflict with the HBM was that mothers who were compliant were more likely to feel that doctors do 'not know best in treating health problems' and that they 'do not know a great deal about asthma' yet they also reported that they felt better when heeding doctors' advice.

Two demographic variables were significantly associated with adherence – mother's marital status and level of education (married most likely to comply; better educated more likely to comply).

Discussion: The authors note the general support this study provides for the HBM. The finding that mothers who adhere most closely to the prescribed medication regime for their child are also the most critical of doctors was viewed by the authors as unsurprising given a) the limited efficacy of the treatment and b) the fact that although the mothers had complied with the medication regime, their child had still ended up in the emergency room with an asthma attack. The conflicting results may reflect the mothers' attempts to reconcile general belief in medical treatment with disappointment that the medicine failed to prevent a serious attack. The HBM is based on hypotheses formulated about people's beliefs prior to receiving medical care, whereas this study was conducted after a period on the medical regimen, therefore results should be interpreted in this light. Another explanation for the finding that compliant mothers were quite negative in their views towards doctors is that it is in accordance with the literature which suggests that compliers are both more realistic and knowledgeable about the value of medical intervention. Mothers' adherence may be interpreted as the outcome of a probabilistic assessment of the prescribed regimen. In other words mothers who comply may not have that high a belief in the efficacy of the treatment but comply anyway as they are keen to seek any possible remedy for their child.

Evaluation

Reliablity/usefulness

The fact that most of the findings of this study show an association with factors that the HBM predicts as important is evidence that there is a degree of **reliability** in both the model and the study's data. However, in most cases the associations found were not particularly strong and on the crucial issue of trust in doctors, the result was not as predicted by the model. It may be that the model is not sufficiently explanatory when dealing with a chronic disease which is not particularly amenable to treatment.

The **usefulness** of this study may be limited by the fact that the authors are researching compliance to a medical regime whose efficacy they doubt themselves. However, as they point out, it is important that we understand why patients fail to adhere not just to medical regimes that are judged to be effective, but also to regimes where efficacy is less certain and also where symptoms are not always evident. We can conclude that this study is **useful** because it provides an opportunity of examining what occurs when compliance does not control disease. The results showed no major changes in health beliefs deriving from the medicine's failure other than an increased level of scepticism about doctors and medical care. The authors welcome this finding as they suggest that it is better to have thinking, critical patients than patients who blindly follow all the medical advice they receive.

5.1 Healthy living: Theories of health belief

Key Study: 5.1.2 Locus of control

Nancy M. Wineman (1980), 'Obesity: Locus of control, body image, weight loss and age-at-onset', *Nursing Research*, 29 (4)

Approach: Cognitive

Aim: To investigate locus of control, body image and weight loss in obese individuals

Method: Self-report; retrospective correlation

Type of sample: Self-selecting sample

Participants: 116 adult members of Overeaters Anonymous (12 males, 104 females). Respondents had a mean age of 40 (sd = 10); were all Caucasian (white) from a range of social class backgrounds.

Procedure:

Sampling procedure

Volunteers were sought at an Overeaters Anonymous (OA) workshop attended by 400 OA members. Participation in the study was listed on the workshop's agenda. 264 questionnaires were distributed at the workshop; 120 of which were completed and handed in at the workshop and 144 were taken home, of which 45 (31 per cent) were sent back to the investigator. From the 165 completed questionnaires, data was analysed from the 116 participants who met all the sampling criteria (aged 21+; 6 months+ membership of OA; at least 20 per cent overweight at time of joining OA; not on diet medication).

Measurement tools

Participants responded to three questionnaires: a demographic data questionnaire; Rotter's Social Reaction Inventory Scale, and Secord and Jourard's Body Cathexis Scale. The demographic data collected included age, sex and age at onset of obesity. Rotter's Social Inventory Scale is a series of 29 forced-choice questions relating to beliefs about the world that measure internal and external control. Secord and Jouard's Body Cathexis Scale is an objective measure of personal body perception that uses a 5-point Likert scale to measure satisfaction with various parts and functions of one's body. Both tests had been tested for reliability (Rotter's using test–retest and the Body Cathexis Scale split–half reliability).

Research methods

Testing the reliability of self-report measures

A measure is judged reliable if it is consistent. There are different ways of testing consistency.

1. **Test retest**

   Rotter's Social Inventory was tested using test–retest. This is where the same respondents are asked to respond to a self-report measure more than once, usually with a gap of several months between tests. If the results are very similar each time, this shows that the test is consistent. Correlations between responses to Rotter's Social Inventory were high – ranging from 0.49 to 0.83. The study does not state mean correlation.

   In reliability testing, a correlation of above 0.8 is ideal. This test appears to barely reach reliability as far as we can tell from data provided. No explanation is given as to why a range and not mean correlation is stated. This omission suggests that the mean was not high therefore casting doubt on the scale's reliability as measured by test–retest.

2. **Split-half reliability**

   An alternative way to test reliability of a self-report measure is to split the statements/questions randomly in two halves and score responses on each half separately. You then correlate the two sets of responses to see whether the measure is consistent.

   The Body Cathexis Scale is a large scale with approximately 50 items which makes it suitable for split-half reliability testing. It was found that split-half reliability coefficients for the BC scale were 0.78 for males and 0.83 for females.

   As the reliability testing on this scale reached the level of 0.8 this suggests good internal reliability of the test.

Results: The demographic data revealed that of the 116 participants, the majority had childhood onset of obesity (59 per cent) and the remainder were more or less evenly divided between those who experienced adolescent onset and those who became obese as adults.

Multiple regression analysis was performed on the three age at onset categories separately in order to analyse the relationship between locus of control and weight loss. Locus of control significantly predicted body image in the adult group but there was no relationship between locus of control and either body image or weight loss in the sample overall. Body image and weight loss correlated in the adolescent group. Analysis by gender was also conducted using *t*-tests. These indicated that males had a higher degree of satisfaction with their bodies than did females. Males also had a greater weight loss than females.

Discussion: Wineman concluded that it was unclear why the hypothesis that locus of control would be a significant predictor of body image and weight loss was not supported in results relating to the group as a whole. She concluded that external cues may influence persons' eating habits specifically yet not be reflected in those persons' general belief about locus of control. From this they suggest that perhaps the Rotter Scale was not the most suitable measure of locus of control with regard to eating habits specifically. The author also concluded that the sampling procedure (mix of opportunity and volunteer participants) and the fact that the participants were all Obesity Anonymous members may have affected results. She also admitted that crucial variables such as date of onset and weight loss may have been affected by memory and honesty issues.

Evaluation

Methodological issues and how they are dealt with

This is a good example of why findings that are not significant should be published as well as those that are. The researcher in this case was clearly not convinced by her own generally non-significant results. She expected locus of control to correlate with body image and weight loss generally but their only significant finding was that in the adult group. Locus of control predicted body image results (not weight loss) and it did not predict either body image or weight loss across the whole sample. Rather than reject the experimental hypothesis in favour of the null hypothesis, the author however criticised the methodology of her own study, including basic premises such as the admission that weight loss measure (being based on self report only) was subject to vagaries of memory and **social desirability** factors.

Key Study: 5.1.3 Self-efficacy

J. Zalewksa-Puchala, M. Majda, A. Galuszka and J. Kolonko (2007), 'Health behaviour of students versus a sense of self-efficacy', *Advances in Medical Sciences*, 32

Approach: Cognitive

Aim: To assess health behaviour of college students, to evaluate their sense of self-efficacy and to specify the relationship between health behaviour presented by participants and their sense of self-efficacy

Hypothesis: That self-efficacy scores would correlate with healthy patterns of diet, low alcohol consumption, not smoking and engaging in physical exercise

Method: Self-report; correlation

Type of sample: Not stated – either opportunity or self-selecting

Participants: 164 students enrolled on Year 1 of a nursing degree at two Polish universities, Krakow and Bielsko-Biala. Participants were mainly female (153 female, 11 male), mean age 21 and from varied socio-economic backgrounds.

Procedure: Research was conducted using two self-report measures, the Generalized Self-Efficacy Scale Revised and a Questionnaire of Health Belief designed by one of the authors specifically for this study which included questions relating to diet, drinking alcohol, smoking and physical activity. One physiological measure was also administered, the Body Mass Index: this is a statistical measure used to estimate a healthy body weight based on a height versus weight calculation.

Results: Most participants were found to be underweight (83 per cent), with 14.5 per cent of correct body weight and 2.5 per cent overweight. Participants were found to have mainly high self-efficacy (54 per cent) or average (38 per cent), with only 8 per cent being characterised by low self-efficacy. It was not found that any socio-economic variables influenced self-efficacy levels.

Diet

- Fats – only 3 per cent of participants declared overconsumption of fats in daily diet
- A statistically significant correlation was found between self-efficacy and declared low fat diet ($p < 0.05$)
- No significant relationship was found between amount of fat in daily diet and BMI
- Fibre – only 3 per cent of participants declared they ate appropriate amounts of fibre (most ate too little)

- Sixty per cent of participants paid no attention to amount of fibre in daily diet
- There was no correlation found between self-efficacy or BMI and stated fibre consumption

Smoking

- Seventy-one per cent of participants stated they had never smoked and only six per cent admitted smoking on a daily basis
- There was no correlation found between self-efficacy or BMI and smoking

Alcohol consumption

- Nineteen per cent of participants declared they had never drunk alcohol; 51 per cent drank only once a month or less frequently; 26 per cent reported drinking two to four times a month; 4 per cent reported drinking two to three times per week
- A relationship was found between self-efficacy and drinking with those with high self-efficacy drinking alcohol more often!
- No relationship was found between BMI and drinking alcohol

Physical exercise

- Participants reported good levels of physical exercise with no participant stating that they never engaged in physical exercise and 80 per cent reporting that they regularly participated in sport
- There was no significant relationship between self-efficacy and physical activity but there was a statistically significant relationship between reported physical activity and BMI, with participants with low BMI taking up sport often or very often

Discussion: The theory of self-efficacy predicts that sense of self-efficacy will influence life choices such as education. The authors of the study assumed that students would be characterised by high self-efficacy and this was confirmed by the research. Sense of self-efficacy is related to health behaviours such as prevention of uncontrolled sexual behaviour, taking up physical activity regularly, controlling weight, eating habits, low consumption of alcohol/nicotine.

The study confirmed the hypothesis about self-efficacy only with relation to fat consumption. The authors concluded that this was related to the cult of the slim body and participants' preoccupation with appearance. Self-efficacy was not found to influence fibre consumption, showing that health reasons are less important than appearance in dictating young people's dietary habits. The authors concluded that low consumption of nicotine and alcohol was not surprising in female students who had chosen to study nursing. The surprising finding that high self-efficacy related to higher alcohol consumption may be explained by young people with high levels of self-efficacy believing that they can safely control their consumption. The study did not reveal a relationship between self-efficacy and reported physical exercise but it did find a relationship between level of physical activity and BMI which the authors concluded was probably a cause–effect relationship that regular participation in sport reduces BMI. The authors did not discuss further the limited support for the influence of self-efficacy on healthy behaviours found in their study.

Evaluation

Sample bias

Although the expected relationship between self-efficacy and healthy behaviours was not found, the results are nevertheless valuable. What is disappointing is that the authors do not discuss the methodological limitations presented by the fact that their sample is a **biased** one – almost entirely female and trainee nurses (suggesting they will be more aware than the general population of health concerns). The BMI readings should have rung warning bells with the authors. The strong bias towards underweight/normal readings made it unsurprising that the findings regarding the relationship between self-efficacy and healthy behaviours were not significant. Another very important issue not discussed by the authors is the problems involved in self-report measures where **social desirability** is always an issue to be faced. In a sample of trainee nurses responding to a questionnaire distributed by their faculty lecturers involving questions of healthy life style, one can assume that even if anonymity was guaranteed (and the authors do not state that it was) social desirability would have been a highly limiting factor. The figures on alcohol consumption appear particularly low – it is known that people nearly always underestimate the amount of alcohol they consume. It seems likely social desirability factors will have influenced the nurses and this is probably true for most of the responses to the Healthy Behaviours questionnaire with the possible exception of the fibre question, where it appears that even trainee nurses did not appreciate the social desirability of reporting high fibre consumption!

The findings of this study are therefore limited by lack of random sampling, lack of a **representative** sample and likelihood of answers that are more a reflection of what the respondents knew to be socially acceptable or desirable rather than a truthful reflection of their behaviour.

5.2 Healthy Living: Methods of health promotion
Key Study: 5.2.1 Media campaigns

Joseph Keating, Dominique Meekers and Alfred Adewuyi (2006), 'Assessing effects of a media campaign on HIV/AIDS awareness and prevention in Nigeria: results from the VISION Project', *BMC Public Health* 6

Approach: Cognitive

Aim: To assess the extent to which a mass-media campaign (VISION) focusing on reproductive health and HIV/AIDS prevention resulted in increased awareness and prevention of HIV/AIDS

Method: Self-report

Type of sample: Stratified systematic sample

Participants: There were 3278 participants aged 15–49 from various ethnic groups represented in three Nigerian states who were interviewed and responded to a questionnaire. Mean age of respondents was 28. Approximately 60 per cent were married and mean numbers of sexual partners in the last year was 1.2. Religious affiliation included both Christians and Moslems.

Procedure:

Sampling method

In 15 local government areas in each of three Nigerian states, 40 enumeration areas were randomly selected and within each enumeration area 27–28 households were selected using **stratified random sampling**. All adults aged 15–49 in each household were listed and one eligible member was selected using a random method. Interviewers obtained verbal informed consent from the selected participants. This gave a total of 3278 respondents across all three states who completed the questionnaire.

> Stratified sampling: **This is an example of a stratified sample. Stratification is the process of grouping members of the population into relatively homogeneous subgroups before sampling. Then random or systematic sampling is applied within each stratum. This often improves the representativeness of the sample by reducing sampling error. Instead of all eligible members of the population having their names put into a hat (or a computer dataset) and being selected randomly, the researchers ensured that they had a representative balance of states (in Nigeria this is important for ethnic balance); a representative sample of enumeration districts in each state and a representative sample of households in each district from which one individual per household was randomly selected.**

Data collection

Data were collected by trained interviewers who interviewed respondents using a questionnaire which was based on a nationally conducted Demographic and Health Survey conducted in 2002 and 2004 but which had additional questions on family planning, sexual activity and behaviour, and exposure to various media campaigns. Respondents were asked whether they had listened to specific radio programmes, watched particular television campaigns, seen any HIV/AIDS or reproductive health advertisements in newspapers or received any information from clinics of community health workers about HIV/AIDS or reproductive health. Outcome measures were responses to the following questions (fixed choice yes/no):

1) Have you ever talked with a partner about ways to prevent getting the virus that causes AIDS?
2) Can people reduce their chances of getting the AIDS virus by using a condom every time they have sex?
3) Did you use a condom during your last sexual encounter?

Data analysis

Chi-square analysis and regression analysis were conducted.

Results: It was found that males were exposed to more media programmes than females but that females were exposed to more clinic-based information. Seventy-seven per cent of respondents reported listening to the radio at least once a week and 47 per cent reported watching TV at least once a week. Exposure to the VISION mass media campaign was high. Fifty-nine per cent were exposed to at least one radio programme, 47 per cent to at least one printed advertisement and 24 per cent to at least one TV programme. Outcome variables between 2002 and 2004 were small. However those who reported high exposure to the VISION programme were one and a half times more likely than those with no exposure to have discussed HIV/AIDS with a partner and over twice as likely to know that condom use can reduce risk of HIV infection. However exposure to the VISION programme had no effect on condom use during last occasion of sexual intercourse.

Discussion: The VISION Project was effective in that it reached a high proportion of its intended audience and increased HIV/AIDS awareness and communication. It also showed that different media are important channels of communication to different sections of the population. For example, clinic–based advice can be expected to reach females better than males. However it was clearly disappointing that increased levels of knowledge, understanding and discussion of HIV/AIDS according to this study had no effect on sexual habits with regard to condom use. The authors concluded that different strategies for reaching subgroups in the population, for example, rural inhabitants, females and singles might be needed in order to disseminate information on where to obtain condoms. The authors saw this as a valuable pointer to the design of future HIV/AIDS awareness programmes that they should integrate information about HIV/AIDS with practical advice about obtaining condoms. They also argued that the small differences found in HIV/AIDS awareness showed the importance of increasing efforts in the direction of providing more multimedia programmes like VISION.

Evaluation

Questionnaire design

The questionnaire used in this study appears to have successfully highlighted the important key points under investigation using a few quick, straightforward questions with closed answers. This is important for **reliable** results: the questionnaire would have been easy to complete accurately and honestly. It is also important for facilitating quantitative analysis from the data. With hindsight it is possible to see that just one more question after the one about whether a condom had been used on the last occasion of sexual intercourse might have proved invaluable for the researchers. The question might have been phrased like this:

If you did not use a condom last time you had sex, was this because:

a) You did not want to (yes/no)

b) Your partner did not want to (yes/no)

c) You did not have one available at the time (yes/no)

d) You do not know how to obtain a condom (yes/no)

Hindsight can show what questions should have been asked in a self-report study. For this reason it is always useful to run a small pilot study before running the full study. However it is not always feasible to run a pilot in advance as there may be external constraints that are not under the control of those conducting the research.

In terms of this study, this is only a minor suggestion for improvement to what appears to have been an extremely effective media campaign and subsequent analysis.

5.2 Healthy Living: Methods of health promotion
Key Study: 5.2.2 Legislation

Melanie A. Wakefield, Frank J. Chaloupka, Nancy J. Kaufman, C. Tracy Orleans, Dianne C. Barker, Erin E. Ruel (2000), 'Effect of restrictions on smoking at home, at school and in public places on teenage smoking: cross-sectional study', *British Medical Journal*, 321

Approach: Cognitive

Aim: To determine the relation between extent of restrictions on smoking at home, in school and in public places and smoking uptake and prevalence among school students

Method: Self-report

Type of sample: Ramdom sample

Participants: 17 287 high school students at 202 schools in the United States

Procedure

Sampling method

One school (grades 9–12; age 14–17) in each county of the mainland United States was randomly selected (probability of selection proportional to number of students in grades specified) and one class from each grade; all the students in these classes were invited to participate in a survey. Seventy-three per cent of schools selected (either those first approached or a matched reserve school) agreed to participate and 80 per cent of students in sampled classes completed the questionnaire giving a total of 17 287 respondents.

Questionnaire measures

Questionnaires contained demographic data and information on whether adults in the home and siblings in the home were smokers. Respondents were then classified by stage of smoking uptake on the basis of responses to questions on smoking history and intentions that have been found to predict current smoking at 3–4 year follow-up. Participants were classified into the following categories:

- 'non-susceptible non-smokers' (never smoked; no intention of doing so)
- 'susceptible non-smokers' (never smoked a whole cigarette but had weak intentions to stay non-smokers)
- 'early experimenters' (had puffed a cigarette more than 30 days before the survey and had strong intentions not to smoke in future)
- 'advanced experimenters' (had smoked a whole cigarette more than 30 days before the survey and had weak intentions not to smoke in the future or had smoked in the past 30 days but had not smoked more than 100 cigarettes

- 'established smokers' (had smoked more than 100 cigarettes in their lifetime, irrespective of future intentions or recent smoking activity
- Current smoking was defined as the traditionally accepted measure of having smoked during the past 30 days

Home smoking restrictions were defined by responses to the question 'How is cigarette smoking handled in your home?' with closed choices of no one is allowed/special guests allowed only/smoking allowed in certain areas in my home/smoking is allowed anywhere in my home.

Two measures of school smoking were ascertained – whether there was a ban or not, and if there was a ban, how strongly the ban was enforced.

Based on school identifiers, the researchers added information on state, county and city laws relating to restrictions on smoking in public places for the 202 school sites in the survey. Strong public place restrictions were defined as restrictions in private worksites and public restaurants; moderate public place restrictions were defined as restrictions in either private worksites or public restaurants; weak public places restrictions were defined as restrictions in neither of these environments.

Statistical analysis

Logistic regression analysis was used to examine the association between smoking status and smoking restrictions. Each analysis was adjusted for school grade, sex, whether adults/siblings at home smoked.

Results: It was found that legal restrictions in public places, parent-enforced restrictions at home and enforced school bans were significantly associated with being in an earlier stage, that is not developing an early smoking habit. However there were differences in the impact on smoking of the different types of restrictions. More extensive restrictions on smoking in public places were more associated with a reduction in the probability of transition between later rather than earlier stages of uptake. Home smoking bans had a much greater effect than legal restrictions on smoking in public places on uptake of smoking. The existence of a school ban was not associated with smoking uptake until the last threshold (the move from advanced experimenter to established smoker) where it was found to increase likelihood of transition to the latter stage. However, strongly enforced school bans were associated with 11 per cent reductions in uptake of smoking across all stages of uptake.

Discussion: The authors acknowledged that there were methodological limitations with their study. The cross-sectional nature of the study limited attributions about causality between variables and the authors hypothesised that there might be other factors that influence teenage smoking apart from restrictions on smoking and these might lead to an artificial relation between restrictions and youth smoking as the study did not control for other factors. Also the authors were unable to establish the level of compliance or enforcement of the restrictions discussed. Nevertheless they concluded that their findings were consistent with other research which has shown that parental opposition to smoking and banning smoking in the home reduce uptake of smoking in teenagers. Legal restrictions in public places and school bans, in the view of the authors, have a more modest effect and in the latter case only when strictly enforced.

Evaluation
Random sampling

This study involved a very large sample of teenagers across the United States (age 14–17). It was not a systematic sample as it did not select, for example, every xth student on a list. Nor was it stratified as there was no attempt to compare subpopulations. However a simple random sampling method in this case was sufficient to produce a large, **representative** sample of the teenage population.

Key Study: 5.2.3 Fear arousal

Robert A. C. Ruiter, Gerjo Kok, Bas Verplanken and Johannes Brug (2001),
'Evoked fear and effects of appeals on attitudes to performing breast self-examination: an information–processing perspective', *Health Education Research*, 16 (3)

Approach: Cognitive

Aim: To examine the effect of fear arousal on attitude toward participating in early detection activities (breast self-examination for cancer)

Method: Laboratory experiment

Design: Independent measures

Type of sample: Volunteer sample

Participants: 88 female first-year undergraduates at the University of Maastricht in the Netherlands with a mean age of 20

Procedure: Participants were randomly assigned to a 2 x 2 condition between-participants design – conditions being low versus mild fear; weak versus strong argument. Participants completed a questionnaire measuring their pre-experimental attitude toward breast self-examination. They were then told they would evaluate the effectiveness of several educational messages about breast cancer. The experiment was computer controlled. Participants first read a message about the threat of breast cancer (containing manipulation of fear). This was followed by a self-report measure of fear arousal. Next, participants read a persuasive message about performing monthly breast self-examination, supported by eight weak or eight strong arguments. Finally, a questionnaire was administered with the post-experimental attitude towards breast-self examination as the dependent variable. The fear manipulation consisted of different levels of implied severity of breast cancer and susceptibility of participant. Argument strength varied between arguments such as 'breast self-examination was a nice way to be intimate with yourself' to 'by performing breast-self examination you are able to detect breast cancer in an earlier and therefore more treatable stage'.

Measures: Level of fear arousal was measured by reaction to ten mood adjectives, for example nervous, frightened on a 4–point scale; then averaged into a fear arousal index. Attitude towards performing a monthly breast self-examination was assessed by four 7–point word pairs, for example unimportant–important averaged into a single attitude index. Two items asked participants whether they knew someone who had suffered from breast cancer or another kind of cancer. Participants were fully debriefed and offered information on breast cancer and how to perform breast self-examination.

Results: The main effect of manipulated fear was not statistically significant, nor was the predicted interaction between fear and argument strength. However there was a significant main effect of argument strength suggesting argument-based message processing, irrespective of the level of evoked fear. There was also a significant interaction between reported fear and argument strength. Participants who expressed low fear did not differ in their attitude towards breast-self examination after reading either the weak or strong persuasive message, whereas participants who reported mild fear indicated they were more positive towards breast-self examination after reading the strong persuasive message than the weak message ($p < 0.01$).

Discussion: In contrast to earlier studies that reported effects of manipulated fear on argument-based processing, this study found only an effect of reported fear. The authors conceded that in future it might be more reliable to use physiological measures of reported fear rather than relying on self-report measures. They concluded that their study supported the hypothesis that evoked fear motivates people into more argument-based processing. However, they accepted that their findings might only be generalisable to breast self-examination or similar detection behaviours and should not be generalised to primary prevention behaviours such as using condoms to prevent HIV infection.

Evaluation

Method

This is a **well controlled** experimental study which shows the value of the experimental method. Although the fear manipulation aspect of the study was unsuccessful, the thoroughness of the approach taken by the experimenters enabled them to gain valuable data on the effects of strength of message on individuals who reported fear of breast cancer at the start of the study.

5.3 Healthy Living: Features of adherence to medical regimes

Key Study: 5.3.1 Reasons for non-adherence

C. J. Lowe and D. K. Raynor (2000), 'Intentional non-adherence in elderly patients: fact or fiction?', *The Pharmaceutical Journal*, 265 (7114)

Approach: Cognitive

Aim: To assess the extent to which intentional non-adherence to medical regimes is present in elderly patients

Method: Self-report

Type of sample: The paper states a random sample but no random sampling method is described

Participants: A sample of 161 patients aged 65+ and taking three or more drugs recruited from a general practice. Mean age of participants was 76 years (range 65–96); Fifty-three (33 per cent) were male and 71 per cent lived alone. Mean number of medicines prescribed was four.

Procedure: All participants were visited at home and interviewed using a structured questionnaire. Participants were asked which medicines they took, dose taken and frequency. Responses were compared with the medical records and patients were questioned about any discrepancies between their responses and their records.

Results: There was a discrepancy in 86 cases (53 per cent of sample). In 28 cases the discrepancy was due to administrative error and in three cases it was due to patient confusion. However the remaining 55 patients had made a rational decision to alter their medication. In all, 92 medicines were involved: 51 medicines were no longer being taken by the patients, while in 19 cases dosage was adjusted and in 22 cases frequency was adjusted. Table 5.1 shows reasons given by patients for non-adherence.

Discussion: According to this study, the stereotypical image of elderly patients and their non-adherence to prescribed medications due to confusion is inaccurate. The authors of this study argue that the elderly patients weighed up costs and benefits of taking particular medicines and that a third of the elderly patients showed intentional non-adherence. The most frequently cited reasons were the experiencing of side-effects and adjustment in response to symptoms. In common with younger adults, the patients made reasoned decisions and acted in a way that appeared rational to them, even if medical professionals would not have shared their opinion. The authors conclude that it is concerning that patients did not communicate their decision to their doctor. On the other hand, this behaviour may be understandable given that it can take some time to make a non-urgent appointment. Also elderly patients may have felt that it would have been wasting their doctor's time to make an appointment for this reason.

Table 5.1 Stated reasons for discrepancy

Reason	Number of drugs (n = 92)
Side-effects	17
Adjustment according to symptoms	17
Drug not working	12
Adjustment to suit daily routine	10
Drug not needed	10
Did not like taking tablets	9
Self-limiting condition	9
Misunderstanding	5
Concern about cost	3

Source: adapted from Lowe and Raynor (2000)

Evaluation

Usefulness

This is an interesting study because it deals with the issue of non-adherence in an open-minded way and does not assume that patients who stopped taking their medicine were acting irrationally even though they were not acting in accordance with medical advice. The reasons expressed by the elderly patients made sense on their own terms. Unfortunately the authors did not describe their sampling method, nor do they give many details about the demographics of the general practice involved, which reduces the usefulness of the study.

5.3 Healthy Living: Features of adherence to medical regimes

Key Study: 5.3.3 Improving adherence

P. M. Watt, B. Clements, S. G. Devadason, G. M. Chaney (2003), 'Funhaler spacer: improving adherence without compromising delivery', *Archive of Disease in Childhood*, 88

Approach: Cognitive

Aim: To assess the effect of adherence to prescribed asthma drugs of a 'Funhaler' or incentive toy

Method: Self-report and physiological measures

Type of sample: Not stated

Participants: 32 Australian children (10 male, 22 female) mean age 3.2 years (range 1–6). Average duration of asthma was two years and participants were on prescribed drugs delivered by pMDI (paediatric metered dose inhaler) and spacer.

Procedure: Medicine was administered using a standard inhaler for two weeks followed by the Funhaler for two weeks. The Funhaler is an inhaler with incentive toys (spinner and whistle) incorporated that function best when a deep breathing pattern is used by the child. A questionnaire was responded to by parents after each device had been used. The basic idea of the Funhaler is that the child will find use of it reinforcing hence encouraging adherence to the medication.

Results: The experimenters measured delivery efficiency of the Funhaler as compared to the standard inhaler and found no significant difference. Results of a linked study found that adherence was improved when using the Funhaler. When surveyed at random, 38 per cent more parents were found to have medicated their children the previous day when using the Funhaler than when using the normal spacer. Sixty per cent more children took the recommended four or more cycles per aerosol delivery when using the Funhaler compared to the standard spacer.

Discussion: The authors concluded that although there was no significant difference between efficiency of medication delivery using the Funhaler, there were marked improvements in both parental usage and children's effective use of the Funhaler, so the Funhaler could lead to improved clinical outcomes and reduced morbidity from asthma.

Evaluation

Method

This study appears to have been conducted over a fairly short time span. It would be important to do follow-up studies after several months to see whether the Funhaler continued to be reinforcing. For both parents and children, there may have been a novelty effect of using the Funhaler. Also behaviourist research shows that constant reinforcement is less rewarding than partial reinforcement so after a period of constant reinforcement the rewarding effect of using the Funhaler may reduce.

6.1 Stress: Causes of stress
Key Study: 6.1.1 Work

Gunn Johansson and Gunnar Aronsson (1984), 'Stress reactions in computerized administrative work', *Journal of Occupational Behaviour*, 21 (5), 159–81

Approach: Biological

Aim: To analyse the effects of working with visual display units (VDUs) on white-collar worker stress levels

Method: Field experiment

Design: Independent measures

Type of sample: Opportunity sample

Stage 1

Participants: 95 respondents (mean age = 41 years) to a questionnaire distributed at an office in Gothenburg, Sweden, in which there was extensive employee use of VDUs. This study was carried out in the late 1970s when computer use was in its infancy. The company was quite advanced in having a computer system at all.

Procedure: Participants responded anonymously to a questionnaire consisting of questions about demographics, recent job content and perceived mental strain. Respondents were divided into four groups according to the proportion of time they reported spending working with VDUs (no/little/moderate/extensive VDU work).

Results:

- Two-thirds of participants reported they needed further training in the computer system.
- Only 12 per cent felt they had sufficient influence over the changes computers brought to their jobs.
- Ninety-one per cent of those who worked extensively with VDUs reported some kind of discomfort, in particular eye strain, concentration and posture problems.
- The main differences in reported stressors between groups were computer breakdown, phone call interruptions, and work piling up during computer breakdowns for those who worked extensively with VDUs.
- The group with the highest reported psychosomatic symptoms was the group where little or moderate VDU work was combined with complex tasks involving responsibility.
- Data-entry users reported more strain and environmental issues than the customer-service group.

Stage 2

Participants: Ten volunteers from the group who had little or no contact with the computer system (control group) and 11 volunteers from the group who reported spending more than 50 per cent of work time at VDUs (VDU group) participated in the second stage. All were female, of similar mean age and with similar period of employment in the company.

Procedure: The study occupied two work days and one day off at home. On work days at 8 a.m., 10 a.m., 12 noon, 2 p.m. and 4 p.m. participants went to the company health centre where they made self-ratings of tiredness and mood, and left urine samples. Heart rate and blood pressure were measured. At 6.30 p.m. and 9.30 p.m. the same measures (apart from blood pressure) were collected from participants at home. The same tests were also conducted on the day at home during which participants were asked to behave as if on a normal day off. Urine samples were tested for catecholamine excretion – an indicator of mental stress.

See *Psychology A2 for OCR* Textbook, p. 130 for information on excretion of catecholamine.

Results:

- Differences in adrenaline excretion between work days and the day at home were significant for the VDU group but not for the control group.
- On work day mornings, the VDU group had higher adrenaline excretion than the control group but this was reversed in the afternoon.
- Self-rating results showed the highest strain ratings were reported in the morning for the VDU group but in the afternoon for the control group, reflecting different workload distributions. The VDU participants stated they worked fast in the morning in anticipation that the computer system might break down in the afternoon, whereas the control group participants reported a build up of work by the afternoon.

- The main persistent effect was for adrenaline excretion. The VDU group continued to show higher values in the evening after work, whereas the control group's level of adrenaline returned to baseline in the evening. For the VDU group, ,adrenaline levels were twice as high in the evening after a day at work than after the day at home.

- Corresponding self-ratings of rush, strain, irritation and fatigue remained higher in the VDU group.

- The health questionnaire revealed no significant differences between groups but the content of triglyceride in the blood, which is assumed to be associated with cardiovascular disorders, was significantly higher in the VDU group.

- Six members of the VDU group were examined during a computer breakdown, during which participants showed higher than normal adrenaline, blood pressure and heart rate. Although no 'work' was done during this period while participants were waiting for the system to restart, they felt more irritated, tired and rushed than normal.

> **Triglycerides: Triglycerides** are formed by combining glycerol with three molecules of fatty acid. They play an important role in metabolism as energy sources and transporters of dietary fat. They contain more than twice as much energy as carbohydrates. High levels of triglycerides in the bloodstream have been linked to risk of heart disease and strokes

Discussion: Those doing extensive VDU work were found to experience most strain, especially those whose work was data inputting. Results indicated that the VDU group took longer to relax after work, their physiological arousal was higher and they felt more mental fatigue after work than controls. However at the date at which this study was conducted, the major stress lay in the unforeseeable breakdowns that regularly occurred in computer systems. A modern equivalent might be irritation caused by loss of internet connection, but this would not cause the same level of anticipatory stress.

Food for thought

One interesting observation made by the authors is that whereas in the days before computers it was not uncommon to have to wait a few minutes for a response while information was retrieved from paper files, most study participants stated that they preferred not to wait more than five seconds for an answer from the computer. Nowadays most computer users would not expect to wait more than five milliseconds for a response!

What do you think would be the major stressors for high frequency computer users in the workplace today?

Evaluation

Combined measures

This is a **holistic** study because it incorporates many aspects of the work situation and tested people at work and home. Also it combines self-report measures with physiological measures of stress. This triangulation of data enables results using one type of measure to be confirmed or disconfirmed by comparison with data from another measure. Participants who self-reported that they did not unwind easily after work showed higher levels of adrenaline in the evening after work, confirming self-report findings.

6.1 Stress: Causes of stress

Key Study: 6.1.2 Hassles

Kerry Chamberlain and Sheryl Zika (1990), 'The minor events approach to stress: support for the use of daily hassles', *British Journal of Psychology*, 81 (4), 469–81

Approach: Cognitive

Aim: To analyse the effects of daily hassles on stress levels

Method: Self-report

Design: Longitudinal study

Type of sample: Self-selecting sample

Participants: There were four different samples:

1) 161 adult students, mainly part-time (86 male, 75 female; mean age 32 years)
2) 120 randomly selected adults from one city (47 male, 73 female; mean age 39 years)
3) 194 mothers with at least one child under 5 years and not in paid employment (mean age 29 years)
4) 150 elderly people (66 male, 87 female; mean age 69 years), of whom 43 per cent lived alone

Procedure: For Samples 1 and 2, data were collected using an identical questionnaire about daily 'hassles'. For Samples 3 and 4 data were collected on three occasions – at Time 1 through a structured questionnaire on hassles completed in the presence of a researcher and then at Times 2 and 3 (3 months apart) responded to and returned by post. Return rates (Time 2) were mothers – 95 per cent, the elderly – 91 per cent; (Time 3) mothers – 91 per cent, the elderly – 86 per cent. Additional data relating to life events, mental health and subjective well-being in these two samples were analysed.

Measures:

● Minor stressors were assessed with the Hassles Scale which asks respondents to rate 117 potential hassles on a 3–point severity scale.
● Life events data were obtained from mothers and the elderly at Time 3 using the Life Events Inventory, which assesses potentially stressful life events such as bereavement, moving house, financial problems.
● Mental health was measured at Time 3 with the Mental Health Index, which provides separate sub-scores on psychological well-being and psychological distress.
● Life satisfaction was measured at Time 3 using the question: 'How do you feel about your life as a whole?' answered on a 7-point scale.
● Positive and negative affect (feelings) were assessed with the Affectometer Scale which provides both positive and negative affect scores.

Table 6.1 Six most frequently endorsed hassles by group

Students (n = 161)	%	Community (n = 120)	%
Not enough time	86	Troubling thoughts about future	73
Too many things to do	82	Health of a family member	69
Troubling thoughts about future	79	Misplacing or losing things	69
Too many interruptions	75	Not enough time	67
Misplacing or losing things	73	Rising prices	66
Health of a family member	66	Not enough personal energy	64
Mothers (n = 194)		Elderly (n = 150)	
Not enough time	78	Crime	90
Rising prices	78	Rising prices	77
Planning meals	78	Pollution	75
Preparing meals	75	Misplacing or losing things	66
Not getting enough sleep	73	Declining physical abilities	65
Home maintenance	71	Concerns about news events	65

Source: adapted from Chamberlain and Zika (1990)

Results:

Hassles:

- Some hassles were common to at least two groups, for example, rising prices, not having enough time.
- Other hassles such as planning and preparing meals were of high hassle value to one group (mothers) and not to others.
- Stability of hassles in mothers and the elderly was investigated by assessing severity and intensity over 3 months and 6 months using test/retest correlations which showed considerable consistency in frequency and intensity of hassles.
- Analysis of variance showed no significant difference across time for hassle severity in either group.

Hassles and life events

- Hassles were found to relate to mental-health and well-being at moderate levels, showing stronger associations to the negatively oriented measures of psychological distress and negative affect than to the positively oriented measures.
- Relatively low associations between life events and hassles suggested that these variables provide different types of stressors.
- Life events had relatively low associations with mental health and well-being and appeared less influential than hassles.
- Multiple regression analysis showed that life events were a significant predictor for all outcomes in mothers but only for psychological distress in the elderly.
- Hassles were a significant predictor of all outcomes in both samples after life events had been partialled out.
- When life events were entered with hassles partialled out, they failed to predict any of the outcome variables in either sample.
- Hassles and life events were not found to produce a joint effect on mental health and subjective well-being beyond the effects of each independently.
- Hassles related (negatively) to well-being and positive outcomes almost as strongly as they relate to negative outcomes and they out-performed life events in predicting these measures.

Partialling out in multiple regression: Multiple regression analysis allows the researcher to calculate the amount of variance explained by one factor or set of factors when you remove (partial out) the effect of another factor. In this case, after removing the amount of variance explained by life events, hassles still explained a significant amount of the variance. However after removing the variance explained by hassles, life events did not predict a significant amount of the remaining variance.

Discussion: The findings support the value of assessing minor events (hassles) rather than life events to evaluate stress and predict outcome in physical and mental health. It has been suggested that hassles are the 'downstream' effects of major life events, but the results of this study confirmed the hypothesis that hassles are independent predictors of outcomes and do not function to moderate the relation between life events and health outcomes. The study also found the stability of hassles to be high, which suggests either that the environment provides a consistent source of stressful demands or that the individual is susceptible to particular hassles. A role for environment is suggested by the fact that the nature of hassles experienced by each group was found to be different yet consistent over time within groups. The authors concluded that their findings present strong support for the minor events approach to stress, and confirm the hassles scale as a reliable tool for the assessment of stress.

Evaluation

Self-report

The findings of this study are based entirely on self-report. We know from this study what people think are their chief causes of hassle and stress, but we have no objective data to support the theory that these hassles actually cause physiological symptoms of stress. This may limit the **usefulness** of the study.

1.2 Stress: Causes of stress
Key Study: 6.1.3 Lack of control
James H. Geer and Eileen Maisel (1972), 'Evaluating the effects of the prediction-control confound', *Journal of Personality and Social Psychology*, 23 (3), 314–19

Approach: Cognitive/biological
Aim: To analyse whether the effects of being able to control aversive stimuli are principally due to being able to predict the occurrence of those stimuli
Method: Laboratory experiment
Design: Independent measures
Type of sample: Opportunity sample
Participants: 60 undergraduate students at the State University of New York
Procedure: Participants were randomly divided into three groups. Colour photographs of victims of violent death (the aversive stimuli) were presented by projector. Electronic timers were used to control the duration of the stimulus presentation and a warning signal (60 decibel tone). Participants were seated in a sound-proofed room and galvanic skin response (GSR) and heart rate electrodes were attached.

A headset was placed over the participant's ears for delivery of the warning tone. All subsequent communication was delivered via an intercom. Participants were instructed to rest for 5 minutes, then background data were collected for 2 minutes on all participants. The experimenter then read the instructions to the participant. A further 1 minute rest period preceded presentation of the aversive stimuli. Instructions differed between groups.

- Participants in the 'actual control' group (those who could actively control the stimuli rather than a normal control group) were told that they would be shown a series of 10 photographs of dead bodies and that each photograph would be preceded by a tone of 10 seconds duration. They were told that they could terminate the photograph by clicking whenever they wished. In fact a viewing limit of 35 seconds was imposed if participants had not clicked to remove the photograph but participants were not made aware of this time limit.
- Participants in the predictability group were not given a button to press but were 'yoked' to the control group. That is to say that each participant was shown the photographs for the mean length of time that one of the control participants had chosen to view the photographs for. These

participants were told how long the tones and photographs would be presented for but they had no control and could not terminate presentation.

- Participants in the no control group could neither control not predict the occurrence of the tones or the photographs. They were told that from time to time they would be shown photographs of dead bodies and from time to time they would hear tones.

Stimuli were presented so that the total interstimulus interval between tones and photographs was equal to the same period for the yoked subject in the actual control group. Participants in all conditions were instructed to be certain to look at each photograph.

Results: Heart rate data were dropped as recording difficulties precluded accurate scoring of portions of most records. All analyses reported were therefore skin measures of skin response. All groups began with roughly similar levels of autonomic activity. The principal analyses were of the skin conductance responses to the stimuli. The dependent variable was change in conductance (square root of the sum of skin conductance responses). There were three different responses measured:

- Response to tone's onset
- Response during the latter half of the tone
- Response during presentation of the photograph (between 0.5 and 3 seconds following photograph onset)

It was found that the predictability group responded at a higher level to tone onset than either of the other two groups. Thus participants who could predict the occurrence of the aversive stimuli were more strongly affected by the warning signal preceding the stimuli than the participants who had the same prediction but knew that they could control the stimulus. In the no-control group the signal did not function as a warning since it was randomly presented in relation to the aversive stimulus. There was no significant change in conductance at the second point – during the latter half of the tone. Analysis of variance of skin conductance response on onset of aversive stimulus was highly significant

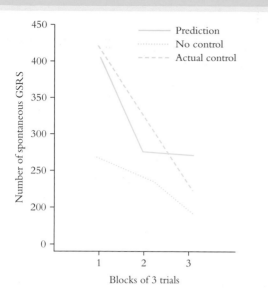

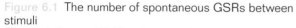

Figure 6.1 The number of spontaneous GSRs between stimuli
Source: J. Geer and E. Maisel (1972), 'Evaluating the effects of the prediction-control confound', *Journal of Personality and Social Psychology*, 23(3), 314–19. Published by the American Psychological Association and reproduced with permission.

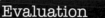

Evaluation

Psychology as science

This is well-controlled experiment that supports the contention that psychology is a science. However, it could be criticised for **reductionism** as the physiological measure is a measure of arousal, but the way in which that arousal is processed by participants cannot be determined without salf-report data.

($p < 0.001$). The prediction and no–control groups showed a higher level of response but this declined over trials while the actual control group showed lower level responses throughout.

These data indicate that the response to the aversive stimuli was similar for participants who could not control the aversive stimuli, whether or not they could predict their occurrence.

A further finding reported was the analysis of spontaneous conductance fluctuations that occurred between trials. The no-control group showed lower spontaneous fluctuation throughout the study, whereas the actual control and the predictability group showed a decrease in spontaneous activity as trials progressed.

Discussion: The results of this study indicate that the effects of control cannot be satisfactorily accounted for in terms of the control-prediction confound. Participants with control over an aversive stimulus exhibited lower GSR reactivity to that stimulus than those subjects who could predict but not control the stimulus. While the study failed to clarify the mechanisms involved, the results strongly indicated that the effects of control were not simply the effects of control and prediction being confounded. Instead there is something about being able to terminate aversive stimuli that reduces the impact of those stimuli.

6.3 Stress: Techniques for managing stress
Key Study: 6.3.1 Cognitive approaches

J. Gaab, N. Blättler, T. Menzi, B. Pabst, S. Stoyer and U. Ehlert (2003), 'Randomized controlled evaluation of the effects of cognitive-behavioral stress management on cortisol responses to acute stress in healthy subjects', *Psychoneuroendocrinology*, 28, 767–79

Approach: Cognitive/behaviourist

Aim: To assess the effect of cognitive-behavioural stress management training on endocrine stress responses and cognitive appraisal under acute psychosocial stress among healthy participants

Method: Laboratory experiment

Design: Independent measures

Type of sample: Self-selecting sample

Participants: 48 healthy non-smoking male students at the Swiss Federal Institute of Technology, Zurich. Volunteers enrolled online and responded to a screening questionnaire and were interviewed by phone. Exclusion criteria were used to reduce confounding variables known to affect physiological measures. Females and smokers were excluded as well as any participants reporting an acute or chronic physical or psychiatric disorder.

Procedure: Participants were randomly assigned to receive group-based cognitive-behavioural stress management before or after undergoing a standardised psychosocial stress test (Trier Social Stress Test – TSST). Participants gave a basal sample of salivary free cortisol then they were introduced to the TSST and were given ten minutes to complete a questionnaire to assess cognitive appraisal processes (PASA) regarding the anticipated stress situation. Afterwards participants took part in a simulated job interview followed by a mental arithmetic task in front of an audience of two people. A saliva sample was taken immediately before and after the TSST with further samples taken at 10, 20, 30, 45 and 60 minutes to assess salivary free cortisol.

All participants attended group-based cognitive-behavioural stress management training following the principles of stress inoculation training (SIT) developed by Meichenbaum (1985). Participants were divided into four groups and were allocated two day-long therapy sessions at two week intervals. Therapy focused on three cognitive and one behavioural stress-reducing techniques:

Cognitive techniques

- Cognitive restructuring
- Problem-solving
- Self-instruction

- Relaxation training – progressive muscle relaxation

At the end of the first therapy session participants were given a manual and flash cards and were required for homework to permanently carry and use the flash cards and to apply the techniques between sessions. Role play was also used. Two of the groups completed the SIT training prior to undergoing the TSST (treatment groups) while the other two groups underwent the TSST while waiting for SIT training (control groups).

Physiological measure

Saliva was collected from participants and cortisol concentration was determined using immunoassay with fluorometric detection.

> For information on determination of cortisol concentration using immunoassay with fluorometric detection, see *Psychology A2 for OCR* textbook, Stress 2.1, p. 129

Psychometric pre-post evaluation of the SIT and the control condition were analysed using the following questionnaire:

- Perceived Stress Scale (Cohen *et al.*, 1983) – used to assess the degree to which situations in life experienced during the past month are perceived as stressful.

Anticipatory cognitive appraisal processes in the TSST were assessed with the following questionnaire:

- Primary Appraisal Secondary Appraisal Scale (PASA). This is composed of four situation-specific subscales assessing 'challenge; 'perceived threat'; 'self-concept of own competence' and 'control expectancy'.

The PASA was administered between introduction to, and conduct of, the TSST.

Results: Results of the two treatment and the two control groups respectively were merged as neither the two treatment groups nor the two control groups differed significantly on any of the assessed demographic, psychometric or endocrine variables. Groups did not differ significantly in mean age (SIT group, mean age 24; control group, mean age 24.5), body mass index or any of the descriptive and pre-treatment psychometric questionnaires.

Principal Component Analysis with varimax rotation was employed in evaluation of the data.

> **Principal Component Analysis (varimax rotation):** This is a type of factor analysis which involves a mathematical procedure that transforms a number of possibly correlated variables into a smaller number of uncorrelated variables called principal components. The first principal component accounts for as much of the variability in the data as possible, and each subsequent component accounts for as much of the remaining variability as possible.
>
> Most of the modern methods for nonlinear dimensionality reduction can be traced back to mathematician Karl Pearson whose original idea was to take a straight line (or plane) which will be 'the best fit' to a set of data points. This can now be calculated using a computer programme and the results represented visually in a three-dimensional diagram.

Endocrine stress responses

The TSST resulted in a significant difference in endocrine response with participants in the SIT group showing reduced cortisol responses in pre- and post-SIT tests and a lower integrated response than the control group. The results including the PASA results in the calculation as co-variates reduced the cortisol differences to insignificant. This suggests that the endocrine differences were a close reflection of the psychological appraisal of the stressfulness of the TSST.

Psychometric measures

Groups differed significantly in their anticipatory cognitive appraisal of the TSST. Participants in the SIT group had lower primary stress appraisal and higher self efficacy appraisal and higher 'self concept of own competence' than the control group.

Discussion: This study demonstrates that short group-based cognitive-behavioural stress management training reduces the salivary free cortisol stress response to an acute stressor in healthy male participants. As indicted by analysis of covariance endocrine responses were influenced by the observed differences in the cognitive appraisal of the situation. Participants in the treatment group appraised the situation as less stressful and displayed more competence in coping with the situation. As there were no significant differences in results from personality and stress scales at the beginning of the study, it can be assumed that the reported results were not influenced by pre-existing differences between the groups. As the cortisol response differences between the treatment and control group were mediated through differences in the cognitive anticipatory appraisal processes, it can be concluded that the SIT influenced the cognitive and affective processing of stressful stimuli. The use of exercises, role-play and encouragement to practise stress-reducing techniques at home were effective in increasing self awareness of relevant cognitive schemas, enabling participants who had undergone SIT to deal better with the stressful situation of the TSST.

Evaluation

Validity of factor analysis

This is a thorough, **well-controlled** study that uses **random** allocation of participants and a relatively high degree of training for the experimental group (two days). It uses a sophisticated statistical method for analysing the variables but it should be pointed out that not all psychology researchers are convinced that factor analysis produces **valid** results whereas analysis of variance is universally agreed to produce clear statistical results (differences between groups). A problem with Principal Components Analysis is that its validity is dependent on the effectiveness of the questions asked of the data by the researcher and the manipulation (rotation) of the dataset to produce principal factors (in this case, varimax rotation). However as this study appears to have been carefully conducted and the data triangulate (the results of the physiological and appraisal test explain the same variance), there is no reason to cast doubt on the **reliability** or validity of the findings of this particular study.

Thomas Budzynski, Johann Stoyva and Charles Adler (1970), 'Feedback-induced muscle relaxation: application to tension headache', *Journal of Theoretical and Experimental Psychology*, 1, 205–11

Approach: Behaviourist

Aim: To assess the effect of a behavioural technique 'bio-feedback' in reducing tension headaches

Method: Case study

Type of sample: Clinical sample

Participants: Five patients who suffered from tension headaches. Full details provided for only one patient, a 29-year-old-female who had suffered regularly from tension headaches since childhood.

Procedure: Tension headache is associated with sustained contraction of the scalp and neck muscles. A technique was developed by the authors for training individuals in deep muscle relaxation in order to alleviated tension headaches. The basic function of the instrumentation is to assist patients in reaching deep levels of muscle relaxation by means of analogue information feedback – patients hear a tone with a frequency proportional to the electromyograpic (EMG) activity in the relevant muscle group.

> **Frontalis muscle:** The **frontalis muscle** runs vertically on the forehead, originating in tissues of the scalp above the hairline and inserting into the skin in the forehead and near the eyebrows. Contraction of the entire frontalis draws the eyebrows and skin of the forehead upwards and forms horizontal wrinkles running across the forehead.

> **Electromyography (EMG):** Electromyography is a technique for evaluating and recording the electrical activity produced by skeletal muscles, which produces a record called an electromyogram.

The patient has EMG electrodes applied to the skin surface over a particular muscle and has to keep the feedback tone low by relaxing that muscle. As the patient gets better at doing this, the loop gain of the feedback system is increased, thus requiring the participant to maintain a lower EMG level in order to hear the low tone.

Patient 1 spent the first two sessions in the laboratory practising relaxing the frontalis muscle without biofeedback. Her EMG levels were exceptionally high. The patient subsequently had two or three 30-minute feedback training sessions per week and worked at bringing her frontalis EMG to low levels.

Over the weeks as she grew more proficient at relaxing, silent trials were interspersed with feedback trials. These were designed to help her maintain the relaxation response even in the absence of the feedback tone. Also the patient was encouraged to practise relaxation training at least once a day at home. The patient also kept a daily record of her headaches.

Results: Analysis of the daily headache record showed a gradual decline in headaches from the first week of training although the patient did not notice the decline until the third week of training. In all Patient 1 received nine weeks of training during which she showed declining EMG and headache activity levels. A follow-up interview three months after termination of training showed that tension headaches had virtually disappeared.

Patient 2 was a middle-aged woman who had suffered from frequent tension headaches during the previous three years. She received 11 weeks of training and headache activity showed a substantial decrease from the first week of training. This patient had originally shown a tendency to overreact to minor stresses. After training she reported that such lesser events no longer upset her. The three-month follow-up revealed an all but complete elimination of headaches.

Patient 3 was a young female teacher who had suffered with tension headaches since graduating from college two years previously. She received five weeks of intensive training (three times per week). Headache activity dropped off rapidly and remained low through the training period. However a move and new job brought back the headaches. Patient 3 reported that she had not taken the time to follow the relaxation programme. After she reinstated the daily relaxation period, headache activity declined again and remained low for the three-month post-training period.

Patient 4 was a 33-year-old housewife who reported a moderate level of headache activity over a period of three years. She learned quickly to produce low frontalis EMG levels and headache activity remained low for the three-month training period. Patient 4 also reported an improvement in sleeping patterns.

Patient 5 was a middle-aged businessman who had suffered from frequent and severe tension headaches since early adolescence. He had previously received training in deep relaxation and learned quickly to relax his frontalis muscle and maintained low EMG levels during training. Although his baseline headache activity was very high, it decreased rapidly during the second week of training and remained low during training. After his fourth week of training, Patient 5 took a five-week vacation. On his return he experienced high tension and the return of his headaches. However after receiving two more feedback sessions and advice to schedule a period of daily relaxation, his headache activity returned to low and remained low for the rest of the three-month training period.

Discussion: The results of this pilot study showed that chronic tension headache sufferers can be trained to voluntarily lower their striate muscle tension in the face of daily life stresses and to reduce the incidence of tension headaches. The muscle relaxation response described in this study suggests that operant conditioning techniques might be successfully applied to particular events within the skin of the organism as well as to externally visible responses. The authors suggested that this technique – precise measurement and amplification of a particular response, information feedback and 'shaping' - might potentially be applicable to a wide variety of physiological events.

Evaluation

Generalisability

This study that showed significant improvements in patient response to stress and frequency of tension headaches after behavioural training. However this study was based on a small number of individual case studies and therefore it is not possible to **generalise** the results. The study did not apply the experimental method (no control group) and patients were aware of the goal of the study, so placebo effect was a possibility. However Budzynski *et al.* subsequently conducted an independent measures experiment using an experimental group, a placebo group and a control group. They found that the biofeedback group became less dependent on drugs and reported greater improvement in symptoms than either the placebo group or the control group.

6.3 Stress: Techniques for managing stress
Key Study: 6.3.3 Social approaches

Sahab P. Sinha, P. Nayyar and Surat P. Sinha (2002), 'Social support and self-control as variables in attitude toward life and perceived control among older people in India', *Journal of Social Psychology*, 142 (4), 527–40

Approach: Social

Aim: To assess the effects of social support and self-control in older adults in India

Hypothesis: That social support and self-control would act as moderators for a more positive attitude toward life and increased perceived control

Method: Self-report

Type of sample: Representative sample

Participants: 300 older adults (150 male), mean age 73 years (range 60–85 years) who were members of extended families and lived in high-density households in an urban area of Agra city, India. All participants were university graduates and had retired from government service.

Measures: Participants were assessed using the Self-Control Schedule, the Social Support Questionnaire, the Perceived Control Scale and the Life Attitude Profile.

The Self-Control Schedule (Rosenbaum, 1980) has four subscales relating to:

- cognitions to control emotional and psychological responses
- the use of problem-solving strategies
- the ability to delay gratification
- self-efficacy

The Social Support Questionnaire (Sarason *et al.*, 1983) contains 27 items and measures social support and satisfaction with that support. For the purposes of this study, only availability of support was measured. Participants were asked to list all the people (maximum of nine per question) who could assist them in various scenarios.

The Perceived Control Scale (Nayyarm 1993) contains 14 items rated on a Likert scale from 1 (never) to 7 (always). An example question was, 'How often do you feel you can exchange your room for another one if you wish to?'

The Life Attitude Profile (Recker and Peacock, 1981) contains 44 items. It is a multidimensional measure of attitude toward life. It has seven dimensions:

- Life purpose
- Existential vacuum
- Life control
- Goal seeking
- Death acceptance
- Desire for meaning
- Fulfilment in future

Respondents rated each item on a 7-point Likert-type scale.

Procedure: Details were collected from 950 participants concerning their age, education level, income from pension, family members living in the house, and total area of the house they had lived in for the past two years. A total of 300 participants were selected on high household density. Then participants were divided into groups according to age (old-old/young-old; social support (high/low) and self-control (high/low). The dependent variables were scores on the Perceived Control Scale and the Life Attitude Profile.

Results:

Control

Analysis of variance revealed a significant effect of age with old-old participants reporting less perceived control than young-old participants. The high self-control participants reported more perceived control than did the low self-control participants. Social support also affected participants' perceptions of control with the high-social support participants perceiving more control than the low-social support group. There was a significant interaction for age x social support with those in the young-old high-support group reporting highest perceived control, followed by young-old with low-social support, then old-old with high-social support and lastly old-old with low social support. There was also a significant interaction for age x social support x self control. Least control was perceived by the old-old group with low social support and low self-control.

Life Attitude Profile

Scores on the LAP were significantly affected by age (young-old participants being more positive than old-old); the high self-control group were more positive than the low self-control group and the high-social support group were more positive than the low-social support group. There was a significant age x social support interaction with young-old participants with high social support viewing their lives most positively. There was also a significant interaction for age x social support x self-control.

Discussion: The authors selected for study older adults in high density living conditions for whom they assumed restriction of freedom and perceived loss of control would be important sources of stress. They found that social support acted as an important buffer protecting older adults from stress and loss of control. They recommended that providing social support and enhancing self-efficacy are intervention strategies that can be used to enhance older people's perceived control and to change negative attitudes to life and improve life satisfaction.

Evaluation

Method

It is no surprise that younger old people feel more in control and more positive than older old people. Nor is it a surprise that scores on a self-control scale predict perceived control. However the interesting result here is that amount of social support predicted perceived control and life attitudes. This shows that the stresses brought by old age and overcrowding can be lessened by having a number of people with whom problems and stressors can be shared. However the value of this study is limited by the fact that there may be other hidden variables operating here that were not controlled for by the researchers. Also the measures were solely self-report and the research would have benefited from the addition of physiological measures of stress.

7.1 Dysfunctional behaviour: Diagnosis of dysfunctional behaviour

Key Study: 7.1.1 Categorising dysfunctional behaviours (DSM-IV and ICD-IO)

Diagnostic and Statistical Manual IV (APA, 1994)

1. At least one of the following three abnormal moods which significantly interfered with the person's life.
   a. Abnormal depressed mood most of the day, nearly every day, for at least two weeks.
   b. Abnormal loss of all interest and pleasure most of the day, nearly every day, for at least two weeks.
   c. If 18 or younger, abnormal irritable mood most of the day, nearly every day, for at least two weeks.

2. At least five of the following symptoms have been present during the same two-week depressed period.
   a. Abnormal depressed mood (or irritable mood if a child or adolescent).
   b. Abnormal loss of all interest and pleasure.
   c. Appetite or weight disturbance, either:
      - Abnormal weight loss (when not dieting) or decrease in appetite.
      - Abnormal weight gain or increase in appetite.
   d. Sleep disturbance, either abnormal insomnia or abnormal hypersomnia.
   e. Activity disturbance, either abnormal agitation or abnormal slowing (observable by others).
   f. Abnormal fatigue or loss of energy.
   g. Abnormal self-reproach or inappropriate guilt.
   h. Abnormal poor concentration or indecisiveness.
   i. Abnormal morbid thoughts of death (not just fear of dying) or suicide.

3. The symptoms are not due to a mood-incongruent psychosis.

4. There has never been a manic episode, a mixed episode, or a hypomanic episode.

5. The symptoms are not due to physical illness, alcohol, medication, or street drugs.

6. The symptoms are not due to normal bereavement.

Essential features

By definition, major depressive disorder cannot be due to:

- Physical illness, alcohol, medication, or street drug use
- Normal bereavement
- Bipolar disorder
- Mood-incongruent psychosis (for example schizophrenia or schizophreniform disorder or psychotic disorder not otherwise specified)

International Classification of Diseases 10 (WHO, 1992)

Depressive episode

In typical depressive episodes of all three varieties described below (mild, moderate, and severe), the individual usually suffers from depressed mood, loss of interest and enjoyment, and reduced energy leading to increased fatigability and diminished activity. Marked tiredness after only slight effort is common. Other common symptoms are:

(a) reduced concentration and attention
(b) reduced self-esteem and self-confidence
(c) ideas of guilt and unworthiness (even in a mild type of episode)
(d) bleak and pessimistic views of the future
(e) ideas or acts of self-harm or suicide
(f) disturbed sleep
(g) diminished appetite

The lowered mood varies little from day to day, and is often unresponsive to circumstances, yet may show a characteristic diurnal variation as the day goes on. As with manic episodes, the clinical presentation shows marked individual variations, and atypical presentations are particularly common in adolescence. In some cases, anxiety, distress, and motor agitation may be more prominent at times than the depression, and the mood change may also be masked by added features such as irritability, excessive consumption of alcohol, histrionic behaviour, and exacerbation of pre-existing phobic or obsessional symptoms, or by hypochondriacal preoccupations. For depressive episodes of all three grades of severity, a duration of at least two weeks is usually required for diagnosis, but shorter periods may be reasonable if symptoms are unusually severe and of rapid onset.

Some of the above symptoms may be marked and develop characteristic features that are widely regarded as having special clinical significance. The most typical examples of these 'somatic' symptoms are: loss of interest or pleasure in activities that are normally enjoyable; lack of emotional reactivity to normally pleasurable surroundings and events; waking in the morning two hours or more before the usual time; depression worse in the morning; objective evidence of definite psychomotor retardation or agitation (remarked on or reported by other people); marked loss of appetite; weight loss (often defined as 5 per cent or more of body weight in the past month); marked loss of libido. Usually, this somatic syndrome is not regarded as present unless about four of these symptoms are definitely present.

The categories of mild, moderate and severe depressive episodes described in more detail below should be used only for a single (first) depressive episode. Further depressive episodes should be classified under one of the subdivisions of recurrent depressive disorder.

These grades of severity are specified to cover a wide range of clinical states that are encountered in different types of psychiatric practice. Individuals with mild depressive episodes are common in primary care and general medical settings, whereas psychiatric inpatient units deal largely with patients suffering from the severe grades.

Acts of self-harm associated with mood (affective) disorders, most commonly self-poisoning by prescribed medication, should be recorded by means of an additional code from ICD-10 (X60-X84). These codes do not involve differentiation between attempted suicide and 'parasuicide', since both are included in the general category of self-harm.

Differentiation between mild, moderate, and severe depressive episodes rests upon a complicated clinical judgement that involves the number, type, and severity of symptoms present. The extent of ordinary social and work activities is often a useful general guide to the likely degree of severity of the episode, but individual, social, and cultural influences that disrupt a smooth relationship between severity of symptoms and social performance are sufficiently common and powerful to make it unwise to include social performance amongst the essential criteria of severity.

The presence of dementia or mental retardation does not rule out the diagnosis of a treatable depressive episode, but communication difficulties are likely to make it necessary to rely more than usual for the diagnosis upon objectively observed somatic symptoms, such as psychomotor retardation, loss of appetite and weight, and sleep disturbance.

Includes single episodes of depression (without psychotic symptoms), psychogenic depression or reactive depression).
www.mentalhealth.com/icd/p22-md01.html

Evaluation

Validity of classification

Compare the DSM-IV and ICD-10 classification of major depressive disorder (depressive episode).

Do you think the two systems of classification show the extent of overlap you would expect for both to be valid?

Key Study: 7.1.3 Biases in diagnosis

Maureen R. Ford and Thomas A. Widiger (1989), 'Sex bias in the diagnosis of histrionic and antisocial personality disorders', *Journal of Consulting and Clinical Psychology*, 57 (2), 301–5

Approach: Cognitive

Aim: To assess the effects of sex of patient on diagnosis of histrionic/antisocial personality disorder

> **Histrionic disorder:** This is defined by DSM-IV as a personality disorder characterised by a pattern of excessive emotionality and attention-seeking, including an excessive need for approval and inappropriate seductiveness, usually beginning in early adulthood. These individuals are lively, dramatic, enthusiastic, and flirtatious. They may be inappropriately sexually provocative, express strong emotions with an impressionistic style, and be easily influenced by others. Associated features may include egocentrism, self-indulgence, continuous longing for appreciation, feelings that are easily hurt, and persistent manipulative behaviour to achieve their own needs.
>
> **Antisocial personality disorder (APD):** This is defined by DSM-III as 'a pervasive pattern of disregard for, and violation of, the rights of others that begins in childhood or early adolescence and continues into adulthood'. To be diagnosed, an individual must be age 18 or older, as well as have a documented history of a conduct disorder before the age of 15. People having antisocial personality disorder are sometimes labelled 'sociopaths'.

Method: Self report

Design: Independent measures

Type of sample: Self-selecting

Participants: Participants were a self-selecting subgroup of 354 psychologists who responded to a questionnaire sent to over 1000 randomly selected psychologists from the southeastern United States listed on the National Register of Health Services Providers in Psychology. Seventy-six per cent of the participants were male and the mean age of participants was 47 years.

Procedure: Participants were provided with either one of nine possible case histories or with one of three possible lists of individual behaviours. All were assigned on a random basis. The design was a 3 x 3 factorial design (histrionic/antisocial (APD)/balanced) with sex manipulated three ways (male/female/sex unspecified). The balanced case history was that of a patient who exhibited features of both APD and histrionic disorder but did not meet the DSM-III criteria for either. The APD case history was the same but with additional features so that the patient met the DSM-III criteria for antisocial personality disorder. Likewise the histrionic case study contained the same details as the balanced case but with additional features that ensured the patient met the criteria for histrionic disorder. Two hundred and sixty-six psychologists responded to the case histories. Participants rated on a 7-point scale the extent to which the patient appeared to have each of four Axis I disorders (dysthymic; adjustment; alcohol abuse; cyclothymic disorder) and five Axis II disorders (narcissistic; histrionic; passive–aggressive; antisocial; borderline personality disorder). A variety of diagnoses was included to minimise demand characteristics (awareness of the goal of the experiment). A forced choice format was not used so that participants could provide multiple diagnoses for the same case history. An independent group of 88 psychologists rated the extent to which each of a list of ten individual behaviours extracted from the case histories was an example of a respective DSM-III histrionic or APD criterion (for example prone to manipulative suicidal threats). Sex of the patient was again varied three ways.

Results: Borderline personality disorder was the diagnosis made most often across all three case histories when sex was unspecified. APD diagnosis was the second most prevalent for the neuter APD case history and histrionic disorder was the second most prevalent diagnosis to borderline personality disorder in the neuter histrionic cases. Narcissistic personality disorder followed borderline personality disorder as the most popular diagnosis for the neuter balanced case history. Chi-square tests showed that ratings of APD and histrionic disorder for the balanced case histories were not significantly influenced by sex of patient. However for the histrionic case history, the participants significantly more often failed to diagnose histrionic disorder in male patients (44 per cent diagnosed correctly) than in female patients (76 per cent diagnosed correctly). For APD, participants significantly more often failed to diagnose APD in female patients (15 per cent) than in male patients (42 per cent). In fact antisocial female patients were significantly more likely to be diagnosed with histrionic disorder than APD (46 per cent compared to 15 per cent). None of the four Axis I diagnoses and none of the other three Axis II diagnoses were significantly affected by sex of patient. It was found that in rating behavioural characteristics, clinicians did not differentiate between male and female patients with regard to presence of each individual diagnostic criterion. None of the findings was substantially affected when the data were analysed separately for male and female clinicians, but it should be noted the sample of female participants was low (24 per cent of total sample).

Discussion: It was found that practitioners were biased by stereotypical gender views as there was a significant tendency to diagnose females with histrionic disorder and males with APD, irrespective of the reported characteristics of the cases. Sex biases had previously been attributed to the particular content of individual criteria (Kaplan, 1983) and efforts were made to remove such biases from DSM-III but the results of this study suggested that it was not that the individual items were sex biased but the absence of such bias at criterion level does not inhibit bias in final diagnosis. The results further suggested that efforts to eliminate sex bias should focus on expectations and assumptions connected with the disorders themselves rather than on the individual criteria.

Evaluation

Ecological validity

This is a **well-controlled** study that uses a relatively large sample. This study is relatively high in **ecological validity** because participants were given realistic synopses of real life case studies to assess. This is quite similar to the data they would have available to them in their clinical work with the exception, of course, that they could not observe or interview the patients.

7.2 Dysfunctional behaviour: Explanations of dysfunctional behaviour

Key Study: 7.2.1 Behavioural explanations

J. B. Watson and R. Rayner (1920), 'Conditioned emotional reactions', *Journal of Experimental Psychology*, 3, 1–14

Approach: Behaviourist

Aim: To assess whether a baby could be emotionally conditioned to produce a fear response in reaction to a previously neutral stimulus

Method: Case study

Type of sample: Opportunity sample

Participant: One baby boy who was eight months old at start of study. 'Little Albert' was chosen by the researchers because he was the baby of a wet nurse at the Harriet Lane Hospital for Invalid Children and had been brought up in the hospital virtually since birth. Further he was selected because he was 'one of the healthiest babies ever to have been brought to the hospital' and he was 'unemotional and stolid' so they did not anticipate that the research would upset him.

Procedure and results:

Phase 1: Initial testing (9 months)

Little Albert's fear reactions were tested by presenting various possible fear-inducing stimuli such as a rabbit, a dog, a rat, and so on. It was established that Albert did not show a fear response on being presented with the stimuli. When Albert was nearly nine months old the researchers then induced a fear reaction by hitting a large steel bar immediately behind his head. They did this three times. On the second hit his mouth puckered and on the third hit he cried. Watson and Rayner therefore decided to proceed with their experiment using the steel bar. They proposed to examine the following four questions:

- Could fear of a white rat be conditioned by presenting the rat at the same time as hitting the steel bar?
- Would this fear be transferred to other animals?
- How long would this conditioned response last?
- Would it be possible to devise a laboratory method to remove the conditioned response?

The experiment was conducted when Albert was eleven months old. A white rat was presented to Albert and when he reached out one hand to touch it, the steel bar was struck. Albert fell forward but did not cry. Then when Albert reached out his other hand, the bar was struck a second time. Albert again fell forward and he whimpered but did not cry. The researchers halted the experiment at that point as they did not want to upset Albert too much.

Phase 2: Conditioning (11 months, 3 days)

A week later the rat was again presented in silence. At first Albert did not try to touch it then he falteringly stretched out his hand, withdrawing it when the rat sniffed at it. Albert was then presented with blocks (building bricks) which he played with as normal.

Next, the rat was presented at the same time as the steel bar was struck. Albert fell over but did not cry. This was done several times and Albert gradually became more fearful until he cried. After this, when the rat was presented alone Albert cried and crawled away.

In order not to disturb Albert too much, experimentation was halted for one week.

Phase 3: Testing (11 months, 10 days)

The rat was presented alone, Albert whimpered and turned away. On second presentation of the rat alone, Albert crawled away. Then a rabbit was presented alone and Albert moved away and burst into tears. A dog was presented: Albert's response was not as strong but he moved away. When the dog's head was presented close to Albert's face he cried and fell over.

Some inanimate hairy items such as a seal coat, people's hair and a Santa Claus mask were presented and Albert responded with varying degrees of negativity.

Phase 4: Retesting and reconditioning (11 months, 15 days)

Five days later the rat was presented alone. Albert turned away but did not cry. At this point the researchers felt that the conditioning needed to be renewed. They therefore presented the rat again, this time hitting the steel bar at the same time. Albert reacted violently. Again the rat was presented alone and Albert fell to one side but did not cry. A similar reaction followed presentation of the rabbit alone.

Phase 5: Reconditioning (11 months, 20 days)

The rabbit was presented to Albert: as soon as he touched it, the steel bar was struck – a violent fear reaction occurred. Rabbit presented alone: Albert whimpered but still seemed to want to touch it. A dog was presented alone: Albert whimpered and kept his hands as far from the dog as possible. The dog was then presented again and the steel bar was struck when the dog touched him: a violent negative reaction was shown by Albert. Until this point the tests had been conducted in a small well-lit darkroom. Later the same day the same procedure was carried out in a large well-lit lecture room with an audience of four people. The rat was presented alone and at first Albert showed no fear reaction. Then the rabbit was presented and Albert showed a slight fear reaction. The dog was presented and Albert turned away but did not cry. At this point the researchers decided again to renew the conditioning. The rat was presented and immediately the steel bar was struck: Albert jumped violently but did not cry. When the rat was presented alone Albert did not initially show a negative reaction but when the rat was placed nearer him he whimpered and tried to move away. Next the rabbit was presented and Albert startled violently. The dog was then presented alone: at first Albert did not show much reaction. Then the dog barked loudly three times just inches away from Albert's face. Albert fell over and wailed until the dog was removed. However, Watson and Rayner noted that the adults present also showed a fear reaction when the dog barked. At this stage it was decided to wait a month before continuing with the experiment. At the next testing time (1 year, 21 days), a similar pattern occurred.

Discussion: Watson and Rayner concluded that the experiment on Little Albert showed 'as convincing a case of a completely conditioned fear response as could have been theoretically pictured ...that these experiments would seem to show conclusively that directly conditioned emotional responses as well as those conditioned by transfer persist, although with a certain loss in the intensity of the reaction, for a longer period than one month' (pp.5–12) They further concluded that 'our view is that they persist and modify personality throughout life' (p.12). Little Albert subsequently left the hospital (no explanation was given for this departure) so the intention of the researchers to try to remove the conditioned response could not be carried out. It is not known what became of Little Albert afterwards and whether indeed the conditioned fear response to hairy animals remained with him 'throughout life'

Evaluation

How would you evaluate Watson and Rayner's study from the following viewpoints?

Ethics

Validity

Reliability

7.2 Dysfunctional behaviour: Explanations of dysfunctional behaviour

Key Study: 7.2.2 Biological explanations

Kenneth S. Kendler *et al.* (1991), 'The genetic epidemiology of Bulimia Nervosa', *American Journal of Psychiatry*, 148 (12), 1627–37

Approach: Biological

Aim: To clarify from a genetic and epidemiological point of view the major risk factors for bulimia nervosa and to understand the relationship between narrowly defined and bulimia-like symptoms.

> **Epidemiology:** Epidemiology is the study of factors affecting the health and illness of the population. It is concerned with the incidence of disease in populations and does not address the question of the cause of an individual's disease.

> For more information on bulimia nervosa, see *Psychology A2 for OCR* textbook, p. 158

Method: Self-report

Type of sample: Clinical sample

Participants: 1033 female twin pairs from a population-based register.

Procedure: Personal structured psychiatric interviews were conducted with 2066 female twins from a population-based register of births in Virginia in the United States. DNA tests were conducted to establish definitely whether each pair was monozygotic (MZ – identical) or dizygotic (DZ – non-identical).

> For more information on MZ and DZ twins, see *Psychology A2 for OCR* textbook, p. 157

The sample consisted of 590 MZ, 440 DZ pairs with 3 pairs where zygosity could not be established. Psychiatric symptoms were identified using DSM-III-R. Participants were asked questions about their childhood environment (for example whether they were in the same class at school) and responded to the Eysenck Personality Questionnaire.

> For more information on the Eysenck Personality Questionnaire, see *Psychology A2 for OCR* textbook, p. 193

Participants were asked questions about weight, exercise, and body image. The latter was assessed by showing participants body silhouettes and asking which silhouette most resembled their body shape and which represented their ideal body shape. Logistic regression analysis was used to analyse the data.

Results: Of those interviewed, 32 individuals were diagnosed as having definite bulimia with 28 as having probable bulimia and 64 possible bulimia. Lifetime prevalence (those who had at some time had a diagnosis) of narrowly defined (definite and probable) bulimia nervosa and broadly defined (possible) bulimia were 2.8 per cent and 2.9 per cent respectively. Lifetime risk (the percentage who would be expected to have a diagnosis at some point before they reached age 50) was estimated at 4.8 per cent (narrowly defined) and 8 per cent (broadly defined) respectively.

Research methods

Distinguishing between lifetime prevalence and lifetime risk

Epidemiologists use two approaches to the investigation of the incidence of diseases:

- **Lifetime prevalence:** This is an estimate of the number of people in the population who have a diagnosis at time of survey or who have previously been diagnosed with the disease in question.

- **Lifetime risk:** This is an estimate of the individual's risk of developing a particular disease in the future which can then be extrapolated to provide population risk (in this survey the researchers' estimate is based on risk of individuals being diagnosed in the future by age 50).

Methods used to control weight gain were primarily exercise followed by strict dieting and self-induced vomiting. The cohort was divided into groups according to date of birth and it was found that those born more recently were more likely to be diagnosed with bulimia.

Major risk factors identified were:

1) Birth after 1960
2) History of wide weight fluctuations, dieting or extreme exercise
3) Low paternal care
4) Slim ideal body image
5) Low self-esteem
6) External locus of control
7) High level of neuroticism

Significant co-morbidity was found:

1) Depression (51 per cent)
2) Phobias (42 per cent)
3) Alcoholism (16 per cent)
4) Generalised anxiety disorder (11 per cent)
5) Anorexia nervosa (10 per cent)
6) Panic disorder (9 per cent)

There was no co-morbid diagnosis in only 23 per cent of cases.

The risk in a monozygotic co-twin of an affected twin was more than eight times the risk found in the general population. Probandwise concordance in broadly-defined bulima was found to be 26 per cent for monozygotic and 16 per cent for dizygotic twins; in narrowly-defined bulimia it was 23 per cent versus 9 per cent.

Pair-wise concordance: For a group of twins, *pairwise concordance* is defined as C/(C+D), where C is the number of concordant pairs and D is the number of discordant pairs. For example, a group of 10 twins have been selected for study where one member of the pair has a particular disease. During the course of the study four other previously non-affected twins become affected, giving a *pairwise concordance* of 4/(4+6) or 4/10 or 40 per cent.

Probandwise-concordance: For a group of twins in which at least one of each pair of twins is affected, *probandwise concordance* is a measure of the proportion of twins who have the illness who have an affected twin and can be calculated with the formula of 2C/(2C+D), in which C is the number of concordant pairs and D is the number of discordant pairs. For example, a group of 10 twins have been selected for study where one member of the pair is affected. During the course of the study, four other previously non-affected members become affected, giving a *probandwise concordance* of 8/(8+6) or 8/14 or 57 per cent.

Discussion: Results indicated that family aggregation (clustering) was solely accounted for by genetic factors and these indicated a heritability liability of 50 per cent.

Heritability liability: Heritability estimates reflect the amount of variation in genotypic effects compared to variation in environmental effects. Heritability liability means the (genetic) risk an individual has of inheriting a particular disease.

This is not to say that there were no shared environmental factors but that they were not strong enough to be identified separately beyond the genetic factors. The results also indicated that narrowly-defined and broadly-defined bulimia were conditions on the same spectrum and differed only in severity. The researchers pointed out that their findings were correlational rather than causational. That is to say that excessive exercise may not cause bulimia, but rather it might be that individuals with eating disorders take up excessive exercise. They also pointed out that research conducted on twins may not reflect patterns in the wider population.

Evaluation
Usefulness
This is a large study that incorporates a wide range of data and uses sophisticated statistical techniques to estimate prevalence and risk of bulimia nervosa, hence it is a useful study.

Key Study: 7.2.3 Cognitive explanations

Graham J. Pickup and Christopher D. Frith (2001), 'Theory of mind impairments in schizophrenia: symptomatology, severity and specificity', *Psychological Medicine*, 31, 207–20

Approach: Cognitive

Aim: To explore theory of mind impairments in patients with diagnosis of schizophrenia

This study used Theory of Mind task to analyse cognitive impairments in schizophrenia that appear to be similar to those found in people on the autistic spectrum. This links to the Core Study by Simon Baron-Cohen *et al.*, 'Reading the Mind in the Eyes' (1998). The current study did not use the 'Reading the Mind in the Eyes' task but used similar false belief tasks devised during the 1980s by Wimmer and Perner (1983; 1985; 1987).

See *Psychology A2 for OCR* textbook, p. 161 for a brief discussion of Theory of Mind (ToM)

Method: Laboratory experiment

Type of sample: Clinical sample

Participants: Forty-one patients with a DSM-IV diagnosis of schizophrenia took part in this study. They were in the age range 16–65; had an IQ of 70 or over and had no history of drug/alcohol abuse, neurological disability (brain damage) or leucotomy (brain surgery). About half the participants were in-patients at London psychiatric hospitals and the other half lived in the community. All but one of the patients were taking neuroleptic drugs (tranquilisers) prescribed to control their schizophrenia. Tests showed that at the levels at which the drugs were prescribed there was no impairment in memory function. There were two control groups. One group consisted of 35 healthy people with no history of psychiatric problems and the other group was a clinical control group composed of 18 individuals with diagnoses of affective disorders such as depression but not history of psychotic disorders.

Procedure: Schizophrenic patients were divided into groups according to their symptomology on the day of testing. Sixteen patients were allocated to the behavioural signs group (divided into positive and negative behavioural signs); sixteen were allocated to the positive signs of paranoia group, one participant showed passivity (without behavioural signs or paranoia) and the remainder (eight) showed no symptoms on that day. Two first-order and one second-order false belief tests of Theory of Mind (ToM) were given to participants with schizophrenia and the control groups. All participants were also given three 'non-mental' representation control tasks that were similar in structure to the ToM tasks but did not require theory of mind. Tasks were read aloud and enacted by the experimenter using props like 'Playmobil' characters. Most stories were set in a hospital, or involved familiar objects, in order to increase ecological validity for institutionalised patients. Memory control questions were also asked. The test question in each task was the measure of representational understanding (ToM).

Statistical analysis: The relation between ToM and symptomatology was explored using regression analysis.

See p. 4 for an explanation of regression analysis

Results: It was found that schizophrenic patients with behavioural signs were impaired relative to controls on ToM, and that remitted patients and the single case with passivity symptoms performed as well as controls. Regression analysis showed that severity ratings of behavioural signs predicted impaired ToM in schizophrenia. There was weak evidence that a subgroup with paranoid symptoms had ToM impairments, although these were associated with low IQ. Schizophrenic patients only showed ToM deficits on the second-order task. No impairments appeared on the matched control tasks which did not require ToM.

Discussion: The authors concluded that there is a clear association between ToM impairment and behavioural signs in schizophrenia. Deficits in paranoid patients were harder to detect and it may be that any deficits were compensated for by IQ–dependent problem–solving skills. They found that ToM impairments in schizophrenia were less severe than in autism, but were nevertheless specific to those with current symptoms of schizophrenia and were not a reflection of general cognitive deficits.

Evaluation

Validity

This is a well-controlled study that uses ToM tests that have shown to be **valid** in detecting ToM deficits in autism. However the tests were devised for use with children whereas the participants with schizophrenia were adults. This might explain why the deficits were shown only on the second-order (more difficult) task. This suggests that it would be useful to test people with schizophrenia on Baron-Cohen's 'Reading the Mind in the Eyes' task. One issue is why those not showing behavioural symptoms at time of testing did not have difficulty with the ToM tasks. Individuals with autism show consistent deficits. This would appear to indicate that in schizophrenia (unlike autism) the deficit is not consistent but is evident only when symptoms are severe. Do you think that this suggests that the TOM deficits are symptoms of, rather than an explanation for, schizophrenia?

7.3 Dysfunctional behaviours: Treatments for dysfunctional behaviours

Key Study: 7.3.1 Behavioural treatments

Linda Teri, Rebecca G. Logsdon, Jay Uomoto, and Susan M. McCurry (1997), 'Behavioral treatment of depression in dementia patients: A controlled clinical trial', *Journal of Gerontology: Psychological Sciences*, 52B (4), 159–66

Approach: Behavioural

Aim: To assess outcomes of two behavioural treatment programmes for patients with depression and their carers

Method: Laboratory experiment

Design: Independent measures

Type of sample: Self-selecting sample

Participants: Seventy-two patients (38 male, 34 female; mean age 76 years) diagnosed with dementia and depression and their carers.

Procedure: The diagnosis of dementia was based on a thorough physical and neurological exam and confirmed by neuropsychological assessment and diagnostic information obtained during interviews with both patients and carers. Patients were diagnosed with either major depressive disorder or minor depressive disorder according to the diagnostic criteria set out in DSM-III-R. Carers were also assessed for their own levels of depression. The primary outcome measures were the Hamilton Depression Rating Scale and the Cornell Scale for Depression in Dementia.

Patients were randomly assigned to one of four conditions: 'pleasant events'; 'behaviour-therapy problem-solving'; or two control conditions – typical care control or waiting list control. Treatment in the experimental conditions consisted of nine 60-minute sessions, once per week.

Pleasant events treatment involved sessions:

- identifying and planning pleasant events for the patient
- addressing carer problems such as stress and depression
- identifying specific patient behaviour problems and devising problem-solving strategies for modifying behaviour problems.

Behaviour-therapy problem-solving involved:

- a systematic approach to problem-solving
- education, advice and support to carers
- problem-solving patient depression behaviours of specific concern to carers.

Typical care control: patients and carers were given advice and support provided in typical services available in the community.

Waiting list control: patients were informed they would receive no active intervention for the nine-week period of the study.

Results: A significant overall treatment effect was obtained for patient depression ($p < 0.001$). Improvement in the active treatment groups was significantly greater than in the two control conditions. No significant changes were hypothesised for carers as the focus of the intervention was the patient. However an overall treatment effect was found for carer depression levels ($p < 0.01$). Carers in the active conditions improved significantly more than carers in the control conditions.

The significance of improvement post-treatment referred to above is improvement that is statistically significant. For a clinical group of participants it is important also to consider whether the difference pre- and post-treatment is a meaningful one in clinical terms. Patient participants who met criteria for major depression at pre-treatment and no longer met major depression criteria post-treatment were considered to have experienced clinically significant improvement. Likewise patient participants who met criteria for minor depression pre-treatment were considered significantly clinically improved if they no longer met criteria for either minor or major depression. Using this definition, 60 per cent of patient participants showed clinically significant improvement in the active treatment condition while only 20 per cent showed improvement in the control conditions and 10 per cent worsened.

A six-month follow-up assessment was conducted on participants in the active treatment groups but not on those in the control group who for ethical reasons were offered treatment as soon as possible after the end of the nine-week treatment period for the experimental groups. Both patients and carers maintained statistically significant improvement after six months over pre-test scores

Table 7.1 Group Mean Pre- and Post-Treatment Scores on Hamilton Depression Rating Scale (HDRS) and Cornell Scale for Depression in Dementia (CSDD) and group mean changes in outcome measures

	Pleasant events N = 23	Problem solving N = 19	Typical care N = 10	Waiting list N = 20
Patient				
HDRS Pre-T	16.3	16	14.1	14.5
HDRS Post-T	11	12.2	13.8	14.8
Change	**−5.3**	**−3.8**	**−0.3**	**0.3**
CSDD Pre-T	14.8	15.1	13.9	14
CSDD Post-T	10.6	11.4	13.9	14.9
Change	**−4.2**	**−3.7**	**0.0**	**0.1**
Carer				
HDRS Pre-T	8	9	6.7	6
HDRS Post-T	6.3	5.8	7.3	6.6
Change	**−1.7**	**−3.2**	**0.6**	**0.6**

Source: adapted from Teri *et al.* (1997)

(patients on both outcome measures, $p < 0.001$; carers on HDRS, $p < 0.05$). Using the same definition of clinical improvement discussed above, it was found that after six months, 69 per cent of patient participants who had shown improvement post-treatment maintained their improvement, while 31 per cent had relapsed.

Discussion: The results of this study support the effectiveness of behavioural treatment of depression in patients with Alzheimer's Disorder. Both patients and their carers receiving either pleasant–event or problem-solving training experienced significant reductions in their level of depression after treatment and at follow-up. The authors recommended that in the light of the results obtained in this study, behavioural interventions should be offered as an alternative to drug treatments when treating depressed patients with dementia.

Evaluation

Significance of results/usefulness

Most studies in psychology discuss results in terms of statistical significance. This is an important aspect of methodology as it indicates the probability that the results obtained would not have been obtained by chance. Normally this criterion is sufficient for judging whether the hypothesis has been supported.

In the case of a clinical sample, it is just as important to find out whether the intervention has brought a meaningful level of improvement to the individual participant in alleviating their symptoms as it is to discuss the results in terms of statistical significance. This study shows that most participants (both patients and carers) benefited from the behavioural treatment in terms of lowered depression levels which shows that it really was a **useful** study, not just in research terms, but also directly useful to those involved.

Key Study: 7.3.2 Biological treatments

Craig J. Whittington, Tim Kendall, Peter Fonagy, David Cottrell, Andrew Cotgrove and Ellen Boddington (2004), 'Selective serotonin reuptake inhibitors in childhood depression: systematic review of published versus unpublished data', *The Lancet*, 363, 1341–45

Approach: Biological

Aim: To assess benefits and risks of prescribing selective serotonin reuptake inhibitors (SSRIs) to children with depression

Method: Meta-analysis

Procedure: Four bibliographic databases were searched for published trials in which any antidepressant was compared with placebo in participants aged 5–18 years diagnosed with depression. Every effort was made to obtain results of unpublished trials as well. Data were extracted for the following efficacy outcomes: remission (significant reduction in symptoms) and response and mean depression level. Data were also extracted with regard to safety of treatment: any serious adverse event (including suicidal behaviours) and discontinuation of treatment due to adverse event.

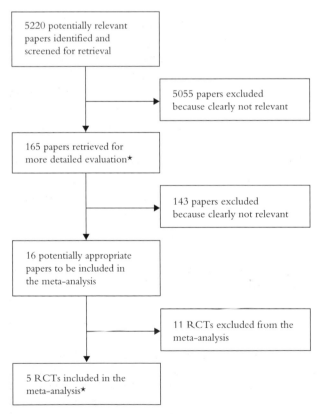

RCT=randomised controlled trial

*Includes trials reported in several publications

Figure 7.1 Trial flowchart for published data
Source: C. Whittington *et al.* (2004). Reprinted with permission from Elsevier

Results: From an original total of over 5000 potentially relevant studies, the researchers were left with 22 studies of which only five met inclusion criteria. Most of the others used an alternative treatment (tricyclic antidepressants instead of SSRIs).

Fluoxetine

Two published randomised controlled trials provided data on 315 participants (7–18 years) with depression that showed that:

- Fluoxetine was more likely than placebo to bring about remission after seven to eight weeks of treatment.
- Fluoxetine led to a small reduction in mean depressive symptoms.
- Fewer adverse events were reported in the fluoxetine group than the placebo group.
- Rate of discontinuation because of adverse events was similar in both groups.
- No data on suicidal behaviour were reported and no deaths were recorded in either trial.
- No unpublished trials of fluoxetine were identified but data from the Expert Working Group of the Committee on the Safety of Medicines (CSM) on suicidal behaviour showed no increased risk of this behaviour for young people on fluoxetine or placebo.
- The researchers concluded that fluoxetine has a favourable risk–benefit profile.

Paroxetine

One trial of paroxetine was identified which provided data on 180 participants (12–18 years) diagnosed with depression.

- By the end of eight weeks' treatment, more patients given paroxetine met the criteria for remission than those given placebo although there was no meaningful reduction in symptoms for the sample as a whole.
- Patients on paroxetine had increased risk of having a serious adverse event, and of suicidal ideation (thoughts) or attempting suicide.
- The CSM review included two unpublished trials of paroxetine on 478 participants (7–18

years) with depression which provided little evidence of efficacy of paroxetine.

- The researchers concluded that the risks associated with paroxetine outweigh the benefits.

Sertraline

Two published randomised controlled trials of sertraline provided data on 376 participants (6–17 years) with depression found that:

- Sertraline was more likely than placebo to bring about response by the end of ten weeks of treatment.
- Sertraline gave little improvement in mean depressive symptoms.
- Slightly more sertraline-treated patients reported serious adverse events including suicide and suicidal thoughts.
- The CSM review provided additional data on remission levels for the participants in the published trials which did not lend support to the efficacy findings.
- Without the unpublished data, the risk-benefit profile would have marginally favoured use of sertraline, but taken together the questions over efficacy and the possible slight increase in suicidal ideation and attempts suggest an unfavourable risk-benefit analysis.

Citalopram

No published trial that met the criteria of this study was found. However the CSM review provided data from two unpublished trials on 422 participants (7–18 years).

- Efficacy data were limited but suggest that citalopram was unlikely to produce a clinically significant reduction in symptoms by the end of eight to twelve weeks of treatment.
- Citalopram increased the risk of attempted suicide and was associated with a small increased risk of adverse events caused by treatment.
- With no good evidence for efficacy and the potential for increased risk of suicide, the risk-benefit balance for citalopram is unfavourable.

Venlafaxine

One small randomised controlled trial of venlafaxine provided data on 40 participants (8–18 years) with depression.

- The limited data suggested that venlafaxine did not improve symptoms by the end of six weeks of treatment.

- No serious adverse effects were reported, although one patient receiving venlafaxine developed a manic episode and had to be admitted to hospital.
- Two unpublished trials of venlafaxine were included in the CSM review involving 334 participants (6–17 years).
- Patients on venlafaxine had an increased risk of discontinuation due to adverse events and a raised risk of suicide-related events.
- The data suggest that venlafaxine has an unfavourable risk-benefit profile.

Discussion: A favourable risk-benefit profile was found only for fluoxetine as a drug treatment for depression in children. Data on the other SSRIs suggest no/weak evidence of improvement and possible increased risk of adverse events. The researchers concluded that given the lack of evidence of benefit and the high risk of attempted suicide in children and young people with depression, the use of any prescribed drug that might increase that risk without clear benefit should be discouraged.

A second important issue raised by this study is the non-reporting of negative trials. Published data for paroxetine, sertraline and venlafaxine provided some evidence of efficacy and little or no evidence of harm. However the unpublished data highlighted potential risks. The authors argued that the pharmaceutical industry should be urgently required to make public all trial data. They commented: 'The fact that the drugs reviewed here have previously been recommended for use in children on the basis of a very restricted published evidence base can only serve to increase that sense of urgency' (p.1345).

Evaluation

Usefulness

This is an extremely useful report. Extensive searches, a rigorous selection procedure and use of both published and unpublished data enabled the authors to distil the current state of knowledge about the effect of SSRIs currently prescribed to children and young people suffering from depression and led to important recommendations concerning their possible lack of efficacy and potential adverse side effects.

7.3 Dysfunctional behaviours: Treatments for dysfunctional behaviours

Key Study: 7.3.3 Cognitive treatments

Goldapple *et al.* (2004), 'Modulation of cortical–limbic pathways in major depression. Treatment-specific effects of cognitive behavior therapy', *Archives of General Psychiatry*, 61, 34–41

Approach: Cognitive/Biological

Aim: To examine changes in brain activity in patients with depression following Cognitive Behaviour Therapy (CBT)

Method: Laboratory experiment

Design: Mixed method

Type of sample: Self-selecting sample

Participants: Seventeen patients (6 male, 11 female) diagnosed with depression were recruited through newspaper advertisements to the Mood and Anxiety Disorders Program in Toronto. They were volunteers and written informed consent was obtained. Only 14 patients completed the full course of treatment as three withdrew due to worsening of symptoms or inability to comply with CBT instructions.

Procedure: The 14 patients who completed the course of treatment were PET scanned before and after a 15–20 session course of outpatient CBT. Patients in individual sessions received treatment by one of two trained CBT therapists, with eight and ten years of experience respectively. The CBT sessions were conducted according to Beck's manual and were audiotaped to enable ratings of treatment fidelity. Participants were introduced to a number of therapeutic strategies intended to reduce negative thoughts and attitudes. Behavioural activation was used to address the disruption of routine that can be brought by depression. Participants were encouraged to increase the frequency of pleasant events in their lives and events which they could control, especially where they were showing avoidance and withdrawal. They were introduced to the concept of cognitive monitoring, and shown how to dismantle complex chains of thoughts into separate components that could be evaluated for evidence of negatively biased information processing.

Measures: Clinical measures included weekly monitoring using the Beck Depression Inventory and the Hamilton Depression Rating Scale before and after training and once midway through training.

PET scans

Positron Emission Tomography measures of regional cerebral glucose metabolism were obtained at start and end of study using standard imaging methods. All scans were conducted with patients lying down, awake in a resting state with eyes closed and ears uncovered. Patients were asked to refrain from food, coffee and alcohol for at least six hours before the scan session. Patients were given no explicit cognitive instructions but were asked to avoid thinking about any one topic during the uptake period. Image acquisition began after 40 minutes and emission data were acquired during a 35-minute period in which wakefulness was monitored every 10 minutes.

Data analysis: All scans were normalised and corrected for differences in the whole brain global mean and smoothed using a Gaussian kernel. Statistical analyses were performed using dedicated software. Response-specific CBT effects were the focus of the study.

For further information on PET scans, see *Psychology A2 for OCR* textbook, p.18

Analysis of PET scans: The process of correcting for difference and smoothing using a Gaussian kernel is a mathematical operation used in generating multi-scale representations in computer-vision and image-processing. This process enables the image of one individual's brain to be superimposed on another so that identical regions of activation can be imaged as identically located despite individual differences in brain size and shape.

Based on previous studies of antidepressant medication effects, five regions were targeted (ventral subgenual cingulated, dorsal anterior cingulated, dorsolateral prefrontal cortex, hippocampus, and posterior cingulate. As well as pre-and post-treatment scans, patterns of activation were also compared with activations in a separate paroxetine treatment group (n = 13) using the same camera and an identical scanning procedure. In the absence of a controlled randomised trial of CBT and medication, this group served to aid interpretation of the effects of CBT training.

Results:

Clinical effects

For the 14 patients who completed CBT, scores on the HDRS showed a mean reduction from 20 before treatment to 7 after treatment. Of the 14 completers, 9 patients met the 50 per cent decrease criteria for full response. The remaining 5 patients had no less than a 35 per cent decrease in their HDRS scores. All participants were included in the pre-treatment to post-treatment analysis. Patients in the paroxetine-treated comparison group had similar severity symptoms at baseline (start of study) with a mean score of 23 on the HDRS. They also showed a comparable clinical response with mean post-treatment score of 6 on the HDRS.

Regional metabolic change effects:

- Analysis of the data from the PET scans showed significant regional metabolic changes in pre- and post-treatment activation that differed for the CBT group and paroxetine-treated group in several regions.
- Dorsolateral prefrontal, inferior parietal and hippocampal differences represented an inverse pattern for CBT and paroxetine.
- Between-treatment differences in dorsal midcingulate, ventromedial frontal, and posterior cingulate were related to unique changes with CBT treatment and not with paroxetine.
- Differences involving subgenual cingulate, insula, brainstem and cerebellum were due to unique paroxetine effects.
- There were decreases in ventral prefrontal cortex following both treatments.

Discussion: Limbic increases and cortical decreases were identified following successful treatment with CBT. These regional changes involved sites similar (in some case, identical) to those seen in studies of effects of paroxetine and other drug therapies, **but the changes were in the opposite direction.** These results provide tentative neural correlates of the theorised top-down mechanisms that mediate

CBT response. This suggests that CBT affects attention to personally relevant emotional and environmental stimuli, possibly reducing cortical processes involved in encoding and retrieving negative memories and thoughts about irrelevant information. Activation of regions previously associated with emotional processing tasks in nondepressed controls was also associated with CBT treatment.

Taken together, the treatment-specific change patterns in CBT and paroxetine groups support the hypothesis that each treatment targets different sites with differerential top-down and bottom-up effects involving both limbic and cortical regions. The overall modulation of this complex system rather than any one particular regional change may be most critical for symptom remission. A possible confounding variable is the behaviour of patients as, at the time of scan, patients were studied in a relatively uncontrolled state. Previous studies during a variety of cognitive tasks demonstrate that medial frontal activation decreases relative to rest. Medial frontal increases in activity seen at baseline in both sets of participants relative to healthy controls suggesting increased attention to self in those with depression do not change much in response to treatment, suggesting that the change effects related to the disorder rather than a confounding short-term behavioural state.

Evaluation

Method

The researchers acknowledged that although the two independent groups met identical inclusion criteria and were recruited in the same way, selection bias may still exist. For that reason they suggest that a similar study be carried out but on the basis of randomised controlled trial with **random** allocation to a CBT and medical intervention condition.

8.2 Disorders: Explanations of an affective disorder – depression
Key Study: 8.2.1 Behavioural explanations

Thomas M. O'Rourke, Warren W. Tryon, Charles S. Raps (1980), 'Learned helplessness, depression and positive reinforcement', *Cognitive Therapy and Research*, 4 (2), 201–9

Approach: Behavioural

Aim: To test whether learned helplessness could be induced using contingent positive reinforcement and also to compare Seligman's and Lewinsohn's models of depression

Method: Laboratory experiment

Design: Independent measures

Type of sample: Self-selecting sample

Participants: College students were approached and asked to participate in two experiments, a word problem and the other described as working with a machine that ejects nickels 'when students do certain things'. Volunteers would keep any money received from the machine as well as being paid at least one dollar. Fifty-six volunteers participated; age range of participants was 17 to 55; gender ratio 5 male: 3 female.

Procedure: The experiment was based on classical conditioning and operant conditioning techniques. On arrival, volunteers responded to the Beck Depression Inventory and then were assigned to appropriate conditions. The eight participants with the highest scores on the BDI were allocated to the depression group. The remaining 48 were divided into six groups (five males and three females in each group).

Apparatus: The apparatus involved a machine that ejected nickels (equivalent to 1p). At the beginning of each trial, a nickel was illuminated in a window. Two oblong reflector lights were placed to the right of the window with the word 'earned' and 'gift' on them. Nickels were automatically ejected through a slot. Buttons numbered 1, 2, 3 were mounted on a response platform. When the participant pressed a button, a reinforcement schedule was controlled by a system of electronic gates, which automatically monitored for correct active or passive responses. Rewards (nickels) were given at the end of each trial; the reflector with the word 'earned' (contingency training) or 'gift' (non-contingency) training was illuminated, then a nickel was ejected.

Conditions: Participants were allocated to the following conditions:

- Group A earned money via an active response (contingent reward)
- Group P earned money via a passive response (contingent reward)
- Group N60 received money noncontingently on 60 per cent of trials
- Group N30 received money noncontingently on 30 per cent of trials
- Group N0 received no money
- Group C served as a control group and experienced a waiting period
- Group D was the group of depressed patients who also experienced the waiting period

After completing the BDI, the Group C (Control) and Group D were asked to wait approximately 15 minutes and were then sent to Experimental Room 2 for anagram testing (testing phase). All other participants were sent to Experimental Room 1 for the training phase.

Training phase

In Experimental Room 1, participants were seated in front of the machine and given instructions. They were told that the aim of the experiment was to see how intelligently students go about making money from the machine. They were told they had three seconds in which to make a choice: pressing button 1, 2 or 3 or doing nothing. If their response was correct, they would get a nickel. However if the light showed 'gift' rather than 'earned', it meant that the machine had given them a gift, they had not earned the money.

Groups A and P were rewarded on a frequent reinforcement schedule on every second correct response (FR2) – making the appropriate active or passive response. The correct active response (Group A) was pushing button 3; the correct passive response (Group P) was doing nothing. Groups N60, N30 and N0 were exposed to 80 trials during which noncontingent reinforcement (rewards delivered irrespective of participant actions) occurred 60 per cent of the time, 30 per cent of the time or not at all.

After completion of the contingency or non-contingency training, participants were sent to Experiment Room 2 for anagram testing.

Test phase

Materials for the test task consisted of 20 anagrams presented individually in a standard sequence 3-4-2-5-1 (that is, PATIO was presented as TIAPO). Participants were told they were to solve the anagrams as quickly as possible and that there might be a pattern or principle by which to solve the anagrams. Response latencies were timed by a stopwatch. Following the test phase, participants were debriefed.

Results: The dependent variable was mean number of anagram failures. Group D (depressed) failed significantly more anagrams than Group C (control). Group N60 also failed more anagrams than Group C. Groups N30 and N0 were found not to be different from Group C. The contrast between Groups A and P (active/passive actions rewarded) was not significant.

Discussion: The results did not support Lewinsohn's rate of reinforcement hypothesis. In the noncontingent training conditions, increasing helplessness should have varied with the decreasing probability of reinforcement but helplessness occurred when reinforcements were delivered on 60 per cent of trials, and not on the lower reinforcement of 30 per cent or 0 per cent. Results were more in line with predictions based on classical conditioning in that:

1) Depressed participants showed cognitive performance deficit in comparison to controls.
2) There was no performance deficit in contingent–passive participants.
3) Helplessness was induced by noncontingent positive reinforcements.
4) The performance of helpless participants closely mirrored the performance of depressed participants.

Results were not consistent with predictions based on the original learned helplessness formulations. The authors acknowledged that their study did not take account of Abramson *et al.*'s revised learned hopelessness theory with its inclusion of the role of attributional processes as the latter revision was published after the study had been conducted. O'Rourke *et al.* concluded that neither Lewinsohn's theory nor Seligman's could readily account for their findings but that their results supported the theory that helplessness could be induced by using positive reinforcement; that contingent nonresponding is not a sufficient condition for helplessness, and that helpless and depressed participants are measurably similar.

Evaluation

Usefulness

This is a **well-controlled** study the results of which ran slightly counter to expectation. It supports the hypothesis that when people feel helpless (that they cannot control events), their behaviour is similar to that of people with depression. However the fact that people in the higher noncontingent reward condition felt more helpless in the anagram test than those in the low- or no-reward noncontingent condition might suggest further, that feeling that you should be able to control things but cannot, may lead to a greater sense of helplessness than simply knowing that you can't control things.

8.2 Disorders: Explanations of an affective disorder – depression

Key Study: 8.2.2 Biological explanations of depression

Avshalom Caspi *et al.* (2003), 'Influence of life stress on depression: moderation by a polymorphism in the 5-HTT gene', *Science*, 301 (5631), 386–9

Approach: Biological

Aim: To investigate a gene-by-environment interaction in which an individual's response to environmental insults is moderated by their genetic makeup

Method: Independent groups

Design: Prospective longitudinal study of a representative birth cohort

Type of sample: Representative sample

Participants: Birth cohort of 1037 children from Dunedin, New Zealand who were involved in the Dunedin Multidisciplinary Health and Development Study. Study members were assessed at age 3, 5, 7, 9, 11, 13, 15, 18, 21 and 26 years.

Procedure: At age 26, study members were divided into three groups on the basis of their 5-HTTLPR genotype: those with two copies of the short (*s*) allele; those with one copy of the *s* allele of the 5-HTT gene and one of the long (*l*) allele, and those with two copies of the *l* allele (*l/l* homozygotes). The *s* allele is associated with lower efficiency of serotonin reuptake than the *l* allele.

Participants were assessed for past-year depression using the Diagnostic Interval Schedule. Also informant reports about symptoms of depression for 96 per cent of study members were obtained from close friends/relatives.

Results: Regression analysis was performed. The interaction between 5-HTTLPR and life events showed that the effect of life events on self-report of depression symptoms at age 26 was significantly stronger among individuals carrying an *s* allele than among *l/l* homozygote carriers. Individuals carrying an *s* allele whose life events occurred after their twenty-first birthday experienced increases in depressive symptoms from the age of 21 to 26 years,

while those with the *l* allele did not. The gene x environment interaction also showed that stressful life events predicted a diagnosis of major depression among carriers of an *s* allele but not among *l/l* homozygotes. Life events occurring after their twenty-first birthday predicted depression at age 26 among carriers of an *s* allele who did not have a prior history of depression but did not predict onset of new depression among *l/l* homozygotes. Stressful life events predicted attempted suicides among individuals carrying an *s* allele but not among *l/l* homozygotes. The gene x environment interaction also showed that the effect of life events on informant reports of depression was stronger among individuals carrying an *s* allele than among *l/l* homozygotes.

Discussion: The authors concluded that the evidence that the 5-HTTLPR variation moderates the effect of life events on depression does not constitute unambiguous evidence of a gene x environment interaction because exposure to life events may itself be influenced by genetic factors (which would give a gene x gene interaction). However if the measure of life events used in the study represents environmental stress, the timing of the life events relative to depression must follow cause-effect order. The authors also analysed the relationship between childhood maltreatment and adult depression and found that childhood maltreatment predicted adult depression only among individuals carrying an *s* allele, not among *l/l* homozygotes.

The authors suggested that most genetic research has been guided by the assumption that genes *cause* diseases, whereas this research suggests that as far as complex psychiatric disorders are concerned, the genetic variants maintained at high prevalence in the population probably act to promote organisms' *resistance* to environmental pathogens (agents of disease).

> The same birth cohort is reported on by Caspi *et al.* (2002) in an investigation on serotonin and aggression. See Key Study 1.3.2.

Evaluation ✓ ✗

Reductionism

Although biological approach studies are often assumed to be **reductionist**, this is a good example of a study that takes a **holistic** approach, using biological techniques to investigate gene x environment interactions.

8.2 Disorders: Explanations of an affective disorder – depression

Key Study: 8.2.3 Cognitive explanations of depression

Peter M. Lewinsohn, Walter Mischel, William Chaplin and Russell Barton (1980), 'Social competence and depression: the role of illusory self-perceptions', *Journal of Abnormal Psychology*, 89 (2), 203–12

Approach: Cognitive

Aim: To disentangle the role in clinical depression of two personal variables: social competences (as perceived by others) and self-perception of social competence

Method: Laboratory experiment

Design: Independent measures

Type of sample: Self-selecting sample

Participants: Seventy-one depressed patients (mean age 34 years, 68 per cent female) receiving treatment at the University of Oregon Psychology Clinic, 59 psychiatric controls (mean age 26 years, 58 per cent female) , and 73 normal controls (mean age 30 years, 51 per cent female).

Screening: A two-stage screening process was employed. First, using cut-off scores on a personality inventory and interviewers' ratings of depression, participants were selected for the three groups. Second, semi-structured interviews were conducted and participants rated on 25 items of the Feelings and Concerns Checklist (Grinker, 1961).

Procedure: Participants took part in four 45-minute group interactions (five to six people in a group) at each of four-monthly assessment periods. Participants were selected to make sure that they did not know each other and had not met in any earlier group interaction. The seating arrangement was circular. Each participant was asked to give a three-minute self-introduction monologue. Following the monologues, the experimenter left the room and the group continued conversing for about 20 minutes.

Coders: Fifty-eight undergraduates were trained as observers/coders for group interactions. The coders were blind to the diagnostic categorisation of the participants and the exact design of the experiment, although they were aware of the fact that the study was exploring depression and interpersonal behaviour.

Measures: Two to four coders stationed behind observation windows rated the behaviour of participants facing them in each group session on a list of 17 desirable attributes. Twelve items were assumed to measure social skill (for example

friendly, socially skilful, interested in other people) while five items were assumed to reveal cognitive style and be sensitive to the cognitive treatment module; thus reflecting thoughts and attitudes that should be interpersonally observable and important (for example confident, positive outlook on life). Immediately following each group session, the participants were asked to rate themselves on the same list of attributes.

Results: Results reported are based on mean self and mean observer scores. Inter-observer reliability was 0.68 which though not an ideal level was regarded as high enough to test the major hypothesis. The 12 items relating to social skill were sufficiently consistent to be combined in one single measure and similarly the five items relating to cognitive style were also regarded as reflecting aspects of the same construct.

The experiment was a 3 x 2 design: diagnostic category (depressed, psychiatric control, normal) x rater (self, observer) analysis of variance.

The first hypothesis, that there would be a significant difference in self-perception of social skill in the depressed group compared to the other two groups was supported ($p < 0.001$). As far as the second hypothesis was concerned, that the less desirable perceptions of the depressed reflect negative distortions of self rather than actual social skill deficit seen in a greater discrepancy between self ratings and observer ratings, with self ratings being significantly lower), was not supported. Contrary to expectation there was a greater discrepancy between self and observer ratings for the control groups than for the depressed group, with the self ratings of the controls being significantly higher than the observer ratings. This was also true of the depressed but the difference was less in the depressed group. In contrast to normal controls who rated themselves higher on every item, the depressed rated themselves as less desirable on six items, two of the cognitive style items and four of the social skill items.

The results showed that

a) Depressed individuals see themselves as less socially skilled than non-depressed people.

b) These less desirable self-perceptions are not irrational negative perceptions but in fact parallel the perceptions of others.

c) Depressed individuals tend to distort (relative to observers) their self-perceptions less than do controls who rate themselves more positively than they are rated by others.

Pre-treatment/post-treatment analysis showed that:

a) By the end of treatment, those with depression had become more benign in their self-perceptions than at the start of treatment.

b) Those with depression however continued to view themselves as less desirable than the controls viewed themselves.

Depression: The major and unexpected finding was that self-perceptions of the depressed participants were less discrepant with observer ratings than were the self-perceptions of both the psychiatric and normal controls. Non-depressed people may thus be characterised with a halo or glow that involves an illusory self-enhancement in which one sees oneself more positively than others see one. Thus a problem in depression appears to be one of realism rather than irrational negative thoughts and self-assessments. That the individuals with depression viewed themselves less critically as a result of cognitive treatment is testimony of the efficacy of the treatment. However this study overturns previous views as it suggests that depression has less to do with negative perceptions and expectations than with falsely positive ones.

Evaluation

Individual versus situational

This research suggests that although environmental factors may play a role in depression, there may also be **individual differences** in self-perception that protect against depression to a lesser or greater degree. Such individual differences may themselves be the outcome of experiences or they may be innate. The data from Crispi *et al.* suggests that there may be a biological vulnerability to depression – that people with different variants of the 5-HTT gene might react differently to life stressors. If that is the case, realistic self-perception may be the outcome of a gene x environment interaction. This would explain the cognitive elements in depression in both **individual** and **situational** terms rather than an either/or dichotomy.

Key Study: 8.3.1 Combined biological and cognitive-behavioural treatment for substance use

Pamela D. Riggs *et al.* (2007), 'A randomized controlled trial of fluoxetine and cognitive behavioral therapy in adolescents with major depression, behavior problems, and substance use disorders', *Archives of Pediatric and Adolescent Medicine*, 161(11):1026–34

This is a study that compares results of a combined biological treatment (fluoxetine) with cognitive-behavioural treatment (CBT) for substance use, as compared to CBT plus placebo. *Note that the CBT was directed at the substance use rather than depression.*

Approach: Biological and cognitive-behavioural

Aim: To evaluate the effect of fluoxetine hydrochloride vs placebo on major depressive disorder, substance use disorder, and conduct disorder in adolescents receiving cognitive behavioural therapy (CBT) for substance use disorder

Method: Randomised controlled study

Design: Independent measures

Type of sample: Self-selecting sample

Participants: One hundred and twenty-six adolescents (13–19 years) recruited from the community, meeting DSM-IV diagnostic criteria for current major depressive disorder, lifetime conduct disorder, and at least one nontobacco substance use disorder

Procedure: Participants were randomly allocated to one of two conditions for a period of 16 weeks: fluoxetine hydrochloride (20 mg per day) plus CBT for substance use or placebo plus CBT for substance use

Measures:

For depression:

- Childhood Depression Rating Scale–Revised
- Clinical Global Impression Improvement

For substance use disorder:

- self-reported nontobacco substance use
- urine substance use screen results in the past 30 days

For conduct disorder:

- self-reported symptoms in the past 30 days

Results:

- Fluoxetine combined with CBT had greater efficacy than did placebo and CBT according to changes on the Childhood Depression Rating Scale–Revised but not on the Clinical Global Impression Improvement.
- There was an overall decrease in self-reported substance use and conduct disorder symptoms but in neither case was difference between groups statistically significant.
- The proportion of substance-free weekly urine screen results was higher in the placebo-CBT group than in the fluoxetine-CBT group.

Discussion: Fluoxetine and CBT had greater efficacy than did placebo and CBT on one but not both depression measures but was not associated with greater decline in self-reported substance use or conduct disorder symptoms. The CBT, which had focused on problems of substance use rather than depression, may have contributed to higher-than-expected treatment response and mixed effectiveness findings.

Evaluation

Comparative effectiveness

As discussed in Key Study 7.3.2, fluoxetine has been identified as one biological treatment that is effective in treating depression while not conferring risk in terms of serious side effects. This study is **useful** because it shows that participating in CBT, even when the focus is not on depression, can be effective in reducing symptoms of depression. The results with regard to fluoxetine are less clear. It contributed to reduction in depressive symptoms on one measure but not the other.

9.2 Sport and the individual: Aggression
Key Study: 9.2.2 Social theories

Leonard Berkowitz and Russell G. Geen (1966), 'Film violence and the cue properties of available targets', *Journal of Personality and Social Psychology*, 3 (5), 525–30

Approach: Behavioural
Method: Laboratory experiment
Design: Independent measures
Type of sample: Self-selecting sample
Participants: Eighty-eight male university students, mainly studying psychology
Procedure: There were three factors in the experiment:

a) Participants were angered/not angered
b) Of those who were angered, half were angered by a person having a name-mediated association; half were not
c) Half the participants in each condition watched a film containing an aggressive scene and half watched a film containing a competitive race

- When each person arrived at the laboratory, he was met by a confederate in the role of another participant. In half the cases the accomplice introduced himself as Kirk and in the other half of cases he introduced himself as Bob.
- The experimenter said the experiment involved the administration of a mild electric shock and gave the participants the opportunity to withdraw.
- Participants were shown two rooms, one containing apparatus that they were told was for giving electric shocks; one containing a film projector.
- The participants were told that the experiment was dealing with problem-solving ability under stress.
- The participant was told that he was to work on the problem while the other person (the confederate) would judge the quality of his solution and would evaluate his performance by giving the participant from one to ten electric shocks (the poorer the solution, the greater the number of shocks).
- The confederate left the room and the participant was given the problem to solve.
- Five minutes later the experimenter returned, took the written solution and strapped the shock electrode on to the participant's arm.
- The experimenter left the room, ostensibly to take the solution to the other person for judging.

- One minute later the confederate administered one shock (non-angered condition) or seven shocks (angered condition).
- After 30 seconds the experimenter returned, asked the participant how many shocks he had received and administered a brief mood questionnaire.
- While the participant was responding to the questionnaire, the experimenter recalled the confederate.
- The experimenter said he would show both participants a brief film in order to study the effects of a diversion on problem-solving effectiveness.
- The experimenter showed one of two seven-minute films. The first clip was a film of a fight involving Kirk Douglas in which Kirk was given a beating. The clip was introduced by the experimenter who drew attention to the name link with the confederate. The alternative clip was an exciting track race between the first two men to run the mile in less than four minutes.
- When the film was finished the experimenter reversed the roles. The confederate was sent away ostensibly to solve the problem.
- Five minutes later the experimenter returned with a standard solution and told the participant to shock the other person as many times as he thought appropriate.
- The experimenter went to the control room to record the number and duration of shocks supposedly given to the confederate.
- After 30 seconds the experimenter returned and gave the participant a final questionnaire on which he indicated how much he liked the confederate.
- The experimenter explained to the participant the deception that had been practised upon him and was asked not to discuss the experiment with anyone else.

Results:

- Participants given seven shocks consistently reported themselves as angrier than the participants shocked only once.

- There was a significant main effect of anger/non-anger on responses to the question of extent to which the participant liked the confederate. Those who had received seven shocks expressed a significantly lower preference for the confederate than those who had received one shock.
- The primary DV was number of shocks supposedly administered to the confederate. The highest mean number of shocks was administered by those who in the angered condition had seen the prize fight film and whose 'partner' had been introduced as Kirk.
- The question about whether the participant liked the confederate was not affected by name of confederate. The researchers explain this by suggesting that the participants felt guilty for administering a high number of shocks and therefore were more restrained in their judgement of their 'partner'.

Discussion: The authors argued that their findings supported their hypothesis that observed aggression does not necessarily lead to open aggression against anyone but that particular targets are most likely to be attacked and these are targets that cue aggression, for example by association of name with the aggressive scene witnessed.

Evaluation

Individual/situational factors

This is a **well-controlled** study that suggests strongly that **situational** factors are key in explaining aggression. Participants were randomly allocated to the different conditions so there is no reason to believe that those who were introduced to Kirk or those who received seven shocks were naturally more aggressive than those in the other conditions. This shows that an aggressive mood may be evoked in most people, given appropriate cues.

Key Study: 9.2.3 Managing aggression in sport

John P. Brunelle, Christopher M. Janelle and L. Keith Tennant (1999), 'Controlling competitive anger among male soccer players', *Journal of Applied Sport Psychology*, 11, 283–97

Approach: Cognitive/Behavioural

Aim: To assess the effect of cognitive/behavioural interventions in anger management among male soccer players

Method: Field experiment

Design: Randomised group design with repeated measures

Type of sample: Self-selecting sample

Participants: Fifty-seven male participants (mean age = 20) from football (soccer) teams

Procedure: Male soccer players enrolled in two sport and fitness soccer classes at an American university were recruited for this study. Players were selected and distributed among four teams in each class based on talent, with the aim of having four evenly matched teams that went on to participate in a round robin of 15 games. Participants from the teams were matched with their teammates and randomly assigned to one of three treatment groups (anger awareness/role-playing/control group).

Anger awareness treatment

Weekly one-hour treatment sessions for five weeks in which participants listened to an educational lecture on anger as the role-playing group. Participants then engaged in discussion of their experiences of anger and anger control. The experimenter suggested alternative reactions to anger-inducing situations without modelling or role playing. Participants were asked to monitor their anger in football competitions over the next five weeks of treatment. Participants were asked to keep a journal recording their experiences, feelings and behaviour. During subsequent sessions, participants shared their journal entries and evaluated their anger control.

Role-playing treatment

Role-playing intervention included weekly one-hour sessions over a five-week period of treatment. Participants began with the same educational lecture as that given to the anger awareness group. Participants were then given live demonstrations of alternative responses to typical anger-inducing situations and then in small groups they assumed the roles of actors or observers. Each group rotated roles in common anger-inducing situations (such as a disagreeable referee decision).

The next two sessions used scripted scenarios to encourage participants to behave appropriately in such situations. The last two sessions involved improvised role play exercises during live football sessions.

Control group

The control group spent the same amount of time as the experimental groups but anger control was not discussed. Instead these participants engaged in activities associated with improving athletic performance, for example confidence building.

Instruments

Angry behaviour rating scale

Research assistants blind to treatment assignment observed participants during each soccer game and recorded participants' reactions to anger provocations. Different provocations and responses were scored on a scale and the mean scores for each participant were calculated.

Anger inventory

State anger was assessed before the first game by the State-Trait Anger Expression Inventory, a 44-item instrument that measures the intensity of anger as an emotional state (state anger), the disposition to experience angry feelings as a personality trait (trait anger). This provided a control measure for the participants' pre-existing anger disposition.

Angry behaviour and self-reported anger of each participant was observed/measured during a 15-game round robin season of competitive soccer games. All 57 participants played in at least four games during the pretreatment phase, four games during the treatment phase and three games during the retention phase. As well as being observed, the games were videotaped to ensure accuracy. Participants were told that the observation was focussed on skill. After each game, the participants completed a disguised version of the State-Trait Anger Expression Inventory. Two dependent variables, angry behaviour and state anger, were analysed separately. Both dependent measures were calculated by averaging anger scores in the games played during the pretreatment, treatment and retention phases of the study.

Results:

Pretreatment anger
There was no significant difference found between groups on pretreatment anger scores.

Observed angry behaviour
The role-playing and anger awareness groups both displayed less angry behaviour than the control group during the treatment phase. During the retention phase, the role-playing group showed less angry behaviour than the anger awareness group and both experimental groups showed less angry behaviour than the control group.

Discussion: It was hypothesised that the role-playing group would demonstrate more effective and enduring anger control than the other groups. This was supported. Both experimental groups showed anger reduction during the treatment phase but the role-playing group continued to achieve lower anger scores at the end of the treatment and in the retention phase. The direct and active involvement in simulated situations allowed the participants to practise the skill of anger control. With active rehearsal, the appropriate behaviour became the dominant response and subsequently appeared in real game situations. After matching the role-play group's anger scores in the early phase of the study, the anger awareness group failed to make any significant additional reductions in angry behaviour. The authors suggested that this was probably because the awareness intervention is primarily a passive learning process that did not encourage a player's ability to control anger during a game. Reports of state anger immediately after games did not follow the reduction in angry behaviour. One explanation for this might be that the players still experienced the same level of anger but controlled it better.

Evaluation

Ecological validity

This is a **controlled** experiment but unlike many laboratory experiments, it has **high ecological validity** because participants' anger was monitored during competitive games. In common with other studies involving cognitive-behavioural treatments discussed in other sections of the book (for example, **Anger management 4.3.2**, this study found such treatment to have effective and long lasting positive effects.

9.3 Sport and the individual: Motivation

Key Study: 9.3.1 Achievement motivation

Judith M. Harackiewicz, Kenneth E. Barron, Suzanne M. Carter and Alan T. Lehto (1997), 'Predictors and consequences of achievement goals in the college classroom: maintaining interest and making the grade', *Journal of Personality and Social Psychology*, 73 (6), 1284–95

Approach: Cognitive

Aim: To analyse predictors of achievement goals in psychology students and consequent achievement

Method: Self-report

Design: Longitudinal survey

Type of sample: Opportunity sample

Participants: Over 300 students in introductory psychology classes at a university in the United States

Procedure: There were five assessment waves.

- Participants' achievement orientation and test anxiety were assessed at the beginning of the semester.
- Participants' goals for the class were measured two to three weeks into the semester.
- One month later, participants were asked to state their goals in their own words.
- Towards the end of the semester, participants' intrinsic interest in the class was measured.
- At the end of the semester, the participants' final grades were obtained.

Individual differences wave

Around 1000 students completed two personality scales as part of a wider study. Achievement orientation was measured with the Work and Family Orientation Questionnaire (Spence and Helmreich, 1983), which assesses three dimensions of achievement motivation: mastery; work/work avoidance and competitiveness on a scale of 1–5. Anxiety was measured with the Test Anxiety Scale (Sarason, 1978) which assesses affective, cognitive and physical reactions to exams.

Goals wave

Two to three weeks into term, 384 students responded to a questionnaire designed to assess students' self-reported adoption of mastery (gaining competence), performance (goal orientation) and work avoidance goals in their introductory psychology class (responses on a scale of 1–7 where 1 was not at all true and 7 was very true).

Open-ended goals wave

A month after the start of the project, 311 students remained in the study and were asked an open-ended question relating to achievement motivation: 'What are your personal goals in Psychology 202?'

Interest wave

Near the end of the semester, participants were asked to consider the extent (on a scale of 1 to 7) to which they were interested in the psychology class and to estimate how well they were doing in the class.

Grades wave

At the conclusion of the semester, students' grades were obtained. Students could receive one of seven possible grades (A = 4; AB = 3.5; B = 3; BC = 2.5; C = 2; D = 1; F = 0). Grade results revealed that the sample was slightly skewed in the direction of the achieving student.

Results:

Factor analysis

Principal components factor analysis using varimax rotation (for explanation, see p.91) was performed on the goals questionnaire and the measure of interest and competence.

Gender differences

Male students were found to be more competitive and female students reported more test anxiety.

Instructor differences

There were three different instructors involved in teaching introductory psychology and an effect of instructor was found as there were significant group differences in interest levels and final grades. This was controlled for in subsequent analyses.

Regression analyses

Multiple regression analysis (for explanation, see p.4) was conducted to examine the effects of individual differences on goals adopted in the class and subsequent effects on interest and grades.

Mastery goals

Students high in workmastery were more likely to adopt mastery goals and female students were more likely to adopt mastery goals.

Performance goals

A significant main effect was found for competitiveness. Those high in competitiveness were more likely to adopt performance goals and female students were more likely to endorse performance goals.

Work avoidance goals

A significant main effect was found for competitiveness with competitive students **more** likely to endorse work avoidance goals. Students high in workmastery were less likely to endorse work avoidance goals. There was an interaction between gender and test anxiety – women who were high on test anxiety were more likely to report work avoidance. Men reported similar levels of work avoidance, whether high or low on test anxiety.

Interest

A main effect was found for mastery. Students who adopted mastery goals reported higher levels of interest in the class. There was a main effect for gender. Female students reported higher levels of interest than males.

Final grade

Main effects were found for performance goals and work avoidance goals. Students who adopted performance goals achieved higher grades and students who adopted work avoidance goals received lower grades. There was a significant effect of gender – female students received higher grades than males. Test-anxious students received lower grades than those who were not test-anxious, but this was qualified by competiveness. Students who were both test-anxious and low on competitiveness were most likely to achieve low grades. No other factors were significant in predicting grades.

Effects of perceived competence

There was a main effect of perceived competence. Students who felt they were doing better in the class reported higher levels of interest. Students who perceived themselves as doing well actually obtained higher grades. However, as the researchers noted, self-report of confidence was conducted late in the semester when the students had already received some feedback with regard to their progress. In terms of final grade there were no significant interactions between perceived competence and goals, which was against expectations.

Discussion: The researchers argued that they found significant effects of all three achievement goals on students' interest and grade achievement. However rather than finding that the goals interacted in predicting interest and performance, they found that mastery and performance goals had independent positive effects on interest and grade performance respectively, whereas work avoidance had a negative effect on grade performance. They concluded that this study contributed to achievement motivation theories by identifying important personality predictors of achievement goals and in showing that both mastery and performance goals are associated with motivation and performance in college. They expressed disappointment with the finding that performance orientation rather than mastery predicted grade performance, but they suggested this might be a consequence of the nature of the college assessment, rather than indicating a lack of relationship in general between mastery and achievement.

Evaluation

Individual versus situational/nature versus nurture

This study found that both **individual** factors (student goals; level of test anxiety) and **situational** factors (which instructor the student had teaching them) had effects on grade performance. What these data do not tell us is the relative importance of **nature** versus **nurture**. The dispositional factors, for example competitiveness or grade orientation, could equally be the outcome of biology or environment.

Key Study: 9.3.2 Sports-specific achievement motivation

Diane L. Gill and Thomas E. Deeter (1988), 'Development of the Sport Orientation Questionnaire', *Research Quarterly for Exercise and Sport*, 59 (3), 191–202

Approach: Individual differences

Aim: To develop a multi-dimensional, sport-specific measure of individual differences in sport achievement orientation

Method: Measure standardisation

Type of sample: Opportunity sample and random sample

Participants: Three samples:

1) Opportunity sample of undergraduates (n = 237), at a US university enrolled in 1984 in both competitive sports activities skills classes (n = 33 males; 64 females) and non-competitive sports skills classes (n = 40 males; 100 females).

2) Two hundred and eighteen undergraduates selected on the same basis enrolled the following year in competitive sports activities (n = 77 males; 33 females) and non-competitive sports activities (n = 24 males; 84 females).

3) High school students (n = 266) randomly sampled across grades 8, 9, 10, 11 and 12. Of these, 126 (77 males; 49 females) were classified as competitive sport participants and 140 (47 males; 93 females) were classified as non-participants.

Procedure: All three samples completed both the Sport Orientation Questionnaire (SOQ, Gill and Deeter, 1984) and the Work and Family Orientation Questionnaire (WOFO, Helmreich and Spence, 1978).

Measures:

WOFO: Twenty-three achievement motivation items from the WOFO were used. Factor analysis revealed four scales: mastery, work, competitiveness and personal unconcern.

SOQ: Items for the SOQ were developed by reviewing the achievement and sport competition literature, consulting with other sport psychologists and by collecting responses from diverse sport participants. As a result, 52 items were produced, of which 32 remained after a process of rating by five independent raters who assessed the items for content and clarity The SOQ was later remodelled in a revised version consisting of 25 items responded to on a 5-point scale (strongly agree to strongly disagree).

A graduate student attended first classes of the semester and asked the university students to respond to the WOFO and the 32-item SOQ on a voluntary basis. With the second sample of 218, the same graduate student returned after four weeks and readministered the SOQ. 205 of the original 218 respondents retook the SOQ and their scores were used for test-retest comparisons.

The WOFO and revised 25-item SOQ were administered to the high school students. Grade 9 students from randomly selected PE classes and students from randomly selected grade 10, 11 and 12 form rooms filled in the questionnaire.

Results:

Exploratory factor analysis

Exploratory factor analysis was conducted based on the data from the first sample and a three-factor solution emerged:

- Factor 1: Competitiveness
- Factor 2: The desire to reach personal goals in sport (goal orientation)
- Factor 3: The desire to win in interpersonal competition in sport (win orientation)

Competiveness items included 'I try my hardest to win'. Personal goal items include 'I set goals for myself when I compete'. Interpersonal competition items include 'The only time I am satisfied is when I win'.

Confirmatory factor analysis

Both exploratory and confirmatory factor analyses were conducted on the SOQ data from the other two samples and the results supported the three-factor solution (competitiveness, goal orientation and win orientation). The data were examined for internal consistency and item-to-total correlations and both were acceptably high. Reliability of the measure was assessed by retest on Sample 2 and the correlations indicated high test-retest reliability.

Correlations with WOFO

The WOFO competitiveness score was found to correlate moderately to highly with both competitiveness and win orientation and also with slightly lower significance also with goal orientation. These data proved evidence of construct validity.

- Goal orientation exhibited higher correlations with the WOFO mastery and work scores, which may suggest that some individuals who are motivated to work hard and meet challenges. carry over that orientation to the sporting arena.
- Win orientation was not correlated with either mastery or work, suggesting that the desire to win in sport is unrelated to general individual achievement orientation.
- Competitiveness had the highest correlation with WOFO competitiveness but was also moderately related to mastery and work.

For each of the three samples, separate gender x competitive/noncompetitive classification analyses of variance were conducted.

Results from Samples 1 and 2 (university students)

SOQ

- A main effect of gender and a main effect of competitive/noncompetitive engagement but no interaction were found.
- Females scored higher than males on goal orientation, males scored higher on competitiveness and males much higher than females on win orientation.
- The competitiveness score revealed a significant difference between those engaged in competitive classes and those in noncompetitive classes. In Sample 2, students in competitive classes also scored higher on win orientation.
- In Sample 2, a gender x competitive/noncompetitive class interaction was observed. Males in competitive and noncompetitive classes had similar competitiveness scores but females in competitive classes scored considerably high on competitiveness than those in noncompetitive classes.

WOFO results

- There was a main effect of gender, with males scoring higher than females on competitiveness and females scoring higher than males on work.
- No differences were found between participants in competitive and noncompetitive activities.

Sample 3: High school students

- Main effects of gender and competitive sport participation were found.
- Males scored higher on competitiveness and win orientation than females.

- The strongest difference with regard to competitive participation in sport was on competitiveness but the competitive participants also scored higher on win and goal orientation.
- The WOFO showed a gender effect similar to that found in the university samples but the high school sample also exhibited a competitive participation effect, with competitive participants scoring higher on competitiveness than nonparticipants.

Discussion: The authors concluded that their data provided good evidence that the SOQ is a reliable and valid measure of sport achievement orientation. Further, they concluded that some highly competitive individuals who enjoy sport competition and strive for sport achievement may be both win-oriented and goal-oriented but not necessarily so.

> ## Evaluation
> ### Validity and reliability
> This is a good example of how a measure is standardised and checked for **reliability** and validity. Checks of **content validity**, **concurrent validity** and **test-retest reliability** were all conducted. Results from the three samples indicated that the measure is reliable. Given the checks, it seems likely that the gender differences found show reliable differences between men and women in achievement motivation in sport.

Key Study: 9.3.3: Techniques of motivation

Edward L. Deci (1971), 'Effects of externally mediated rewards on intrinsic motivation', *Journal of Personality and Social Psychology*, 18 (1), 105–15

Approach: Cognitive

Aim: To examine the effects of external rewards on intrinsic motivation

Method: Laboratory experiment

Design: Independent measures

Type of sample: Self-selecting sample

Participants: Twenty-four psychology students fulfilling a course requirement

Procedure: Participants were randomly allocated to two conditions. The experiment lasted for three one–hour sessions on three different days. During all three sessions, the participants worked primarily on a complex 3-D puzzle called Soma.

This task was selected because it was assumed that most college students would find it intrinsically motivating. During the first session, both groups of participants followed the same routine. They were asked to reproduce four particular configurations while being timed with a stopwatch. There were copies of *New Yorker, Time Magazine* and *Playboy* on the table as well as the puzzle. During the second session, the participants in the experimental group were told they would be paid one dollar for each configuration which they were able to reproduce in the appropriate time (13 minutes). The control group were given the same configurations without pay. In the third session, both groups were given more configurations but neither group received pay. The experimental group were told that there had

Figure 9.1 Soma puzzle

128

only been sufficient funding for payment in the second session. The measure of motivation used in the study was that the experimenter left the room for eight minutes during each session. As he left the room, he said that he would only be gone for a few minutes and that the participant could do whatever he wanted during his absence. The primary measure was the amount of time spent working on the puzzle during the eight-minute absence. This was determined by the experimenter who, having left the room, observed the participant through an observation window. In order to ensure that participants did not successfully complete a configuration during this period, the configuration drawings they were given to follow were actually impossible to construct. The criterion selected for whether the participant was working on the task during the free choice period was that he was manipulating and looking at one or more pieces. If a participant was reading, daydreaming or just had his hand on a piece, he was judged not to be working on the puzzle. At the end of each session, the participants were asked to rate on a 9-point scale the degree to which they found the task interesting and enjoyable. This information was collected in order to verify the assumption that the participants were intrinsically interested in the task.

Results: The first hypothesis was that when money is used as an external reward for an activity, one's intrinsic motivation for that activity decreases. When the external reward was introduced at Session 2, the motivation of the experimental group increased. They spent a higher proportion of their time working on the puzzle in Session 2 than in Session 1, while the people in the control group spent about the same amount of time in the first two sessions. Then when the rewards were removed for Session 3, motivation in the experimental group dropped to a level considerably lower than it had been at Session 1. The difference was not quite significant but gave some support to the hypothesis.

Discussion: The authors argued that even though the difference was not significant at the 5 per cent level, their hypothesis was largely supported. They suggested that the strength of the experimental effect was obscured by a ceiling effect. Two of the participants spent all eight minutes in each session on the puzzle. This suggests that the task was so intrinsically interesting for those participants that their intrinsic motivation was not in fact diminished by the reward effect.

Evaluation
Ceiling effect and reliability

The term ceiling effect has two distinct meanings. It refers either to the level at which an independent variable no longer has an effect on a dependent variable, or to the level above which variance in an independent variable is no longer measured or estimated, affecting **reliability** of the findings. In this case, the task was so intrinsically motivating that the IV produced no variance in the case of two participants. However, one could argue that this shows that the introduction of an external reward does not necessarily affect a person's motivation if they are sufficiently deeply motivated.

John I. Lacey (1950), 'Individual differences in somatic response patterning', *Journal of Comparative and Physiological Psychology*, 43, 338–50

Approach: Individual differences/Biological
Aim: To test the theory of general arousal
Method: Case study
Type of sample: Opportunity sample
Participants: 12 pregnant patients
Procedure: Participants were asked to relax on a bed with instructions to lie motionless, to think of nothing and to go to sleep if possible. After ten minutes of relaxation, autonomic arousal was secured by:

a) Announcing that in one minute, a letter would be given to which the subject would respond by naming as quickly as possible all the words they could think of that began with that letter.

b) Requiring the participant, after the minute of waiting was over, to perform the task of association for a period of three minutes.

The number of different occasions on which each patient was tested ranged from six to twelve. The letter was changed from session to session in a prearranged haphazard sequence and each participant was given the same sequence of letters.

While they were undertaking this task, measurements were made of diastolic and systolic blood pressure, palm conductance, heart rate and heart rate variability. Blood pressure was taken at one-minute intervals. Palm-to-palm conductance was measured by means of a constant current circuit which provided direct reading of the resistance and heart rates were continuously recorded on a mechanical cardiotachometer.

Results:

- Long before the end of the three-minute period, participants ran out of associations and became embarrassed and frustrated (that is, they experienced stress/arousal).
- All participants showed an increase in systolic blood pressure ranging from 3.1 per cent to 22.4 per cent.
- All participants showed an increase in diastolic blood pressure, ranging from 8.6 per cent to 44 per cent.
- Most participants showed a greater absolute increase in diastolic than in systolic blood

pressure but two participants showed marked reversals of this trend.

- The increases in palm conductance ranged from 75 per cent to 637 per cent.
- For ten out of twelve participants, moderate increases in heart rate and increases in heart rate variability were recorded.
- Participants did not show concordant changes in all of these measures when stressed but somatic responses were patterned.
- One participant showed relatively small changes in blood and pulse pressure and palm conductance but recorded the highest heart rate increment and second highest heart rate variability of the group.
- Another participant showed an almost reverse pattern, with the smallest changes of the group in heart rate and heart rate variability but relatively major changes in blood pressure and palm conductance.
- One pattern that emerged was that some participants showed a similar pattern of responses but varied more on one measure than another.
- A second pattern was that actual reversals occurred in the direction of discrimination between two participants.
- Non-parametric tests of significance showed that same-direction differences between participants were not significant but that significant reversals in direction of discrimination between two participants were found.

Discussion: The evidence presented in this study supports the hypothesis that normal individuals exhibit organised patterns of somatic reaction to stress which are reliable. Patterning of somatic reaction is a variable as important as or more important than average reactivity. Both the degree to which two individuals are discriminated and the direction of that discrimination in terms of autonomic response depends upon the physiological variable used. Variables were not from very different areas but involved mainly cardiovascular (heart) variables and patterning appeared among the cardiovascular variables, for example between blood pressure and heart rate or between blood pressure and heart rate or between palm conductance and the cardiovascular variables.

Evaluation

This was not a true laboratory experiment because there was no experimenter manipulated variable. Instead, all the participants were subjected to exactly the same standardised procedure and the dependent variable was the extent of autonomic responses to the same stressor, hence enabling the experimenters to determine the effect of naturally occurring individual differences.

10.2

Key Study: 10.2.1 State/trait anxiety

Martin Eubank and Dave Collins (2000), 'Coping with pre- and in-event fluctuations in competitive state anxiety. A longitudinal approach', *Journal of Sports Sciences*, 18, 121–31

Approach: Individual differences

Aim: To investigate the interrelationship between state anxiety and coping strategies of sport participants

Method: Laboratory experiment

Design: Mixed design

Type of sample: Opportunity sample

Participants: 24 youth sport participants (10 males; 14 females, mean age 18). Ten were from a regional gymnastics club and 14 were talented tennis players. All participants had been actively competing for at least six years, including at regional and national level.

Measures:

- State anxiety was assessed using the CSAI-2 which measures the intensity of cognitive anxiety and somatic anxiety. Martens *et al.* reported high internal consistency of the CSAI-2 (0.8, Cronbach's Alpha).

- A direction scale was added, enabling participants to rate the extent to which they viewed each anxiety response as facilitative (helping) or debilitative (hindering) to their performance.

- The COPE measure was used to determine coping strategies.

Internal consistency and split-half reliability

Internal consistency is assessed by determining correlations between different items on the same test in order to ensure that several items that propose to measure the same construct produce similar scores. Cronbach's Alpha is a statistical test that calculates pair-wise correlations between items. Internal consistency ranges from zero to 1. Correlations of 0.6 and above indicate acceptable reliability and 0.8 and above suggest good reliability.

Split-half reliability is assessed by administering a test then dividing responses into halves, scoring the halves separately and analysing correlations between scores on the two halves. If the test or measure is reliable, scores on the two halves should correlate at a significant level.

Procedure: The COPE measure was sent to each participant a month before the first event. Participants and coaches identified low- and high-importance forthcoming competitions and the CSAI-2 was administered on four occasions: in low stress training, in high stress training (before major competition), in low stress competition and in high stress competition (for example, selection for national team).

On the basis of the results of the directions scale, results from the high competition event participants were divided into two groups – those with negative scores classed 'debilitators' (five gymnasts; five tennis players) and those with positive scores classed 'facilitators' (five gymnasts; seven tennis players). Two participants did not fit either category and their data were removed. Thirty minutes before the start of each training and competition condition, participants responded to the CSAI-2.

Semi-structured interviews were conducted by experienced interviewers within a day of the high stress competition condition and videotaped. Participants were asked to recall the best and the worst performance phase of the event just completed. While watching a video recording of their selected phases, they were asked to give a verbal anxiety direction score and to recall the extent to which the emotions they had experienced were perceived to be negative or positive for their performance. Participants were given a definition of 'coping' and then were asked to identify the sources of coping they had used during the event.

Qualitative methods: Semi-structured interview

In a structured interview, the interviewer has set questions that they have to stick to, but in a semi-structured interview, the interviewer can be flexible and respond with new questions in response to the interviewee's replies.

Data analysis:

Qualitative data

Interview data were analysed using a content analysis procedure. Three investigators (of whom two were naive to the aim of the study) listened to the interviews and read the transcripts then determined themes and categories regarding coping strategies used in good and bad phases of performance. The investigators debated the themes until consensus emerged (triangulation).

Quantitative data

Three-way analysis of variance was conducted on

1) Group (facilitator/debilitator)
2) Condition (training/competition)
3) Stress (high/low)

Results:

Pre-event state anxiety:

- Facilitators and debilitators experienced similar levels of anxiety across the four environments.
- For facilitators, there was no change in anxiety as a function of condition or stress.
- Debilitators experienced more somatic anxiety in the competitive conditions.
- Facilitators had a positive perception of their anxiety intensity in competition, whereas debilitators interpreted a similar anxiety intensity negatively.
- Facilitators maintained a stable perception of anxiety intensity across environments, whereas debilitators interpreted a similar intensity as being negative when the situation was more important.
- Debilitators' perception of somatic anxiety became more negative under conditions of higher importance.

In-event state anxiety:

- Facilitators maintained a facilitative anxiety interpretation through good performance.
- Fifty per cent of debilitators experienced debilitative perceptions of their anxiety even when they felt they were performing well.
- In the bad phase of performance, all members of the debilitative group experienced a negative anxiety interpretation.
- Over 50 per cent of facilitators maintained a positive perception of anxiety direction during their bad phase.

Coping:

- Facilitators had a higher mean total coping score than debilitators.

- Facilitators commonly adopted both problem-focused strategies and emotion-focused strategies.
- Debilitators showed no tendency for any particular coping strategy.

The findings of the content analysis showed that:

- When facilitators perceived their emotion to be positive in good phases of play, they focused on dealing with stressors and coped actively with anxiety.
- Even in a bad phase of play, facilitators were still able to rely on their coping strategies.
- When debilitators perceived their anxiety to be negative in bad phases of play, they appeared to be at a loss as to what to do.
- Even in good phases of play, debilitators appeared to be concerned that the slightest worry would creep in and affect their focus.

Discussion: The main finding is that the nature of anxiety perception creates a bias in interpretation. Facilitators appeared to maintain a positive state anxiety perception in most conditions, whereas debilitators appeared to reverse their perception of anxiety once the competition became more important and were always more debilitative when they felt they were doing badly. In competition, the environment becomes too stressful and debilitators exhibit negative state anxiety. The results indicate the importance of coping mechanisms in dealing with anxiety.

Evaluation

Sample and ecological validity

Sample size was relatively small but the participants were all highly successful (national level) sports participants, which contributed to high **ecological validity**, along with the fact that the participants were tested and interviewed before and after actual training sessions and competitions.

Key Study: 10.2.2 Multidimensional models

Carolina Lundqvist and Peter Hassmen (2005), 'Competitive State Anxiety Inventory-2 (CSAI-2): Evaluating the Swedish version by confirmatory factor analyses', *Journal of Sports Sciences*, 23 (7), 727–36

Approach: Individual differences

Aim: To evaluate the Swedish version of the Competitive State Anxiety Inventory-2

Method: Self-report

Type of sample: Opportunity sample

Participants: Participants were initially 969 students (571 males; 398 females; mean age 17) at specialist sport high schools in Sweden. Participants' competitive standard ranged from subelite to elite and included a range of individual and team sports, including skiing, badminton, volleyball, track and field athletics, swimming, tennis, basketball, ice hockey and soccer. Twenty returned inventories were excluded due to partial completion, reducing number of participants to 949. A further 22 athletes were subsequently taken out of the analysis as they were considered outliers, leaving a total of 927 participants. Informed consent was received from all participants.

Measure: The original CSAI-2 consists of 27 items divided into three 9-item subscales that assess cognitive anxiety, somatic anxiety and self-confidence (Martens *et al.*, 1990). Participants respond on a 4-point scale ranging from 1 (not at all) to 4 (very much). Translation was conducted accorded to a standardised procedure. The CSAI-2 was translated from English into Swedish then sent to two bilingual translators who translated it back into English. Differences were discussed and resolved so that the original meaning was considered to be intact in the final Swedish version.

Procedure: Participants were instructed that while completing the CSAI-2, they should recall the most important competition they had participated in during the previous season, and to refer to their state of mind immediately before that particular competition.

Data analysis: Participants were grouped into samples of elite (n = 253) and non-elite (n = 674) athletes. Elite athletes were defined by Swedish junior or senior national team in their chosen sport. They were also grouped on the basis of involvement in individual (n = 626) or team sport (n = 299). Confirmatory factor analysis was performed after the sample was corrected for non-normal distribution.

Results: The strength and direction of the intercorrelations among the factors in both samples are similar to those reported by Martens *et al.* (1990). Chi-square analysis showed that the elite and non-elite samples were equivalent in terms of the numbers of individual and team sport athletes, and that the distribution of elite and non-elite athletes was similar in the samples of individual and team sport athletes.

Model fit: Three measurement models were evaluated in all samples: the original three-factor correlated model proposed by Martens *et al.* (1990b); a two-factor correlated model for which the self-confidence factor was removed; and a 17-item model suggested by Cox *et al.* (2003). The three-factor correlated model showed a reasonable fit but not a close one. The two-factor model indicated an unacceptable fit to the data. The confirmatory factor analyses of the 17-item model revealed an improved model fit in all samples. Based on the finding that the 17-item model displayed the most acceptable overall fit of the three models, the local-fit was also assessed to determine if any individual parameters in the model might be problematic. A statistical test revealed that model fit would be significantly improved if three items in the sample of elite athletes, six items in the sample of non-elite athletes, six items in the sample of individual sport athletes and four items in the sample of team sport were allowed to cross-load on to more than one factor.

Discussion: The results of this study did not support the reliability of the original 27-item CSAI-2. It provides an explanation for why previous research using the CSAI-2 had indicated only weak relationships between performance and state anxiety and had generally produced contradictory or inconsistent results. Based on the findings of this study, at least 50 per cent of the variance in the CSAI-2 can be explained by error variance rather than by the constructs themselves. Although the revised 17-item model displayed an improved overall model fit, the error variance for the cognitive anxiety and somatic anxiety subscales was still in general higher than the variance captured by the constructs. The authors also accepted the findings of research such as Key Study 10.2.1 (Eubanks and Collins, 2000) that indicate that high state anxiety can be perceived as facilitating performance and not just detrimental to it. This is supported by findings that athletes' ratings of their anxiety direction (positive/negative) have been shown to predict performance better than intensity of anxiety. However Lundquist and Hassman concluded by stating that despite the doubts that have been voiced in the literature regarding the validity of the original CSAI-2 when evaluated by confirmatory factor analysis, the CSAI-2 has proved valuable in enabling sport psychology researchers to measure state anxiety as both a sport-specific and a multi-dimensional construct more accurately than did its predecessors. Nevertheless this study shows that data obtained from the CSAI-2 in its original form cannot reliably be trusted, which the authors of the study suggest is alarming when considering the enormous amount of anxiety research conducted with the scale in the field of sport psychology.

Evaluation

Retrospective self-report of anxiety

The authors of this study themselves highlighted a possible methodological limitation and that is that it was based on retrospective data. Participants were asked to remember a specific and very important competition they had participated in during the previous season. There is some support that athletes can reliably recall pre-competition anxiety levels related to competitions in which they have participated in days, weeks or even months previously. However, it is still plausible that memory error could reduce **reliability** of the results.

Key Study: 10.2.3 Models of anxiety

John S. Raglin and Paul E. Turner (1993), 'Anxiety and performance in track and field athletes: a comparison of the inverted–U hypothesis with zone of optimal function', *Personality and Individual Differences*, 14 (1), 163–71

Approach: Individual differences

Aim: To analyse the relationship between anxiety and sport performance by comparing the efficacy of the inverted-U hypothesis and the Zone of Optimal Function (ZOF)

Method: Self-report

Type of sample: Not stated

Participants: 39 male and 29 female members of the Indiana University Varsity Track and Field teams; participants were assured of anonymity and gave informed consent

Measures: Anxiety was assessed with the State-Trait Anxiety Inventory (Speilberger, 1981), consisting of two, 20-item Likert format questionnaires

Procedure: Three pilot studies were carried out.

- The first pilot study assessed whether athletes could accurately recall anxiety experienced at a previous meet. A subsample of athletes completed a version of the STAI four months after a meet at which they had previously completed the same measure. Correlation between the scores obtained was 0.8, which is an acceptable correlation.

- The second pilot study compared the STAI with the CSAI-2 in order to decide which measure to use. A subsample of athletes completed modified forms of both 72 hours before the meet (predicting how anxious they would feel when the time came to compete) and again one hour before the meet. It was found that the predicted and actual precompetition anxiety was significantly correlated for both scales but for the STAI, the correlation was 0.95, whereas for the CSAI-2, the correlation for the cognitive subscale was 0.66 and for the somatic subscale it was 0.71. It was therefore decided to use the STAI.

- The third pilot study investigated the problems of habituation to the STAI. Twenty-two college students completed the STAI twice weekly for a period of four weeks. Responses were compared and it was found that only one individual showed habituation (scoring the same responses for all items on more than one occasion).

The study: Three men's and women's indoor track and field meets were selected. The athletes completed a predictive version of the STAI (for example, how do you think you will feel one hour before the meet?) 48–72 hours before each meet. Actual precompetition anxiety was tested with the normal version of the STAI an hour before the meet. For each meet, the actual precompetition anxiety values of the athletes were compared to their own optimal precompetition values in order to determine if the achievement of Zone of Optimal Functioning related to athletic performance. Athletes were categorised into those whose precompetition anxiety scores were within their range of optimal functioning (inside) and those whose actual anxiety values were higher or lower than the optimal range (outside). The mean performance of the two groups was contrasted to ascertain if the ZOF was related to athletic success. An optimal precompetition anxiety table based on Oxendine's (1970) theory was used which provided optimal ranges for precompetition state anxiety based on STAI scores for various sporting events. An additional means of determining optimal anxiety was undertaken using an individualised approach to the inverted-U hypothesis. Each athlete's median precompetition anxiety value for the three meets was calculated and those who scored above or below this level were grouped as 'outside'.

Performance variables: Four methods were used to compute performance. Performance values of athletes were standardised as follows:

1) Meet performance values were converted into percentages based upon average performance of each participant during the season (per cent personal average).

2) Each individual's meet performance was expressed as a percentage of his/her own personal best performance (per cent personal best).

3) Each participant's performance was expressed as a percentage of the National Collegiate Athletic Association national qualifying standard for indoor track and field meets (per cent qualifying).

4) Each participant's performance was assessed using the International Amateur Athletic Federation's tables based on world record performances that provide numerical values for athletic performance in various track and field events standardised across all events (multi-event points).

Results: The results showed a significant main effect of gender only on actual precompetition state anxiety (females higher than men) but anxiety did not differ across meets. Trait anxiety was significantly correlated with baseline state anxiety, recalled optimal state anxiety and actual precompetition state anxiety for all three meets. Because significant gender differences were not found on either performance or anxiety responses, male and female data were combined for analysis.

Performance and precompetition anxiety: ZOF vs inverted-U (task-specific)

It was found that for ZOF, the inside group performed significantly better than the outside group for 'per cent qualifying' and approached significance for 'multi-event points'. However significant differences between the inside and outside groups were not found on 'per cent personal average' or 'per cent personal best'. In the case of inside and outside groups for the inverted-U hypothesis (task-based), significant differences in performance were not found for any of the four performance classifications.

ZOF and inverted-U (personalised)

For this comparison the sample was limited to athletes who participated in all three meets. The same result applied for the ZOF groups and again no significant differences were found for the inverted-U (personalised) groups.

A further calculation was made by determining the percentage of participants that fell into low, moderate or high optimal anxiety categories. If only a small percentage of athletes reported performing best at low or high anxiety levels, then the inverted-U hypothesis would apply. Overall 19 per cent of participants possessed optimal levels of precompetition anxiety in the low category, 31 per cent were in the moderate category and 50 per cent in the high category. These findings do not support the inverted-U hypothesis.

Discussion: The findings from this study support Hanin's ZOF theory of the relationship between anxiety and performance. Additionally it was found that the zone of optimal functioning for these athletes varied considerably. Nearly 70 per cent of the entire sample reported that they performed best at either low or high levels of precompetition anxiety, not at moderate levels, as predicted by the inverted-U hypothesis. Whether the optimal level was low, moderate or high appeared to be somewhat related to trait anxiety levels of the particular athlete. The findings indicated, in contrast to past theories, that there is a trend for high trait anxious athletes to have higher optimal precompetition anxiety ranges compared to low anxious athletes. It should be noted however that the significant correlations were found only with the national college performance measure and near significant correlations with the IAA standardised performance measures and not with the individuals' own performance measures.

Evaluation

Measuring performance

As this study shows, it is extremely difficult to measure effects of anxiety on performance as one needs to establish not only an individual's anxiety level but also to have some way of measuring performance. In this study only performance against some kind of external standard appeared to correlate with zone of optimal anxiety. Can you think of any possible explanation as to why there were no significant correlations found between optimal anxiety and individual performance as measured by comparing with personal best or personal average?

10.3 Sport performance: Self-confidence
Key Study: 10.3.1 Self-efficacy

Teri J. Hepler and Melissa A. Chase (2008), 'Relationship between decision-making self-efficacy, task self-efficacy, and the performance of a sport skill', *Journal of Sports Sciences*, 26 (6), 603–10

Approach: Cognitive

Aim: To examine the relationships between decision-making self-efficacy, task self-efficacy and performance

Hypothesis 1: That decision-making self-efficacy and task self-efficacy will correlate with performance on a soft-ball task

Method: Self-report

Type of sample: Self-selecting sample

Participants: 65 undergraduate students with a minimum of two years of baseball- or softball-playing experience participated. Participants had a mean age of 21 and a mean of seven years' baseball/softball experience. Informed consent was received from all participants.

> Softball is a team game played in the United States. It is similar to baseball although some key softballs are larger than baseballs and the pitches are thrown underhand rather than overhand. Despite the game's name, the standard softball is not soft; in fact, it is harder than a baseball.

Procedure: A demographic questionnaire was used to collect background information. Participants were asked to rate how important it was for them to be successful in the softball test. Importance ratings were taken because self-efficacy theory states that self-efficacy only influences performance in the

Figure 10.1 Softball is similar to baseball

presence of incentives. For this reason, participants who marked a low importance rating were dropped from the study, leaving 60 participants remaining in the study.

Each participant performed both the decision-making and physical task. Order of tasks was counterbalanced to avoid order effects. Participants completed a pre-decision-making self-efficacy questionnaire before performing the decision-making task. Decision-making self-efficacy was assessed again following completion of the trials. Scores on all three test situations were summed to calculate total decision-making performance score but participants were given failure feedback. Before performing the physical task, participants completed the task self-efficacy questionnaire. Participants performed the physical task and upon completion of each throw, were given failure feedback. Post-task self-efficacy was measured.

Participants were fully debriefed about the study including the false failure feedback.

Measures:

Decision-making self-efficacy questionnaire

Decision-making self-efficacy was measured through a task-specific questionnaire designed for the study. This measured participants' strength of self-efficacy for making the best decision in an infield defensive situation. Participants rated their degree of certainty that they would make the best decision. Participants' degree of certainty with regard to ten decisions was scored on a 10-point scale from 0 (uncertain) to 10 (very certain) and a mean self-efficacy score was calculated for each participant. A post-decision-making self-efficacy questionnaire was also used.

Decision-making task

The decision-making task used three videotaped softball situations involving a halt to play action. Game conditions and diagrams were used. Participants were presented with a decision-making question and three possible solutions and were asked to make their decision as quickly as possible. The possible solutions were ranked by coaches and participants scored one for the best decision through three for the worst decision. Thus best performance scored three points in total and worst decisions over all three videos scored nine points.

Task self-efficacy questionnaire

Task-self-efficacy was measured by the same format used to assess decision-making efficacy. Participants were asked to rate their self-efficacy to complete successfully a throw from an infield position to a base. The questionnaire asked participants to pretend they were playing an actual game and assess how certain they were that they could complete successfully the required throw. Participants rated their certainty on ten occasions on a 10-point scale from 0 to 100. Self-efficacy strength was calculated in the same way as on the decision-making task and a post-task self-efficacy questionnaire was also used.

Physical task

The physical task required participants to throw a softball to a designated target. A successful trial was defined as a throw that hit the target in the specified time limit and distance ranged from 10 to 20 metres. Physical performance was based on the speed and accuracy of each throw. A throw that hit the target was awarded one point, while two points were awarded for each miss. Throwing performance was calculated by multiplying speed of throw by accuracy score. Low scores reflected greatest accuracy.

Manipulated failure

Both tasks involved manipulated failure. This was done because self-efficacy theory states that self-efficacy has its greatest influence on performance in the face of failure. Participants were told that they had failed all three decision-making trials with the failure feedback provided after each trial. The physical task used failure feedback on nine out of ten trials. Balls that did not hit the target, were automatic failures but when the ball hit the target, the experimenter stated that the throw was not completed in the time limit. This ensured that participants were told they had failed on the physical task 27 out of 30 times.

Results: A multivariate multiple regression analysis was used to evaluate the predictive validity of decision-making self-efficacy and task self-efficacy on the performance of the decision-making and physical tasks.

> **Multivariate multiple regression: This is an extension of multiple regression in which two or more explanatory (independent) variables can be used to predict two or more response (dependent) variables.**

Decision-making self-efficacy and task self-efficacy were both found to be important predictors of physical performance, with task self-efficacy acting as a stronger predictor of physical performance than decision-making self-efficacy. The research hypothesis was partially supported as task-self efficacy predicted physical performance but decision-making self-efficacy did not predict decision-making performance.

Discussion: The authors expressed their surprise that decision-making self-efficacy did not predict decision-making performance, as other studies had reported significant correlations between self-efficacy and sport performance. However, they accepted that limitations in their methods might have led to this lack of support for the alternate hypothesis. Firstly, they admitted that the decision-making task was somewhat artificial and ambiguous. Secondly, they suggested that the study may have contained an inadequate assessment of decision-making performance as accuracy of decision-making without decision speed was assessed, whereas in softball speed is important.

Evaluation

The role of empirical evidence

The authors were reluctant to accept their own findings as self-efficacy theory predicts that both task self-efficacy and decision-making self-efficacy should predict both physical task performance and decision-making performance. Rather than rejecting the theory, they instead sought explanations for their findings in limitations in their study. Should we accept the stated limitations or reject the experimental hypothesis?

10.3 Sport performance: Self-confidence

Key Study: 10.3.2 Sport-specific self-confidence

Jeffrey J. Martin and Diane L. Gill (1991), 'The relationships among competitive orientation, sport-confidence, self-efficacy, anxiety and performance', *Journal of Sport and Exercise Psychology*, 13, 149–59

Approach: Cognitive

Aim: To examine the relationships among trait and state psychological variables and performance

Hypothesis 1: That performance orientation and trait sport-confidence are positively related to self-efficacy and to state sport-confidence and negatively related to cognitive state anxiety

Hypothesis 2: That state sport-confidence and self-efficacy are positively related to performance, whereas cognitive state anxiety is negatively related to performance

Method: Correlation

Type of sample: Not stated

Participants: 73 male middle- and long-distance runners on local high school track teams from 13 different high schools (mean age, 16 years)

Measures:

Competitive orientation measures

Both Vealey's Competitive Orientation Inventory (1986) and Gill and Deeter's Sport Orientation Questionnaire (1988) were used to assess competitive orientation.

Confidence measures

Vealey's Trait Sport-Confidence Inventory (TSCI, 1986) and Vealey's State Sport-Confidence Inventory (SSCI, 1986) were used to assess trait and state self-confidence respectively.

State anxiety measure

The cognitive subscale of the Competitive State Anxiety Inventory-2 (Martens *et al.*, 1990) was used to assess state anxiety.

Self-efficacy measure

The researchers developed a series of questions based on Bandura's self-efficacy theory. As self-efficacy is unique to specific behaviours, there is no generally applicable measure that can be used. The measure was composed of questions that it was believed measured both outcome and performance self-efficacy. An example of an outcome self-efficacy question is 'How certain are you of winning the race?' and an example of a performance self-efficacy question is 'How certain are you of running 15 seconds faster than your personal best time?' Respondents indicated degree of confidence by choosing a percentage from no confidence (0) to absolute confidence (100). Self-efficacy scores were determined by finding separate mean individual scores for outcome and performance self-efficacy.

Performance measures

An athlete's finishing time (standardised) and place from the first race in which they competed represented two measures of performance.

Procedure: One of the researchers made two visits to coaches and students at the high schools, introduced them to the study and gained their informed consent. At a third meeting two to seven days before a midseason track meet, participants completed the TSCI, the SOQ, the COI and an informal questionnaire requesting information such as running experience and personal best times. At a fourth meeting, immediately (25 to 30 minutes) before the start of the race, the athletes completed the SSCI, the self-efficacy questionnaire and the CSAI-2.

Results: Pearson correlations and multiple-regression analyses were performed. It was found that participants were competitive in orientation and were more performance rather than outcome oriented. They were high in both trait and state sport-confidence. They were moderately anxious. They expected to place high and to run faster than their personal best.

Significant correlations were found between trait and state confidence on the COI and between state confidence and win and competitive orientation on the SOQ. Multiple-regression analysis found that trait confidence was the only significant predictor of outcome self-efficacy. The only trait variable that was significantly correlated with performance self-efficacy was SOQ goal orientation.

In terms of relation of psychological variables to performance, it was found that outcome self-efficacy and state sport-confidence were significantly related to finishing time and place. Multiple-regression analysis indicated that only outcome self-efficacy predicted finishing time and place.

Discussion: This study gave partial support to the experimental hypotheses. The researchers concluded that an individual's enduring and consistent level of sport-confidence is a powerful predictor of their more transitory precompetition state sport-confidence, which replicated Vealey's results. However in contradiction to Vealey, they did not find that competitive orientation was related to state sport-confidence. They suggested that this might be because the participants were young and inexperienced. On the other hand, they also suggested that the COI might not be reliable as it asked respondents to consider how satisfied with past performances they were and that satisfaction might not reflect a competitive orientation as much as past performance and outcome goals. The researchers found that win orientation and competitiveness as assessed by the SOW were related to outcome self-efficacy and to sport-confidence.

The researchers expressed their surprise that outcome self-efficacy was a stronger predictor of performance than performance self-efficacy. They concluded that the runners' youth and lack of competitive track experience prevented them from forming accurate performance self-efficacy judgements. In contrast, they concluded that the small and familiar competitive field enabled the boys to form accurate outcome self-efficacy judgements. Their final conclusion was simply that highly confident high school long distance runners run faster and place higher than less confident athletes. No support was found for the theory that highly anxious athletes compare poorly on performance with low anxious athletes.

Evaluation

Reliability

It is difficult to estimate the **reliability** of the findings of this study. While the study produced interesting conclusions, the authors doubted the reliability of some of their findings which conflicted either with previous research or their expectations. Their main explanation for the fact that they failed to replicate other studies was that their sample was young and inexperienced. However this then throws doubt on the other findings of the study which the authors appeared to be satisfied with. This study exemplifies the lack of clarity over the relative roles of arousal, anxiety and confidence in sport performance.

10.3 Sport performance: Self-confidence
Key Study: 10.3.3 Imagery

Krista Munroe-Chandler, Craig Hall and Graham Fishburne (2008), 'Playing with confidence: The relationship between imagery use and self-confidence and self-efficacy in youth soccer players', *Journal of Sport Sciences*, 26 (14), 1539–46

Approach: Cognitive

Aim: To examine the relationship between imagery use and confidence in soccer players.

Method: Self-report

Type of sample: Self-selecting sample

Participants: 122 male and female athletes from recreational and competitive soccer leagues in Ontario, Canada (age range was 11 to 14 years, with a mean of 7 years' experience)

Measures:

Imagery use

The Sport Imagery Questionnaire for Children (SIQ-C) was used which was developed from the SIQ (Hall, 1998), used to assess the motivational and cognitive functions of imagery in adults. The SIQ-C is a 21-item questionnaire with statements measuring frequency of children's imagery use on a five-point scale where 1 = not at all and 5 = very often. The questionnaire contained statements relating to each of five posited functions of imagery:

- Cognitive-general (CG) *(I see myself being mentally strong)*
- Cognitive-specific (CS) *(I can usually control how a skill looks in my head)*
- Motivational general – arousal (MG-A) *(I make up new game plans routinely in my head)*
- Motivational general – mastery (MG-M) *(In my head, I imagine how calm I feel before I compete)*
- Motivational specific (MS) *(I see myself doing my very best)*

Confidence

The CSAI-2 C (Cognitive State Anxiety Inventory for Children) was administered.

Self-efficacy

The Self-efficacy Questionnaire for Soccer (SEQ-S) was used. This was developed by Mills *et al.* (2001) and Munroe-Chandler and Hall (2005) as a specific measure of self-efficacy of soccer players. This is a five-item instrument responded to in 10-unit intervals from 0 (no confidence) to 100 (complete confidence). The five items are as follows:

- *I am confident I can work through difficult situations*
- *I am confident I can remain focused during a challenging situation*
- *I am confident I can be mentally tough throughout a competition*
- *I am confident I can remain in control in challenging situations*
- *I am confident I can appear confident in front of others*

Procedure: After consent was received from parents and players, the players were asked to complete a demographics questionnaire. They then completed the three measures listed above. Data were collected mid-season at the players' respective practice fields.

Results: Separate multiple-regression analyses were performed for the recreational soccer players and the competitive players.

The authors found that imagery, especially imagery of the motivational general – mastery function, was a significant predictor of both self-confidence and self-efficacy in both recreational and competitive soccer players. They concluded that young athletes who want to increase their self-confidence should engage more in imagery techniques.

Evaluation

Generalisability

As the authors admit, the findings of this study are not **generalisable** as the sample was an all-male sample of young Canadian soccer players only. However it suggests that imagery may play an important role in sport confidence and self-efficacy and if replicated with other sportspeople, it could prove useful for coaches and players.

Mark H. Anshel (1995), 'Examining social loafing among elite female rowers as a function of task duration and mood', *Journal of Sport Behavior*, 18 (1), 39–49

Approach: Social

Aim: To examine whether social loafing will occur in a rowing task performed by elite female rowers working as a team as compared to working individually

Hypotheses: It was hypothesised that social loafing would be evident when performing in a group situation in contrast to performing the same task alone. It was also predicted that although a loafing effect was hypothesised for all group performances, the effect would be significantly more pronounced in a longer (10-minute) than shorter (one-stroke) task duration condition.

Method: Laboratory experiment

Design: Repeated measures

Type of sample: Athletes were volunteered by their coach and were required to participate

Participants: Participants consisted of a team of six female elite crew rowers who represented New South Wales, Australia (age range 20–23 years). The subjects were required to engage in this study by their coach. To ensure high motivation and identifiability, the athletes were informed prior to the study that all performance scores in both the alone and group conditions would be used for future goal setting.

Measures: The Profile of Mood States (POMS, McNair *et al.*, 1971), consisting of six factors (tension, depression, anger, vigour, fatigue, and confusion) was administered before the tasks and after completion of each task to ascertain participant mood.

Procedure: The rowing task, measured as average kilometers per hour, was performed on a Five Concept II rowing ergometer.

There were three different tasks, each preceded by a one-minute warm-up:

- One stroke at maximum effort (followed by 10-minute rest)
- Rowing continuously for 1.5 minutes (followed by 20-minute rest)
- Rowing continuously for 10 minutes

Participants performed the rowing tasks under each of two conditions, alone and simultaneously with five teammates, in counterbalanced order. Thus each participant engaged in a total of six performance trials. The sequence in which the three tasks were experienced always occurred from shortest to longest duration to control for physical fatigue.

For group rowing, participants were placed in a manner that simulated actual crew rowing conditions. Participants were not told on whom data were being collected during any particular trial. The tasks were performed without observers (other than the experimenter) to reduce audience effects. The rowing ergometer measured total distance travelled within the prescribed times. To ensure that the task was meaningful, each participant was asked prior to the experiment by the team's head coach to give maximum effort, and participants were told that their scores would be recorded and subsequently reviewed by their coach. Participants were asked immediately after the study to indicate the extent to which they worked at their capacity on the rowing task on a scale from 1 (very low) to 100 (maximal).

Results:

- Overall mean perceived exertion was reported at 89 per cent of capacity. Participants reported perceived expended effort to have been higher in the group condition (mean = 91 per cent) than in the individual condition (mean = 87.0 per cent) but the difference was not significant.

Figure 11.1 Training on Concept II ergometers

- Social loafing was not apparent for the two short duration tasks (one-stroke and 1.5 minutes) but a loafing effect was evident for the 10-minute task. A comparison of mean performance indicated that performance on the 10-minute task was significantly poorer in the group than alone condition, reflective of a social loafing effect.
- Responses to the post-trial POMS showed that reported vigour declined measurably when performing all tasks in the group condition, although performance declined measurably only on the 10-minute task.

Discussion: The author explained the finding that participants performed similarly under the group and alone conditions for two of the three task durations by reference to presumed high self-efficacy in the elite athletes. That social loafing was found on the 10-minute task was ascribed to the fact that the participants did not perceive that individual effort would be monitored in the group task. Anshel suggested that social loafing may be a variable that is affected not only by social factors but also by individual differences in personality, competitiveness and self-efficacy. The conclusion drawn from the changes found in POMS scores was that social loafing is accompanied by emotional factors that may be accompanied by physiological changes. The 10-minute task led to increased fatigue in both conditions. Hence the reported decline in vigour across all group tasks may, when accompanied by higher fatigue levels (in the 10-minute task), have exacerbated the social loafing effect.

Evaluation

Reliability and validity

This study is valuable because it examines social loafing in a sporting context in which measurement of effort can be measured exactly as the rowing machine records consistently precise distance travelled in the prescribed time (assuming that the machines are properly calibrated). Data from this study are therefore presumed **reliable** and the conclusions drawn should be **valid** unless other factors reduce validity. Although the study was not as high in **ecological validity** as it would have been if it were conducted while the rowers were performing on water, neither is it low in ecological validity as rowers regularly use rowing machines in training.

Key Study: 11.1.3 Aspects of cohesion

Albert V. Carron, Steven R. Bray and Mark A. Eys (2002), 'Team cohesion and team success in sport', *Journal of Sports Sciences*, 20, 119–126

Approach: Social

Aim: To examine the relationship between task cohesiveness and team success in elite basketball and soccer teams

Method: Self-report

Type of sample: Self-selecting sample

Participants: 294 Canadian intercollegiate and club athletes from 18 basketball teams and nine soccer teams (154 females/140 males; age range 15–30 years). The participants had considerable competitive experience.

Measures:

Cohesion

The Group Environment Questionnaire (GEQ, Carron *et al.*, 1985) was used to assess cohesion. This is a self-report measure containing 18 items. Four aspects of cohesion are assessed:

- Individual attractions to the group – task
  This reflects a member's feelings about his/her personal involvement with the group's task.
- Individual attractions to the group – social
  This reflects a member's feelings about his/her personal social interactions with the group.
- Group integration – task
  This reflects a member's perceptions of the similarity and unification of the group as a whole around its tasks and objectives.
- Group integration – social
  This reflects a member's perception of the similarity and unification of the group as a social unit.

Responses are provided on a 9-point Likert scale where 1 = strongly disagree and 9 = strongly agree. Higher scores indicate strong perceptions of cohesiveness.

Only the task cohesion dimensions were included in order to reduce study demands on participants. Task cohesion was selected above social cohesion because previous research suggested that team success is more highly correlated with team success than social cohesion.

Team success

Team success was operationally defined as team's total winning percentage for games in their regular schedule. A percentage score was calculated by dividing number of points obtained by maximum possible number of points, where a win = 2, draw = 1, loss = 0.

Procedure: One of the researchers contacted coaches who gave permission for the researcher to ask for volunteers from among the athletes. Informed consent was obtained from all participants and where athletes were under 18 years of age, parental consent was also obtained. The group integration – task and individual attractions to the group – task scales of the GEQ were completed by participants in groups under supervision of the researchers approximately two weeks before the end of the season.

Results: No effect of gender was found so male and female results were combined. Differences were found between sports so it was decided that results were analysed separately for soccer and basketball. For cohesion as manifested by individual attractions to the group – task, a statistically significant relationship was observed between cohesion and success for both basketball and soccer. Analysis of the relationship between cohesion and success using the group integration – task showed a significant relationship for basketball but not quite significant for soccer.

Discussion: The results of the study provide evidence of a very strong relationship between cohesion and success in basketball and soccer teams. The results also showed that perceptions of team task cohesiveness were relatively consistent among members of the same team, suggesting that mean measurement of perceptions of cohesion is a valid indicator of team cohesion.

Evaluation

Reliability and validity

This study is based on self-report which is sometimes seen as lacking **reliability**. However this is an example of **valid** use of self-report as what is being measured is perceptions of team cohesion. It is difficult to see how a team could be measured in any other way that would be **ecologically valid**. The researchers adopted stringent criteria for assessment of statistical significance and they also analysed results for consistency across individuals. This suggests that the results are reliable and that the study has provided valid insights into the role of group cohesion in sporting success.

11.3 Social psychology of sport: Leadership and coaching

Key Study: 11.3.2 Contingency theories

P. Chelladurai and S. D. Saleh (1980), 'Dimensions of leader behaviour in sports: development of a leadership scale', *Journal of Sport Psychology*, 2, 34–45

Approach: Social
Aim: To develop a Leadership Scale for Sports (LSS)
Method: Self-report

Stage 1: Development of the LSS

Type of sample: Not stated
Participants: Participants were 160 students (80 male; 80 female) enrolled on a physical education degree at a Canadian university
Procedure: Participants responded to a questionnaire containing 99 items chosen and modified from existing leadership scales. Each item in the LSS was preceded with the phrase 'The coach should. . .' and five response categories were provided: *always, often, occasionally, seldom, never*. The data were analysed using factor analysis.
Results: A five-factor solution was found to be most meaningful. The factors were labelled *Training, Democratic Behaviour, Autocratic Behaviour, Social Support, Rewarding Behaviour*. Thirty-seven items were selected to represent these five dimensions.

It was noted that none of the 99 items in the original pool tapped the behaviour of the coach in teaching the skills and strategies of the sport, so in the second stage seven more items were included to tap the 'instruction' behaviour of the coach. It was also decided to extend the number of items relating to 'social support', resulting in 50 items in all. Response categories were modified from the subjective responses 'often', 'occasionally' and 'seldom' with percentage estimates of 75 per cent, 50 per cent and 25 per cent respectively.

Stage 2:

Type of sample: Not stated
Participants: 102 physical education students (not the same as in stage 1), (45 males; 57 females) and a male sample of 223 varsity athletes (basketball players, wrestlers, track and field athletes and rowers) from different Canadian universities.
Procedure: The PE students were asked to indicate their preference for specific leader behaviour in relation to their favourite sport. The athletes were asked to express their preference in relation to the sport in which they were currently competing. In addition, the athletes responded to a second version of the scale in which they recorded their perceptions of the actual behaviour of their current coach. For the preference version, the items were preceded by 'I prefer my coach to. . .' and in the second version the items were preceded by 'My coach. . .' The three sets of data were analysed separately.
Results: Because the second stage was an attempt to confirm the five factors found at the first stage, five factors were extracted. However the five factors accounted for only a limited amount of the variance: 41 per cent for PE students; 39 per cent for athletes' preference; 56 per cent for athletes' perceptions. As a result of the factor analysis, some items were cut, resulting in 40 items in total.
Internal consistency and reliability: As an index of internal consistency, Cronbach's Alpha was calculated and the result was considered acceptable. For test-retest reliability, 53 of the PE students responded to the revised questionnaire again four weeks later. Reliability coefficients were adequate (ranging from 0.7 to 0.8).
Factorial validity: The factor structure was found to be very similar across all samples, suggesting that the factor structure was stable.
Content validity: The five factors were determined to be meaningful in terms of coach–athlete relationships. Below are examples from each factor: I would prefer my coach to. . .

- *Training and instruction*
  Explain to each athlete what he should and should not do.
- *Democratic behaviour*
  Let his athletes share in decision making.
- *Autocratic behaviour*
  Keep to himself.
- *Social support*
  Help the athletes with their personal problems.
- *Positive feedback*
  Express appreciation when an athlete performs well.

Discussion: The authors felt that the LSS should provide a valuable tool for coaches and sports psychologists. They concluded that the five dimensions were consistent with theories of leadership, that they are conceptually distinct categories of coaching behaviour, and that each dimension was relatively reliable.

Evaluation

Fit of the model

The authors of this study appear to have followed a rigorous procedure in developing a new measure. However they indicated that the five factors together only explained around 40 per cent of the variance for preferred behaviour and 56 per cent for actual behaviour. This leaves a lot of the variance unexplained, which means that the model is not a very good fit. In other words, there is something missing in the authors' conceptualisation of factors in sports leadership.

12

12.1 Exercise psychology: Exercise and pathology
Key Study: 12.1.1 Exercise and its relation to cancer

Leslie Bernstein, Brian E. Henderson, Rosemarie Hanisch, Jane Sullivan-Halley and Ronald K Ross (1994), 'Physical exercise and reduced risk of breast cancer in young women', *Journal of the National Cancer Institute*, 86 (18)

Approach: Biological

Aim: To determine whether young women who regularly participated in exercise activities during their reproductive years had a reduced risk of breast cancer

Method: Self-report

Design: Case-control design (matched pairs)

Type of sample: Clinical sample

Participants: 545 women from Los Angeles aged 40 and under who had been newly diagnosed with breast cancer were individually matched with 545 controls on age, race (all white), pregnancy history and neighbourhood of residence but who were healthy (no diagnosis of cancer)

Procedure: Contact details of patients were provided by their physicians. Eligible patients were contacted by phone and were interviewed in person by the same female nurse-interviewer. One neighbourhood control participant was found for each patient by experimenters knocking on doors in each patient's neighbourhood until a match was found on variables described listed above. Complete reproductive, contraceptive and physical exercise histories for each participant were obtained. Information was recorded on reproductive factors, oral contraceptive use, other hormone use, family history of cancer and physical activity up to date of patients' diagnosis for both patients and control participants. At the beginning of the study, participants were asked to indicate physical exercise activities at age 10, 16 and 25. This was later revised to include assessment of lifetime history of regular participation in physical exercise. These activities included participation as a member of a sports team, participation in individual sports, walking for exercise, workouts at gyms and participation in dance or exercise classes.

Results: Data were analysed using multiple regression. After adjustment for potential confounding variables, it was found that the average number of hours spent in physical exercise activities per week from menarche (start of periods) to one year prior to diagnosis (in cancer patients) or one year prior to interview (in controls) was a significant predictor of reduced breast cancer risk. The data were controlled for physiological variables, that is

age at first period, age at first pregnancy, number of pregnancies, months spent breast-feeding, family history of breast cancer, weight/height relationship and use of oral contraceptives. The data suggested that women who maintain an activity level of 1–3 hours per week could reduce their risk of premenopausal breast cancer by about 30 per cent and those who maintain an activity level of at least four hours per week might reduce their risk by more than 50 per cent.

Discussion: The results of this study suggest that continued participation in a physical exercise regimen can markedly reduce the risk of breast cancer in premenopausal women and emphasise the importance of beginning an exercise routine when young and maintaining it during adulthood. The authors suggest the need for educational programmes that require participation in physical education classes and encourage lifelong participation in exercise and sport.

Evaluation

Controlling variables

This study adopted an extremely rigorous process of matching clinical participants with controls based on residence. However, other variables may still be influencing the results, such as nature of occupation and diet that are not mentioned as having been controlled for. It is a common problem in medical research that physiological variables are given rigorous consideration but less attention is paid to a wide range of socioeconomic and lifestyle factors.

Key Study: 12.1.2 Exercise and its relation to HIV–AIDS

Judith L. Neidig, Barbara A. Smith and Dale E. Brashers (2003), 'Aerobic exercise training for depressive symptom management in adults living with HIV infection', *Journal of the Association of Nurses in AIDS Care*, 14 (2), 30–40

Approach: Biological

Aim: To evaluate the effects of an aerobic exercise training programme on self-reported symptoms of depression in HIV-infected adults and to examine the convergent validity of two widely used depressive symptom scales

Method: Self-report

Design: Randomised, controlled trial

Type of sample: Clinical sample (opportunity)

Participants: 60 HIV-infected adults

Measures: The study used two depression measures and a mood scale to investigate the convergent validity of the scales when used on HIV patients:

1) The Center for Epidemiological Studies-Depression Scale (CES-D, Radoff, 1977) is a 20-item self-report measure of affective distress. Respondents rate frequency of symptoms experienced in the past week on a 4-point scale.

2) The Beck Depression Inventory (BDI, Beck, 1993) is a self-report depressive symptom index composed of 21 items. Participants rate each symptom on severity.

3) The Profile of Mood State (POMS, McNair *et al.*, 1971) is a 65-item instrument measuring six mood states. Respondents rate the occurrence of adjective items during the past week on a 5-point scale. Excellent reliability has been reported in HIV samples.

Procedure: Participants were assigned to 12-week aerobic training or to a waiting list. Participants gave informed consent and those in the exercise condition were exercise tested in a university health centre and placed on staff and patient fitness programmes. Exercisers were required to attend three supervised one-hour sessions per week. Trained exercise leaders coached participants to exercise a minimum of 30 minutes to individual targets.

Results: Self-report data were collected at weeks 0 and 12. A number of confounding variables were assessed:

- Physical fitness
- Physical activity
- Stress
- Social support
- HIV medical history

Treatment groups were balanced on depressive symptoms and all demographic and clinic characteristics except race. More blacks were assigned to the experiment condition whereas the majority of study participants were Caucasian men. Because the groups were balanced on a number of potentially confounding variables, these variables were not controlled in subsequent analysis.

The scales used were highly correlated, indicating reliability of the measures.

At the start of the study, 20–35 per cent of participants reported significant levels of depression. Participants who completed the exercise course reported improvements in depressive symptoms and depressed mood as compared with controls

Discussion: The authors acknowledged that they had limited control on several variables.

1) Randomisation did not result in racially balanced treatment groups.

2) It was not possible to exclude individuals on antidepressants as only people on stable drug routines were admitted to the study, but the researchers hoped that randomisation of the participants should have ensured a balance between the experimental and control group.

3) Exercise was in a 'real-life' setting similar to a gym and participants worked out individually.

4) Only 48/60 participants completed the study and all those who dropped out were in the experiment condition.

Evaluation

Problems of attrition

The high drop-out rate is normal for exercise studies, however it must be taken into account when analysing the results. It seems likely that those who dropped out would not have benefited in the same way as those who continued, otherwise they would have been motivated to continue. If their data had been analysed, then there might not have been the significant difference in results between conditions. It is therefore vital that any exercise intervention assesses those who withdraw and the reasons for their withdrawal.

12.1 Exercise psychology: Exercise and pathology
Key Study: 12.1.3 Eating disorders and sport

Jorunn Sundgot-Borgen and Monica Klungland Torstveit (2004), 'Prevalence of eating disorders in elite athletes is higher than in the general population', *Clinical Journal of Sport Medicine*, 14 (1), 25–32

Approach: Biological

Aim: To examine the prevalence of anorexia nervosa, bulimia nervosa, anorexia athletica and eating disorders not otherwise specified (ED-NOS) in both male and female Norwegian elite athletes

Method: Self-report

Type of sample: Opportunity and random samples

Participants: The entire population of Norwegian male and female elite athletes (n = 1620: 960 males; 660 females) and controls (n = 1696). Elite athlete was defined as one who had placed among the ten best in international competition, was competing in national teams and/or was a member of a recruiting squad for those teams. In addition, the athletes had to be between 15 and 39 years old and had to be training for at least eight hours per week. The athletes represented 68 sports/events classified into eight sport groups: technical, endurance, aesthetic, weight class, ball game, power, antigravitational and motor sports. A random sample of the general population of Norway (matched on age) was obtained through the Norwegian population register. All participants gave informed consent.

Procedure: All participants were sent a questionnaire. Response rate was 93 per cent for female athletes, 76 per cent for male athletes, 78 per cent for female controls and 72 per cent for male controls. Based on the results of the questionnaire, 121 female and 61 male athletes and 81 female and 22 male controls were classified as at risk for eating disorders. A total of 120 female and 58 male athletes and 76 of the female and 19 of the male controls completed the clinical interview. To match the at-risk athletes, a group of athletes from the initial pool were chosen at random and asked to complete the clinical interview. Seventy-five females and 18 males participated in the interviews as healthy controls. In the clinical interviews the DSM-IV was used to classify for eating disorders.

Results: Data were analysed using a χ^2 test. It was found that a higher percentage of athletes (13.5 per cent) than controls (4.6 per cent) had clinical or subclinical eating disorders. The prevalence of eating disorders in male athletes was higher in 'anti-gravitational' sports (for example, high jump) (22 per cent) than in ball game sports (5 per cent) or endurance sports (9 per cent). The prevalence among female athletes competing in 'aesthetic' sports (for example, gymnastics) was higher (40 per cent) than in endurance (24 per cent), 'technical' sports (17 per cent) or ball game sports (16 per cent). It was also found that the prevalence of eating disorders was higher in female athletes than male athletes and more common in slimness-dependent and weight-dependent sports than in other sports.

Discussion: The authors acknowledge the limitations of self-report as a method of obtaining at-risk individuals. However the fact that the questionnaire was followed up by clinical diagnosis ensured reliability of the final results.

Evaluation

Sample

This was a valuable study because it investigated eating disorders in the total population of elite athletes from one country. Although this cannot be **generalised** to athletes in other countries, the findings replicate studies conducted in other countries among athletes and together, these studies have highlighted an international problem for high level sport that requires active attention.

12.2 Exercise psychology: Exercise and mental health
Key Study: 12.2.1 Theories of exercise and mental health
P. B. Sparling, A. Giuffrida, D. Piomelli, L. Rosskopf and A. Dietrich (2003), 'Exercise activates the endocannabinoid system', *Neuroreport*, 14 (17), 2209–11

Approach: Biological

Aim: To test the theory that moderate intensity exercise may activate the endocannabinoid system

Method: Laboratory experiment

Design: Independent measures

Type of sample: Self-selecting sample

Participants: 24 males who met either a running or a cycling criterion (that they had run or cycled for at least 30 minutes on at least four days per week for the previous six months)

Procedure: Participants who fulfilled the running criterion were allocated randomly on a 2:1 basis to either the running or the sedentary (control) condition and those who fulfilled the cycling criterion were allocated randomly to either the cycling or sedentary condition. All participants gave informed consent.

To decrease variability due to arousal levels, all participants reported to the laboratory on the day prior to testing. Information about personal health and exercise training were obtained and the participants were given a familiarisation session. All participants were asked not to exercise on test day and not to eat or consume caffeinated drinks for three hours before reporting. On test day a questionnaire was responded to in order to check compliance.

The exercise protocol was the same for the running and cycling participants. In a temperature-controlled room, the exercise began with a five-minute warm up on either the treadmill or the cycle ergometer. Rate was then increased to obtain a heart rate in the range of 70 per cent to 80 per cent, which corresponds to a moderate training effort for trained runners and cyclists. Once desired intensity was reached, participants ran/cycled for 45 minutes. Participants in the control condition went through the same preparatory procedure but they simply remained seated in the controlled temperature room for 50 minutes. Blood was collected from all participants and samples were tested for endocannabinoids.

Results: A significant interaction was found for group x time. Plasma anandamide levels were significantly raised in runners and cyclists but not in controls. All exercising participants displayed a post-exercise increase in anandamide levels.

> **Anandamide:** Anandamide is an endogenous cannabinoid neurotransmitter.

> See *Psychology A2 for OCR* textbook, p. 258 for explanation of endocannabinoids

Discussion: The researchers concluded that they had shown for the first time that exercise activates the endocannabinoid system and are suggestive of a new explanation for the analgesic (pain reducing) effect of exercise. Anandamide binds to a receptor that is densely expressed in brain regions implicated in motor control, emotion and cognition. Activation of this receptor by exogenous cannabinoids (drugs such as cannabis) causes intense subjective experiences similar to those reported by endurance athletes. Sparling *et al.* theorise as a result of this study that endocannabinoids might interact with other neurotransmitters such as opioids or catecholamines to produce the phenomenon known as runner's high.

Evaluation
Methodology
This study is an example of a **well-controlled** laboratory experiment. Random allocation to groups, careful preparation of participants' routines and control of the experimental tasks all suggest that the results of this study should be **reliable**.

12.2.3 Exercise and mood states

Jennifer Moses, Andrew Steptoe, Andrew Mathews and Sara Edwards (1989), 'The effects of well-being in the normal population: a controlled trial', *Journal of Psychosomatic Research*, 33 (1), 47–61

Approach: Biological

Aim: To compare the effects of two aerobic training programmes of differing intensities on mood and mental well-being with those of a placebo condition

Method: Laboratory experiment

Design: Independent groups

Type of sample: Self-selecting sample

Participants: Over 100 healthy but low exercising residents from the local community out of over 400 volunteers were selected for participation through use of a detailed questionnaire. Those who were included reported no medical problems that would be likely to interfere with training, no hypertension (high blood pressure), no psychiatric history, low scores on a depression scale and who were no more than 25 per cent above ideal weight. Data were collected for final analysis from 75 participants who completed the study.

Psychological measures: The Profile of Mood States (McNair *et al.*, 1981) was administered. In addition, a measure of coping ability and physical well-being was administered, as well as a depression scale in the screening process.

> For details of the Profile of Mood States, see Key study 11.1.2 Social loafing p. 144

Fitness measures: Two measures of aerobic fitness were obtained during the study.

1) Heart rate and oxygen uptake were recorded during exercise.
2) A 22-minute walk-run test was carried out on an all-weather running track before and after training. Participants were asked to walk or run as far as they could within a 12-minute period.

Procedure: Participants were assigned using a randomised matching procedure to one of four conditions: high exercise, moderate exercise, attention-placebo and waiting list.

High exercise

This required exercise three to five times per week with 30 minutes continuous aerobic activity. A walk-jog programme was devised sufficient to elevate heart rate to 70–75 per cent of maximum.

Moderate exercise

This involved aerobic exercise at a level expected to produce only minimal improvements in cardiorespiratory fitness. It was based on 20-minute low intensity walking or jogging devised to elevate heart rate to 60 per cent of maximum.

Attention-placebo

Participants in this condition performed strength, mobility and flexibility exercises that involved slow, discontinuous exercise for 30 minutes that did not elevate heart rate above 50 per cent of maximum.

Waiting list

The final group was placed on a waiting list for an exercise intervention.

There were 12–15 women and 4–6 men in each condition. There were no significant differences between groups in gender profile, age, body weight or pretraining responses on the POMS. Training was carried out over a ten-week period and consisted of one supervised and three unsupervised sessions per week. Participants were individually assessed with psychological evaluations and an exercise test before the intervention and after completion of training.

Results:

Pre-/Post-training (all groups, n = 75)

- Aerobic fitness improved in the high exercise condition more than in the other conditions, but the difference was significant only between the high exercise and the attention-placebo condition.
- A reduction in tension/anxiety was found only in the moderate exercise group. This group was the only group to experience a decrease in confusion.
- No significant differences were found over time or between groups on depression, anger, vigour, fatigue or self-efficacy.
- No significant effects were found on the perceived coping scale but the group x time

interaction was significant on the physical well-being scale.

- All three active treatment groups showed improvements on the measure after training, while those in the waiting list group experienced a decrease in physical well-being.

Three-month follow-up (the three active intervention groups only, n = 58)

- Those in the moderate exercise group (but not the high exercise or the attention–placebo group) experienced a decrease in coping deficit and an increase in perceived coping assets at the end of the three-month follow-up period.
- A similar trend was seen in depression ratings.

Discussion: A positive effect of moderate but not high exercise intervention was found post-training and at follow-up on several mood measures. This is important because it contradicts the hypothesis that improvement in psychological mood would be associated with aerobic conditioning. The authors suggested that perhaps participants in the high exercise group found the training too demanding so that the rigour of the schedule mitigated any improvements in well-being. They also concluded that engaging in physical activity is more important for mood improvement than achieving aerobic fitness.

Evaluation
Generalisability of results

This is another good example of a well controlled experiment using a sample that has higher **generalisability** than many other similar studies that use university students. The measures used have been widely applied in similar studies so there is no reason to doubt **reliability** of the findings. This is interesting as the results do not support the previously held view that only high aerobic exercise would have a positive effect on mood.

12.3

Key Study: 12.3.1 Burnout and withdrawal

P-N Lemyre, H. K. Hall and G. C. Roberts (2008), 'A social-cognitive approach to burnout in elite athletes', *Scandinavian Journal of Medicine and Science in Sports*, 18, 221–34

Approach: Cognitive

Aim: To investigate burnout in elite athletes from a socio-cognitive perspective

Method: Self-report

Type of sample: Opportunity sample

Participants: There were 141 participants in total: 45 were current Norwegian winter Olympic team members and 96 were junior elite athletes studying at national sport academies in Norway; 81 participants were male, 60 were female; age range 17–32 years. Over half had previous World Cup or World Championship experience. Participants were Alpine skiers, Nordic skiers, Nordic combined, biathlon athletes and speed skaters. Participants gave informed consent, and in the case of junior athletes, parents also gave informed consent.

Measures:

Achievement goals

A Norwegian translation of the sports-specific Perception of Success Questionnaire (Roberts *et al.*, 1998) was used to assess achievement orientations.

Perceived motivational climate

A translated version of the Perceived Motivational Climate in Sport Questionnaire (Seifriz *et al.*, 1992) was used to assess performance and mastery.

Perceived ability

A translated version of the Intrinsic Motivation Inventory (McAuley *et al.*, 1989) was used to assess perceived sport ability.

Perfectionism

Athletes' perfectionist dispositions were measured using a translated version of the Multidimensional Perfectionism Scale (Frost *et al.*, 1990).

Burnout

A translated version of the Athlete Burnout Questionnaire (Raedeke and Smith, 2001) was used to measure three key dimensions of burnout:

- Reduced sense of accomplishment
- Emotional and physical exhaustion
- Devaluation of sport participation

Cognitive appraisal

Participants were asked to express their perceived goal attainment.

Procedure:

First data collection

Participants responded at the beginning of the winter sports season to a questionnaire assessing achievement goals, perception of motivational climate, perceived ability and perfectionism.

Second data collection

Participants responded to a follow-up questionnaire investigating athletes' cognitive appraisal of goal attainment and success, as well as symptoms of overtraining and signs of burnout.

Results: Results indicated that motivational dispositions, achievement motivation, perceived ability and dimensions of perfectionism were associated with burnout. The authors also found that athletes could be grouped into two contrasting motivational groups based on their responses to the initial measures. One group they categorised as adaptive and the other maladaptive. At the end of the season, these two contrasting motivational profiles were associated with different signs of burnout.

Discussion: The authors suggested that burnout may not be simply motivation that has gone wrong but that it may be the consequence of having a maladaptive motivational profile.

Evaluation

Sample

The authors acknowledged that the sample size was too small given the fact that less than 10 per cent of elite athletes experience burnout during one season, but the sample was representative of one country's elite athletes and the study was high in **ecological validity** for this reason. **Generalisability** is, however, low because of the restricted range of sports and the fact the athletes are all from one country.

David P. Ausubel (1960), 'The use of advance organizers in the learning and retention of meaningful verbal material', *Journal of Educational Psychology*, 51 (5), 267–72

Approach: Cognitive-behavioural

Aim: To determine whether learning and retention of unfamiliar verbal material can be facilitated by the advance introduction of relevant subsuming concepts (organisers)

Method: Laboratory experiment

Design: Matched pairs

Type of sample: Opportunity sample

Participants: 120 undergraduate students (78 female, 32 male) of educational psychology: participants took part as a required laboratory exercise performed during class

Materials: A specially prepared 2500-word passage dealing with the metallurgical properties of carbon steel. This topic was chosen on the basis that it would be generally unfamiliar to graduates in liberal arts and sciences but sufficiently accessible to be comprehensible and interesting to novices. The criterion of unfamiliarity was crucial because the purpose of the study was to ascertain whether advance organisers could facilitate retention in areas of knowledge new to learners. For this reason, a prior study was conducted by giving the test on steel to a different group of students of similar background who had not read the passage, and it was found that mean scores in the test were not significantly better than chance. The test used was the same 36-item multiple choice test covering principles, facts and applications also administered to the participants.

Procedure:

- Participants were tested on a similar unfamiliar passage, matched on test scores and assigned to either the experimental or control group.
- Each group was then given an introductory passage of approximately 500 words studied twice for five minutes. The first occasion was 48 hours before and the second occasion immediately before the main passage on steel was given to participants to read.
- The introductory passages for the experimental and control groups were different in nature.

- The experimental introductory passage contained background material presented as a higher level of abstraction and generality than the steel passage. This was designed to serve as an organising and anchoring focus for the steel material and to relate it to participants' existing cognitive structures. Emphasis was placed on similarities and differences between metals and alloys, their uses and limitations.
- The control introductory passage consisted of relevant historical background material of the kind often incorporated in textbooks but which contained no conceptual material that could serve as a cognitive framework for organising the substantive body of more detailed ideas, facts and relationships in the learning passage.
- Both groups studied the steel passage for 35 minutes and took the multiple choice test three days later.
- The pilot test had shown that unprepared scores on the steel test, while not being above chance, were related to participants' sex and major field of study so these factors needed to be controlled for. Participants were therefore rematched across the two groups taking these factors into account and as a result, the data from 80 participants (40 in each group) out of the original 120 were retained for data analysis.

Results: Results were normally distributed. Mean score for participants in the experimental group was 16.7 as opposed to 14.1 for the control group. The difference between the means of the two groups was nearly significant at the 0.01 level (significant well within the 0.05 level).

Discussion: Ausubel suggested that the difference would have been even more significant if the learning passage had been closer in subject matter to the steel passage as this would have allowed more effective matching of participants. He also found that the steel material was not completely unfamiliar to some participants so prior knowledge may have reduced the effects of the organising passage.

Ausubel nevertheless concluded that advance organisers probably facilitate the learning and retention of meaningful verbal material in two ways. Firstly, they explicitly draw upon and mobilise whatever relevant subsuming concepts are already established in the learners' cognitive structure. Secondly, advance organisers at an appropriate level provide the best way of anchoring new material. Ausubel defined the optimum level of organiser as being one as proximate as possible to the cognitive demands of the learning task and the learner's pre-existing knowledge. He recommended that the advance organiser approach should be adopted in textbooks and teaching materials in order to avoid the problem of students being 'trapped' into rote learning without fully understanding the meaning of what they are learning.

Evaluation

Reductionism

This is an attempt to test student learning in an experimental situation. The study was **well-controlled** and thorough, hence the results should be **reliable**, even acknowledging the limitations admitted by the experimenter. However, the **ecological validity** of this study is low. In order to control the variables, all students had the same amount of time to read the passage and had no access to other materials. This is not the way in which most students learn so it failed to take into account students' personal approaches. Moreover other studies show that intrinsic interest in material aids student learning. Intrinsic interest is likely to have been low in this task. So Ausubel has shown that in particular conditions, advance organisers can facilitate learning but it would be **reductionist** to assume that such organisers alone are the key to improved learning.

13.3 Teaching and learning: Personal approaches to teaching

Key Study: 13.3.2 Cognitive approaches to learning

David Klahr and Milena Nigam (2004), 'The equivalence of learning paths in early science instruction', *Psychological Science*, 15 (10), 661–7

Approach: Cognitive

Aim: To compare the effects of direct instruction with discovery learning on children's mastery of an elementary-school science objective, the control-of-variable strategy (CVS)

Method: Laboratory experiment

Design: Independent measures

Type of sample: Not stated

Participants: 112 children (33 male, 79 female) in US elementary (primary) schools aged 8–10 years (third and fourth grades).

Procedure: Participants were randomly assigned to the direct instruction of discovery learning condition

Materials: Apparatus included two wooden ramps, each with an adjustable downhill side, and a slightly uphill, stepped surface on the other side, and two types of balls

Day 1: Exploration and assessment Day 1 had two phases: exploration and assessment.

Exploration phase

- The children could choose the steepness of each ramp (high or low), the surface of the ramp (rough or smooth), the length of the downhill run (long or short) and the type of ball (rubber ball or golf ball).
- They were asked to make comparisons to determine how the different variables affected the distance the ball rolled after leaving the downhill ramp.
- At the beginning of the exploration phase, the ramp apparatus was described and the children were asked to set up four experiments: two to determine effect of steepness and two to determine effect of run length on how far the ball rolls. Each child received a score indicating the number of unconfounded experiments (in which other variables were controlled) he or she designed.
- **Direct instruction condition:** in this condition the children observed as the experimenter set up several additional experiments (some confounded, some

unconfounded) to determine effects of steepness and run length. Each time, the instructor asked the children whether or not the design would allow them to 'tell for sure' whether a variable had an effect on outcome. Then the instructor explained why each of the unconfounded experiments uniquely identified the factor that affected outcome whereas the confounded experiment did not.

- **Discovery learning condition:** In this condition the children continued to design their own experiments, focused on the same two variables as the direct instruction children but without any instruction on CVS or any feedback from the experimenter.

Assessment phase

- The assessment phase started immediately after the exploration phase.
- Children in both conditions were asked to design four additional experiments: two to determine the effect of a factor that had been investigated earlier (run length) and two to determine the effect of a factor that had not been investigated before (surface).
- During the assessment phase, no feedback was provided in either condition.

Day 2: Evaluation of science fair posters

- A week later a different experimenter (blind to training condition) asked all children to evaluate two science fair posters by making comments and suggestions that would help to make the poster 'good enough to enter a competition'.
- One poster explored the effect of the number of holes in a ping-pong ball on how far the ball would travel when launched from a catapult. The other poster compared short-term memory of boys and girls. Both posters described highly imperfect experiments.
- As each poster was presented to each child, the experimenter read aloud the information it contained and then conducted a structured interview in which the children were asked to

critique each poster. The number of critiques was an open-ended measure and the children were encouraged to say as much as they could, as well as being asked to respond to specific questions in the structured interview.

- The poster evaluation score for each child was based on total number of valid critiques made about either poster.

Results: The overall aim was to determine whether there were differences in the ability of children who did or did not acquire CVS, either by direct instruction or discovery learning, to reason about the broader domain of evaluating a science fair poster. There were two parts to the analysis:

1) The extent to which children in each condition learned CVS on Day 1
2) The ability of children to assess posters a week later

Extent to which children learned CVS

- Eight children who produced four out of four unconfounded experiments during the exploration phase as 'CVS experts' were excluded from Day 1 analysis.
- Analysis of the data of the remaining 104 participants revealed a main effect for training condition. CVS scores for direct-instruction children increased dramatically from exploration to assessment phase, whereas children's scores in the discovery learning condition improved only slightly.
- In order to examine the impact of training condition on individual children, each child was classified according to their CVS score following training. Those who obtained a score of at least 3 out of 4 were classified 'masters'.
- Direct instruction produced many more masters than discovery learning. Forty of 52 direct instruction children became masters compared to 12 of the 52 discovery learning children.
- The superiority of direct instruction over discovery learning was maintained when data were analysed for only the children who started out with the lowest CVS scores in the exploration phase.

Evaluative skill

The question in this phase was whether there was an effect of learning path on evaluative expertise.

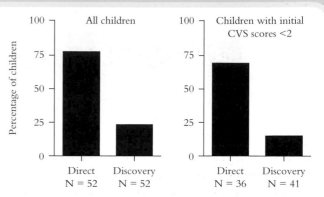

Figure 13.1 Percentage of children (out of the total numbers indicated) in the direct-instruction and direct-learning conditions who achieved master-level performance (at least 3 unconfounded experiments out of 4)
Source: D. Klahr and M. Nigam (2004). © 2004 Sage Publications, reprinted with permission.

There were four training paths: master (discovery), nonmaster (discovery); master (direct instruction) and nonmaster (direct instruction).

- There were no statistical differences on poster evaluation scores for experts, discovery masters and direct instruction masters on poster scores.
- There were no differences in scores of the two groups who failed to master CVS but these were significantly lower than the scores of the three high CVS score groups.

Discussion: Children who became masters via direct instruction were as skilled in evaluating science fair posters as those who became masters via discovery learning. Moreover, a much higher proportion of children became masters as the result of direct instruction than discovery learning. Klahr and Nigam suggest that their results cast doubt on long held, beliefs that discovery learning facilitates skill transfer better than direct instruction methods.

Evaluation

Controlling variables

This is a **well-controlled** experiment which evaluates primary-school age children's ability to learn about experimental control of variables via two alternative teaching methods – direct instruction or discovery learning. It is high in **ecological validity** as the procedure was similar to that carried out in science lessons in classrooms. It is rare to find a study that has both good **control of variables** and high ecological validity.

13.3 Teaching and learning: Personal approaches to teaching

Key Study: 13.3.3 Social constructivism – cooperative learning and scaffolding

Kent A. Rittschof and Bryan W. Griffin (2001), 'Reciprocal peer tutoring: re-examining the value of a co-operative learning technique to college students and instructors', *Educational Psychology*, 21 (3), 313–31

Approach: Cognitive

Aim: To examine the effects of cooperative learning (reciprocal peer training – RPT) on graduate and undergraduate understanding of course material compared to an individualised study task

Method: Laboratory experiment

Design: Independent measures

Experiment 1

Type of sample: Not stated

Participants: 97 graduate students of education at a US university. Mean age was 35 years, 75 per cent were female and 90 per cent were Caucasian (white). The second experimenter taught all sections of the education course.

Measures:

- A 45-item test was developed to serve as a post-test measure of achievement. Content validity was established. A 24-item pre-test was also developed to assess students' initial knowledge of course content.
- Test anxiety and academic self-efficacy were measured using a scale of academic self-efficacy (Pintrich and De Groot, 1990) and the Self-efficacy and Test Anxiety Scale (Griffin, 1994).
- A post-experimental questionnaire was developed to gather reflective self-report of participants' experience of the reciprocal peer training.

Procedure: A pre-test, post-test control group design was used. Participants were assigned randomly to one of three groups. Analysis of the pre-measures showed that the randomly-formed groups did not differ statistically on any of the measures of achievement, self-efficacy or test anxiety.

Treatment and control groups were Out-of-class RPT and In-class RPT.

Out-of-class RPT

Students were

- Randomly assigned a partner.

- Instructed to write ten multiple choice test items (with explanations for correct responses) for each in-class course examination.
- Instructed to administer their ten-item test to their partner prior to the course examination and provided tutoring as needed.
- Instructed to submit their ten-item test and answer sheet on the day of the examination.

This group of students were not monitored by the instructor during the tutoring process but their materials were examined to ensure they had completed the tasks.

In-class RPT

- Students were randomly assigned a partner.
- Students were instructed to write ten multiple choice test items (with explanations for correct responses) for each in-class course examination.
- Students submitted all items to the instructor for review approximately one week prior to the examination for checking.
- Students completed RPT activities (test examination and tutoring) during class time on exam day, immediately before unit examinations.
- Upon completion of RPT prior to an examination, students submitted their tests and written explanations of correct responses to the instructor.
- Participants were allowed as much time as they needed to complete the procedure.
- The instructor monitored each in-class group to ensure individual accountability during tutoring session.

Essentially the in-class RPT and out-of-class RPT differed in that it required students to submit RPT items for instructor review prior to using them, and students administered tests and tutored each other during class time and the instructor monitored tutoring progress.

Control group

- Students were required to keep a journal of their study activities and reflections relative to course content.
- This task was designed to represent useful individualised activity relating to the course that did not involve cooperative interaction between students.

Students participated in RPT three times to match the number of examinations administered in the class.

Experiment 2

Participants: 100 undergraduate students enrolled on a human development course (average age 20; 70 per cent white; 30 per cent black; 84 per cent female). The first experimenter taught all sections of the human development course.

Method: Instruments, procedures and design of Experiment 1 were replicated except that the number of items on the post- and pre-test was 32 and the RPT was carried out four times to match the number of examinations on the course.

Results: There were no significant differences on any of the outcomes in Experiment 1. Neither of the experimental groups obtained means that were consistently better than the control group on any of the five dependent measures:

- Performance test scores
- Situational self-efficacy
- Situational test anxiety
- Trait self-efficacy
- Trait test-anxiety

In Experiment 2 the only significant difference was on situational test-specific self-efficacy. The control group had slightly higher levels of self-efficacy than the experimental groups.

However, the post-experimental self-report measure suggested an overwhelmingly positive response to RPT. Among the four RPT groups across the two experiments, all the respondents reported that writing the test items was helpful. For the undergraduates, goal setting was also cited as useful. In response to whether test taking and tutoring were helpful, the majority indicated they were helpful, with undergraduates being more positive than graduate students. The most consistently provided reasons given by all groups for the usefulness of RPT were the effects of seeking peer-assistance, self-evaluation and application of learning strategies.

Discussion: None of the predictions on effects of RPT (higher test scores, less test anxiety, greater academic self-efficacy) was supported. However, participants overwhelmingly reported that they benefited from RPT. The authors suggested that instructors should weigh up the time/outcome benefits of RPT at student level. They also suggested that when RPT is being used for achievement gains, instructors should evaluate the ecological validity of studies where the findings show expected improvements in test scores. On the other hand, they accepted that the RPT technique appears to enhance enjoyment of learning and that the relationship between student perception, motivational outcome and learning outcome in cooperative environments is worthy of further investigation.

Evaluation

Reporting non-significant results

This study shows the importance of reporting results that do not support the authors' experimental hypotheses. Clearly there was an assumption behind this study that peer tutoring would improve student performance and reduce test anxiety. This assumption may have been based on previous studies with low **ecological validity**, as the authors suggest, or it might be due to the fact that researchers who do not find support for their experimental hypothesis may not always go ahead with publishing their data. The authors of this study do not deny that cooperative learning may be useful for students, but they rightly urge that more studies are needed if assumptions of performance benefits are to be tested.

Shaun Newsome, Arla L. Day and Victor M. Catano (2000), 'Assessing the predictive validity of emotional intelligence', *Personality and Individual Differences*, 29 (7), 1005–16

Approach: Individual differences

Aim: To determine the relationship of emotional intelligence, cognitive ability and personality with academic achievement

Method: Self-report

Design: Longitudinal

Type of sample: Opportunity sample

Participants: 180 students (118 female; 62 male; mean age 21 years) enrolled in introductory psychology courses at a Canadian university. Data reported are based on responses from 137 to 160 students due to incomplete questionnaires or exclusion of outliers.

Measures:

Cognitive ability

Participants completed the Wonderlic Personnel Test (1992), designed as a quick measure of cognitive ability and has been described as a test of academic intelligence. It consists of 50 questions and is reported to correlate with the well-regarded Wechsler Adult Intelligence Test.

Personality

Respondents completed the 16PF (Cattell *et al.*, 1993). Respondents indicated the extent to which 185 items were a true description of themselves. The five global factors of the 16PF (extraversion; anxiety; tough-mindedness; independence; self-control) were used as an indicator of personality.

Emotional intelligence

Respondents completed the EQ-i (Bar-ON, 1997). Emotional intelligence was calculated based on total EQ-i score, as well as scores from five composite factors (intra-personal scale; inter-personal scale; adaptability scale; stress management scale; general mood scale).

Academic achievement

Four months after the end of the study, the researchers obtained the GPAs (Grade point averages) of participants.

Procedure: The above measures were responded to during an introductory psychology course in return for bonus points for course credit.

Results:

- As expected, GPA was significantly correlated with the Wonderlic and with the extraversion and self-control factors of the 16PF.
- Individuals who had higher cognitive ability, who were more introverted and had higher self-control tended to have higher GPAs.
- Correlations between GPAs and measures of EQ-i were very low.
- Neither total score on EQ-i nor the five EQ-i factors were associated with GPA.
- Of all scale scores of the 16PF and the EQ-i, only the extraversion factor of the 16PF was significantly correlated with cognitive ability (high introversion individuals tended to have higher cognitive ability).

Discussion: The original intention of the study was to examine the extent to which emotional intelligence separately from cognitive ability contributed to predictions of academic achievement. However, the results provided no support for claims of the ability of emotional intelligence (as measured by the EQ-i) to predict academic achievement, although the results did provide substantial evidence for the predictive value of cognitive ability and certain personality measures.

Evaluation

Self-report data

The authors accept that there may be a **social desirability** factor operating in responses to the self-report measures. However, as they point out, there was no incentive for participants to try to create a favourable impression as responses were anonymous. They further admit that there was a possibility of unintentional self-deception but they suggest that this would be unlikely to affect outcome predictions. They also point out that the study replicated the well-established relationships between cognitive ability, personality measures and academic achievement, hence indicating that the measures were **reliable**.

14.3 Student participation: Student beliefs and expectations

Key Study: 14.3.2 Learned helplessness

Raymond C. P. Au, David A. Watkins and John A. C. Hattie (2010), 'Academic risk factors and deficits of learned hopelessness: a longitudinal study of Hong Kong secondary school students', *Educational Psychology*, 30 (2), 125–38

Approach: Cognitive-behavioural

Aim: To explore a causal model of academic achievement and learning-related personal variables by testing the relationships between learned hopelessness, its risk factors and hopelessness deficits

Method: Self-report

Design: Longitudinal

Type of sample: Opportunity sample

Participants: 741 Hong Kong secondary school students (age 14–15). The schools were characterised as competitive, dominated by authoritarian teachers tending towards punishment rather than praise. There was often high levels of parental pressure. The schools were selected to be representative of the range of abilities in Hong Kong and students were selected from streaming Bands 1, 3 and 5, representing a cross-section in achievement.

Procedure: Students responded at the beginning and end of the academic year (eleven months apart).

Measures: Chinese versions of nine measures were constructed or adapted to measure the risk factors and deficits of learned helplessness. All measures were found to have adequate estimates of reliability. The scales covered five major domains:

- Prior academic failure
- Learned hopelessness (from Beck *et al.*, 1974)
- Attributional style
  1. Internality
  2. Stability
  3. Globality
  4. Entity conceptions of intelligence
- Affective attributes
  1. Self-efficacy
  2. School values
  3. Self-esteem
- Learning
  1. Learning strategy effectiveness
  2. Academic achievement (data on performance in Chinese, English and Mathematics)

Results:
- Prior academic achievement was a powerful predictor of later academic achievement. Other learning, attributional and affective variables paled in significance compared to this.

- Once prior achievement was removed from the model, the best predictors were perceived learning difficulties and learning strategies.
- Students who received negative feedback at Time 1 were more likely to have lower self-efficacy and self-esteem and an entity concept (fixed/stable concept) of intelligence at Time 2.
- Higher school values led to more internalised attributional style.
- The higher external attributional style, the higher the later levels of learned hopelessness, learning difficulties and the lower self-esteem

Discussion: The researchers found that learned hopelessness was more a consequence of lower achievement than a predictor of it. In other words, the effects of learned helplessness are causal in one direction – from lower achievement to greater hopelessness. Hopelessness may lead to disengagement from schooling. When students experience decline in academic achievement, this can feed 'hopelessness' which leads to beliefs in 'learning difficulties' and this can set off a spiralling of lowering achievement. The researchers suggest that teachers can use strategies to reverse this with effective teaching and an atmosphere that encourages students to ask for help.

Evaluation

Usefulness

This is a thorough study that uses a large, representative sample and takes a longitudinal approach enabling the researchers to indicate the direction of the relationship between variables even though the study is not an experiment. The complex findings reflect the complexity of the learning process. If students had only been examined at one time point, it would not have been possible to determine the relationship between the personality variables, learned helplessness and academic attainment. Using two time points, the researchers were able to establish the pattern of causality. This is a **useful** study because it is **generalisable** due to the nature of the sample and can inform teaching strategies.

15.1 The social world of teaching and learning: Personal and social development

Key Study: 15.1.2 Application of humanist values of acceptance and approval to learning

David W. Johnson and Roger T. Johnson (1983), 'Social interdependence and perceived academic and personal support in the classroom', *Journal of Social Psychology*, 120 (1), 77–82

Aim: To compare attitudes towards social interdependence and attitudes towards relationships with peers and teachers in students who participated in frequent cooperative learning experiences

Method: Self-report

Type of sample: Teachers volunteered their students

Participants: 859 students (421 males, 438 females; 826 white, 33 ethnic minority) from three school districts in the American Midwest

- Grade 5: 79 students
- Grade 6: 171 students
- Grade 7: 180 students
- Grade 8: 146 students
- Grade 9: 46 students

Measures: The *Classroom Life Instrument* was administered which consists of 67 Likert-type questions on attitudes to learning and relationships with peers and teachers

Procedure: About half the teachers had been trained in how to use cooperative learning experiences. The *Classroom Life Instrument* was administered to all the students during the same two month period.

Data analysis: Factor analysis produced 15 factors:

- Liking of cooperative learning
- Positive goal interdependence (perception of joint outcomes)
- Resource interdependence (division of labour)
- Liking for positive competitive learning
- Liking for individualistic learning
- Belief teacher cares about your learning
- Belief teacher cares and likes you
- Belief that other students care about how much you learn
- Belief that other students like you as a person
- Belief that students in the class are friends and like each other
- Belief that working with diverse students is beneficial
- Belief that grades are fair
- Achieving for social approval

The sample was divided into those who reported learning within cooperative groups less than half the time (n = 366) and those who reported participating in cooperative learning groups half or more of the time (n = 431); 62 participants did not respond to this question. Tests of significance were conducted on differences between responses of low and high cooperative groups.

Results:

- Positive attitudes towards cooperative learning were moderately related to perceptions of positive goal interdependence and resource interdependence.
- Positive attitudes towards cooperative learning were negatively related to positive attitudes to individualistic learning.

The more students like to work cooperatively and the more they perceived positive goal and resource interdependence existing between them and their classmates, the more respondents believed that:

- teachers cared about how much the respondents learned and wished to facilitate their learning
- teachers cared about and liked the respondents as people
- other students cared about how much the respondents learned and wished to facilitate their learning
- other students cared about and liked the respondents as people
- students in the respondents' classes were friends and liked each other

Students who perceived themselves as frequently participating in cooperative learning experiences, compared to those who did not, felt that they experienced more caring and affection from teachers and encouragement from peers.

Discussion: The authors concluded that cooperative attitudes and experiences were related to feeling supported and accepted by teachers and peers, both academically and personally. There was some tentative evidence for the hypothesis that students who are positive towards cooperative learning will welcome working with students from diverse backgrounds. Fears that students who engaged in joint work would perceive the grading system as unfair were not upheld as the more positive the students were towards cooperative learning, the more they believed that the grading system was fair. Finally, it was found that the more positive students' attitudes towards competition, the more they wanted to achieve in order to win the social approval of others.

Evaluation

Sample and control

This study used a large sample size and is high in **ecological validity** as it was part of the students' learning process. However, the data hinge on student perception of their experience of cooperative learning and the amount and quality of the cooperative learning experiences appear not to have been controlled or reported.

Key Study: 15.1.3 Moral development and the implications for social rules

Dianna Murray-Close, Nicki R. Crick and Kathleen M. Galotti (2006), 'Children's moral reasoning regarding physical and relational aggression', *Social Development*, 15 (3), 345–72

Approach: Developmental/social

Aim: To analyse children's moral reasoning concerning physical and relational aggression

Method: Self-report

Type of sample: Self-selecting sample

Participants: 639 (336 female; 303 male) fourth and fifth graders were recruited from elementary schools in a large midwestern city in the United States. Students heard a ten-minute presentation and both student consent and parental consent were obtained.

Measure: A measure of moral reasoning about aggression (MRA) was used

Procedure: The MRA was administered to the children. It included three physical aggression scenarios and three relational aggression scenarios to which the participants were asked to respond with moral judgements with regard to how wrong the behaviour was, how often the behaviour resulted in harm and the domain used to judge the behaviour (moral, social conventional, personal or prudential). To explore the latter, children were asked how they would view the behaviour (for example, hitting others) if there were no rule against it. For example, it would be:

a) OK, because there is no rule against it (social convention)

b) OK, because as there is no rule, it is up to you whether you do it or not (personal)

c) Wrong, because the kid might hit you back and hurt you (prudential)

d) Wrong, because it would hurt the kid if you hit them (moral)

Participants' physically and relationally aggressive behaviours were assessed using a multi-informant approach (assessed by both teachers and their peers) and results compared with responses on the MRA.

Results:

Differences in attitudes to physical/relational aggression

- Analysis of variance revealed a significant main effect for aggression type, with children judging physically aggressive behaviour as more wrong than relationally aggressive behaviour.

- Participants reported that physically aggressive behaviours were more likely to result in harm for the victims than relationally aggressive behaviours.

- Children differed in their domain placement of physical and relational aggression. Children more often thought that physical aggression was a prudential issue (they might hurt you back), whereas they more frequently identified relational aggression as a moral issue.

Gender differences

- It was found that girls believed that behaving in aggressive ways was more wrong than did boys.

- Girls reported higher levels of harm resulting from aggressive behaviours than boys.

- The previous finding was qualified by aggression type. Boys and girls equally believed that physical aggression was wrong but girls were more likely than boys to believe that relational aggression resulted in harm to the victim.

- Girls were more likely to judge both relational and physical aggression in moral domain terms, while boys were more likely than girls to judge both relational and physical aggression in terms of social convention or personal domain.

Relationship with aggressive behaviours

- As expected, children's moral judgements of relational aggression were associated with involvement in relationally aggressive conduct. Children who regarded it as wrong were marginally less likely to be identified by peers as engaging in such behaviours.

- However, children's ratings of perceived harmfulness of relational aggression were **positively** related to teacher- and peer-reported relationally aggressive behaviours, with girls exhibiting higher levels of relational aggression than boys.

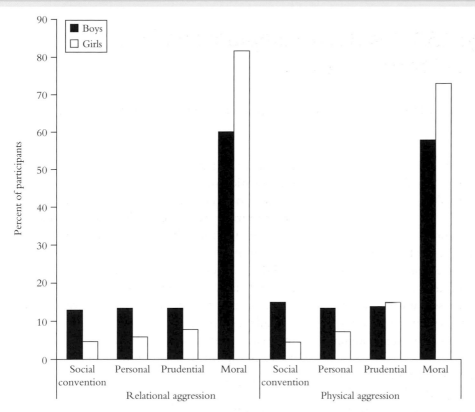

Figure 15.1 Boys' and girls' domain placement of physical and relational aggression
Source: D. Murray-Close *et al.* (2006), reproduced with permission.

- Children's ratings of the harmfulness of physical aggression were **positively** associated with teacher- and peer- reported involvement in such conduct.
- Children's global ratings of the wrongness of physical aggression were **negatively** associated with teacher- and peer-reported involvement in such conduct.

Discussion: The study showed that children overwhelmingly tend to approach both physical and relational aggression from a moral orientation rather than a social convention, personal or prudential domain. However, children tended to assert that physically aggressive behaviour was more wrong than relationally aggressive behaviour. Expected gender differences were found in relation to attitudes to aggression. The study also found as expected a negative relationship between involvement in aggression and wrongness judgements. However, the researchers were surprised by the fact that those rated as most engaged in aggressive conduct judged aggressive behaviours as more harmful than those not involved in them. A focus on social rules and

regulations about aggression and not simply an absence of thinking about the harm caused to others by behaving aggressively is associated with aggressive conduct.

Evaluation

Usefulness

The authors themselves pointed out three limitations with their study:

1) The study only dealt with one developmental period.

2) The study was cross-sectional therefore did not provide evidence of developmental change in moral reasoning.

3) The study was based on self-report and might be limited in assessment of different types of aggression.

However, we can agree with the authors that despite the limitations, this study provides **useful** insights into children's attitudes to bullying and the development of moral rules.

Key Study: 15.2.2 Friendship, bullying and academic success

Kathryn R. Wentzel and Kathryn Caldwell (1997), 'Friendships, peer acceptance and group membership: relations to academic achievement in middle school', *Child Development* 68 (6), 1198–209

Study 1

Approach: Social/cognitive

Aim: To determine relationships between number of reciprocated friendships, peer acceptance/peer group membership and academic achievement

Method: Self-report

Design: Longitudinal

Type of sample: Opportunity sample

Participants: 213 sixth-grade students from a middle school in an American midwestern mainly working-class community were followed for two years (mean age at start of study = 12). Fifty-two per cent of sample was female, 48 per cent male; 70 per cent of the sample was European American, 23 per cent African American and 7 per cent other minorities.

Procedure: Participants were assured that all responses would remain confidential. Data were collected by the first author in normal class.

Measures:

Reciprocated friendship
Students circled names of three same-sex best friends and names were matched to determine reciprocation scores.

Peer acceptance
Students were given a list of 25 randomly generated names of same-sex peers and asked to rate on a 5-point scale (1 = not at all, 5 = very much) how much they would like to be in school activities with each person named. A peer acceptance score was based on the average rating each student received.

Group membership
The friendship nominations used to identify reciprocal friendships were used to identify groups of friends. Groups were determined statistically by means of same-sex matrices constructed to represent the number of times any two individuals occurred together either through direct nomination or through co-occurrence with another student through a mutual friend, for example if Jim named

Mark and Steve, the co-occurrences in the matrix would include Jim and Mark, Jim and Steve and Mark and Steve.

Academic achievement

> **Hierarchical cluster analysis:** Cluster analysis uses statistical methods to classify a set of observations/characteristics into two or more mutually exclusive unknown groups based on combinations of interval variables. The purpose of cluster analysis is to discover a system of organising observations, usually people, into groups where members of the groups share properties/relationships in common. In hierarchical cluster analysis, data can be grouped top-down or bottom-up. The outcome is represented graphically as a dendrogram.

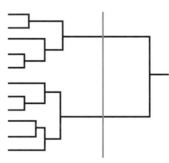

Figure 15.2 Example of a dendrogram generated using cluster analysis that has produced two clear groups from the subgroups

End of year cumulative grade-point average (GPA) based on English, science, social studies and mathematics was used for sixth-grade achievement. In seventh grade, GPA was based on grades from reading, language arts, science, social studies and mathematics.

Results:

- Number of reciprocated friendships did not differ significantly by gender. Thirty-seven per cent of students did not have a reciprocated friendship. Sixty per cent of European American students had reciprocated friendships as compared to 50 per cent of the non-European American students.
- Peer acceptance ratings for girls were significantly higher than for boys.
- Results of the hierarchical cluster analysis were that for males, 28 clusters were identified, of which 24 were clusters of 2 or more (mean cluster size = 5, range 2–16; 4 isolates) and for females a 30-cluster solution was chosen, of which 27 were clusters of 2 or more (mean size = 5, range 2–20, 3 isolates).
- Four boys and three girls did not belong to any identified peer group.
- In both sixth and seventh grades, girls had significantly higher GPAs than males.

Correlations:

- Peer acceptance ratings correlated significantly and positively with reciprocated friendships for both males and females.
- For boys, group membership in sixth grade was correlated significantly (positively) with GPA in sixth and seventh grade.
- For boys, both reciprocated friendship and peer acceptance in sixth grade was correlated significantly (positively) with sixth and seventh grade GPA.
- For girls, group membership in sixth grade was correlated significantly (positively) with GPA in sixth and seventh grades.
- For girls, peer acceptance in sixth grade correlated positively with sixth- and seventh-grade GPA but having a reciprocated friendship was not related significantly to girls' GPA in sixth grade or seventh grade.

Study 2

Approach: Social/cognitive
Aim: To replicate findings of Study 1 and also to examine the role of prosocial behaviour, antisocial behaviour and emotional distress in explaining these findings
Method: Self-report/correlation
Design: Longitudinal (three years)

Type of sample: Opportunity
Participants: 404 sixth grade students were followed for three years in a US mainly middle-class, mid-Atlantic community. Forty-eight per cent of the sample was female, 52 per cent male; 92 per cent of the sample was European American, 2 per cent African American and 6 per cent other minorities.

Procedure: Participants were assured that all responses would remain confidential. Data were collected by the first author in normal class with teachers present.

Measures: The same measures were used in Study 1 for reciprocated friendship, peer acceptance and group membership and academic attainment (sixth and eighth grade). In addition, antisocial and prosocial behaviours were assessed using peer and teacher ratings.

Antisocial/Prosocial behaviour ratings

- Teachers were asked how often each student breaks classroom rules (antisocial behaviour)/helps other children learn/is considerate of others (prosocial behaviour) on a scale of 1–5 (1 = not at all, 5 = always).
- Students were given a list of 25 randomly generated names of same-sex classmates and were asked to circle the name of students who 'break the rules/do things you are not supposed to' (antisocial behaviour) or 'helps others learn/cares for others' (prosocial behaviour). A total was calculated by dividing percentage of nominations of antisocial/prosocial behaviour received divided by number of times the child's name appeared on the list.

Psychological distress

Psychological distress was measured using the Weinberger Adjustment Inventory (short form). Responses are made on a 5-point scale (1 = false, 5 = true) to statements that tap anxiety, depression, low self-esteem, low well-being, for example, I often feel sad or unhappy (depression).

Results:

- In contrast to Study 1, having a reciprocated friendship differed significantly by gender, with girls averaging more reciprocated friendships than boys.
- As in Study 1, peer acceptance ratings for girls were higher than for boys.

- Result of the hierarchical cluster analysis were that for males, 29 clusters were identified, of which 27 were clusters of 3 or more (mean cluster size = 7, range 3–34; 2 isolates) and for females a 30–cluster solution was again chosen, of which 27 were clusters of 3 or more (mean size = 7, range 3–14, 3 isolates).
- Two boys and three girls did not belong to any identified peer group.
- As in Study 1, girls had a significantly higher GPA than boys.

Antisocial/prosocial behaviour

- Males were nominated by same-sex peers as breaking rules more often than females.
- Females were nominated by same-sex peers significantly more than boys for prosocial behaviour.
- Eighth-grade teachers' ratings of antisocial behaviours were significantly lower for girls than for boys.

Correlations:

For both males and females, peer acceptance and reciprocated friendships were correlated significantly and positively to each other.

Girls

- Girls' peer acceptance and reciprocated friendships correlated significantly (positively) with GPA in sixth grade but only peer acceptance was related significantly to eighth grade GPA.
- Peer acceptance was related significantly to antisocial (negatively) and prosocial behaviour (positively) at both time points and to distress (negatively) in sixth grade.
- For girls, having a reciprocated friendship was related significantly to emotional distress in eighth grade but not in sixth grade.
- Sixth- and eighth-grade GPAs of girls were related significantly (negatively) to antisocial behaviour and distress scores at both points in time and positively to prosocial behaviour at both time points.

Boys

- Boys' peer acceptance was related significantly to all variables expect sixth-grade antisocial behaviour and eighth-grade distress.

- Boys' reciprocated friendship was related negatively to antisocial behaviour at both time points.
- Boys' sixth-grade GPA was significantly related to all variables except eighth-grade distress.
- Boys' eighth-grade GPA was related positively to peer acceptance and prosocial behaviour at both time points, and negatively to sixth- and eighth-grade antisocial behaviour.

Group membership

This was related to different variables for boys and girls. For boys, group membership was related significantly (positively) to peer acceptance and antisocial behaviour in sixth grade and prosocial behaviour and distress in eighth grade. For girls, group membership was related significantly to peer acceptance, reciprocated friendship, and sixth grade antisocial behaviour.

Independent predictors of GPA

- When behavioural and distress variables were included in the model, sixth-grade group membership remained a significant predictor of sixth-grade GPA for girls, and group membership and peer acceptance remained significant predictors of sixth-grade GPA for boys.
- Eighth-grade prosocial behaviour and sixth-grade GPA were the only significant independent predictors of eighth-grade GPA.
- For males, all three aspects of peer relationships were related to eighth-grade GPA indirectly (through sixth grade GPA and and eighth-grade prosocial behaviour).
- For females, peer acceptance and group membership were indirectly related to eighth-grade GPA.

Discussion: As the authors indicate and as should be evident from the above results, the peer relationships of young adolescents are related to academic achievement in complex ways. Group membership was the most consistent predictor of GPA. However, when sixth grade GPA and social and emotional characteristics were taken into account, none of the sixth-grade peer variables remained independent predictors of academic achievement two years later. Reciprocated friendships and peer acceptance were related less consistently than group membership to GPA. As the authors suggest, not having a friend might lead to reduced academic motivation, but on the other hand, high levels of friendship might distract from academic pursuits.

Evaluation
Causal relations

This study tells us little about causal relationships between variables. It could be that positive socialisation enhances academic attainment, in which case teachers might intervene and promote the formation of peer groups with a positive orientation toward school. On the other hand, it may be that students' academic achievement influences their social behaviour which in turn affects levels of acceptance by peers and opportunities to make friends and join peer groups.

How might teachers intervene constructively if direction of causation is shown to be that academic achievement or reputation affects friendship opportunities?

15.3 The social world of teaching and learning: Student–teacher social interactions

Key Study: 15.3.1 Comparison of student–teacher communications

Zinaida Ilatov, Shmuel Shamai, Rachel Hertz-Lazarovitz and Shoshanna Mayer-Young (1998), 'Teacher–student classroom interactions: the influence of gender, academic dominance, and teacher communication style', *Adolescence*, 33 (130), 269–77

Approach: Social
Aim: To investigate whether teacher–student interactions are influenced by gender, teacher style and/or academic attainment of students
Method: Observation
Type of sample: Self-selecting sample
Participants: Two female teachers (literature and geography) of two seventh-grade classes in a small town in northern Israel. Both teachers had at least five years' experience. In class 7A there were 19 females and 16 males and in class 7B there were 22 males and 14 females. In 7A the more able students were mainly female, whereas in 7B the genders were more balanced in academic ability.
Procedure: Data were collected by videotaping 13 hours of class lessons (three lessons for each teacher) and interactions were analysed according to the following categories:

Teachers' utterances, categorised according to role:

- Academic instruction – academic presentation, answering students' academic questions, supportive and corrective feedback.
- Motivational – speech acts aimed at activating students, for example, asking academic questions.
- Evaluative – positive and negative feedback.
- Classroom management – discipline instructions and directives, procedural instructions.

Student utterances, categorised according to source:

- Teacher initiated – student utterances directly induced by, and addressed to, the teacher.
- Spontaneous student utterances – academic and procedural questions; calling out of turn.

Traditional forms of teaching were observed to avoid other influences. Videotaping was conducted over a period of three months. All speech acts were coded according to these categories and analysed for frequency, gender distribution, speech direction and initiation.

Results:

Academic instruction
The two teachers talked more with females than with males in both classes. However, there were differences in each teacher's treatment of males/females.

- Teacher 1: The difference between number of interactions with males and females was not large and was the same in both classes.
- Teacher 2: Gap between number of interactions with males and females was considerable in class 7A but not in 7B.

Motivational talk

- Teacher 1: Motivated males more than females, showing same motivational speech activity in both classes.
- Teacher 2: Motivated females more than males in both classes, especially in 7A.

Evaluative comments
Both teachers used positive evaluation more than negative evaluation.

- Teacher 1: Negative evaluations for males and females were similar in 7A and slightly greater for females in 7B.
- Teacher 2: Negative evaluations were greater for females than males in 7A but equal in 7B.

Class management (discipline management, procedural management)
Gender differences were more class-dependent than teacher-dependent.

- Teacher 1: Used less disciplinary management with females than males in class 7A but equal in 7B; with regard to procedural management, was more occupied with male than female students in 7A but more with females than males in 7B.

- Teacher 2: More occupied in terms of disciplinary management with males than females in both classes; with regard to procedural management, was more occupied with females than males in both 7A and 7B.

General teacher differences

Teacher 1 demonstrated a stable manner of treating male and female students in both classes with regard to academic and motivational roles, that is teacher–student interaction was relatively independent of situational factors. However, in motivational role, Teacher 1 was more motivational with males than females. In evaluation and class management functions, Teacher 1 was influenced by specific class situations. She exhibited a more equitable gender pattern than Teacher 2.

Teacher 2 generally interacted more with female than male students. The quantity of her interactions differed considerably between the two classes. In all her school roles, she was student-dependent and she interacted more with males than females in disciplinary situations. Teacher 2 initiated less talk in 7B than in 7A and more talk with females than males in both classes.

Differences in student-initiated talk

In both classes there were gender differences in student-initiated talk. In class 7A, females dominated student-initiated talk. The proportion of student-initiated talk was lower in 7B. For Teacher 2, only males initiated more talk than females in 7B.

Discussion: The 'personality' of each class influenced the whole spectrum of teachers' behaviours. Important differences between the two classes were found in the gender-related patterns of both teachers' and students' classroom talk. Differences were in the direction of providing more help to the weaker group, which happened to be males in class 7A. Females dominated one class academically, while the other was not dominated by either gender. That this influenced teacher behaviour shows that class composition is an important factor in teacher–student interactions. However, personal characteristics and student–student relationships also play a role. Interestingly, neither teacher showed any bias against females so the finding did not support previous studies that have indicated that males get more attention from teachers than females.

Evaluation

Generalisability

This is an interesting study that provides support for the hypothesis that teacher behaviour is influenced by characteristics and composition of the class. Although this study used a structured observational procedure that suggests fruitful ways forward for future research, we cannot generalise the findings as the participants were just two teachers investigated in the context of two classes. The study was conducted in Israel. This does not mean that it is any more or less **generalisable** than a study conducted in any other country. However, it does mean that the study would need to be replicated in a British context if practitioners in the UK were to plan interventions based on the findings.

15.3 The social world of teaching and learning: Student–teacher social interactions

Key Study: 15.3.2 Transmission of teacher expectations to students

Christine M. Rubie-Davies (2010), 'Teacher expectations and perceptions of student attributes: is there a relationship?', *British Journal of Educational Psychology*, 80, 121–35

Approach: Individual differences

Aim: To compare how teachers with very high (or very low) expectations for all their students would rate students' personal attributes and attributes in relation to achievement

Method: Self-report

Type of sample: Self-selecting sample

Participants: Six high expectation (HiEx) teachers and three low expectation (LoEx) teachers and their 220 students

Procedure: At the beginning of the school year, 24 primary school teachers completed a questionnaire in which they rated their expectations for student achievement for each student in their class. Teacher expectations were then compared with student achievement. Six teachers were found to have expectations of their students that were significantly above student achievement at the beginning of the year and three were found to have expectations significantly below student performance. Students with HiEx teachers made much greater progress in reading over one year than students of LoEx teachers. The teachers identified in the earlier investigation were the participants in this study.

Students in HiEx and LoEx classes were divided into equal thirds according to ability and further analyses by ability group in each class showed that the teachers' expectations were for all students as HiEx teachers had high expectations for each ability group and LoEx teachers had low expectation for each ability group.

Measures: Initially teachers rated pupils on a 7–point scale (1 –negative end, 7 – positive end) on 15 wide-ranging attributes including, for example, perseverance, independence, interest in schoolwork, level of disruptiveness, physical attractiveness.

The six HiEx students and three LoEx students who participated in the current study also rated students' attitudes to their schoolwork, their relationships with others and their home support.

One month into the academic year, the 24 original participants were asked to decide the reading level they expected their students to achieve by the end of the year on a 7–point scale, rating to New Zealand curriculum levels. At the end of the year, student achievement was assessed in order to compare expectations with outcome.

Results: Results of teacher ratings were aggregated by teacher type (HiEx or LowEx teacher) in order to perform statistical analysis.

Differences between HiEx and LoEx teachers' ratings

All means for HiEx teachers of their ratings of student characteristics were well above student achievement. Of the 15 student characteristics rated by teachers on 11 of the characteristics, the mean of HiEx teachers' ratings was above the mean for their expectations. The teachers appeared not only to have high expectations for their students but also to rate them highly on all characteristics. Just over half of the means for LoEx teachers' ratings of student characteristics were below students' achievement means but all were above the teachers' class expectation level. So while these teachers had low expectations for their students, they did perceive many of their characteristics positively.

Correlations

A significant difference was found between HiEx and LoEx teachers for their ratings of students' perseverance, independence, reaction to new work, interest in schoolwork, cognitive engagement, participation in class, motivation, confidence, self-esteem, classroom behaviour, peer relationships, parent attitudes to school, home environment and homework completion. In fact for every rating on the scale, HiEx teachers had more positive views of their students than did the LoEx teachers, not only in terms of expectations but also in relation to their perceptions of a range of student characteristics.

For HiEx teachers, there was a significant positive correlation between teachers' perceptions of students' attitudes and expectations. The HiEx teachers had very positive views of their students that reflected their positive expectations.

For LoEx teachers, there were fewer significant correlations between teachers' perceptions of student attitudes and teachers' expectations. There were small negative correlations between teacher expectations and interest in schoolwork, motivation, classroom behaviour, peer relationships and homework completion. These teachers' expectations were low for every student's achievement. The fact that these were small negative correlations shows that while teacher expectations were low, their perceptions were not similarly low. This group of teachers appeared to believe that the students tried hard and were well behaved and related well to others, even though their expectations for attainment were low.

Student achievement and teacher perceptions

In the classes of HiEx teachers, there were positive significant correlations between student achievement and teacher perceptions of student attributes. It seems that HiEx teachers perceived student attributes positively and in line with achievement.

For LoEx teachers, the only significant correlation was small and was between student achievement and teachers' perceptions of student cognitive engagement. Hence LoEx teachers perceived that student achievement was related to student engagement with the task. No other student attributes were associated with student achievement for this group of teachers. One explanation for this is that overall the teachers' perceptions of students' characteristics and achievement were not related.

Discussion: Students in the classes of HiEx teachers made large gains in learning over one year and improved their self-perceptions. Rubie-Davies suggested that it may be that their learning was enhanced because teachers viewed their attributes positively, as well as having high expectations for them. The association for LoEx teachers between expectations and perceptions of student attributes was weaker and negative. Rubie-Davies suggests that in unsupportive classroom environments, students may receive confused messages from their teachers. Teachers may provide positive messages about some of their characteristics but negative messages about their expectations for their attainment.

There was a positive correlation between all teacher perceptions of student attitudes and students, achievements but for LoEx teachers, the correlation was weak. It may be that LoEx teachers have less understanding of their students than HiEx teachers. LoEx teachers' expectations were well below student achievement. As Rubie-Davies has commented, it is unlikely that Lo-Ex teachers were expecting student performance to decline because they had spent a year in their class, therefore it seems likely that teachers would perceive a relationship between students' effort and achievement.

In conclusion, Rubie-Davies has argued that expectations for whole classes may be a more powerful mediator of self-fulfilling prophecy than expectations for individuals within a class. Some teachers may have an important positive effect on student learning while other teachers may have less of an effect or even a negative effect.

Evaluation

Generalisability

This is a **useful** study in that it proposes important lessons for schools in terms of the need for teachers to be positive about their students and their future attainment. It was a thorough study that was high in **ecological validity** and proposes a useful methodology for replication. However, it is based only on a small number of teachers and therefore cannot be **generalised**.

16

16.1 Enabling learning, dealing with diversity: Dealing with additional needs

Key Study: 16.1.3 Provision of remedial support

Sue Burroughs-Lange (2008), 'Comparison of literacy progress of young children in London schools: a Reading Recovery follow up study', published on-line (London, ULIE)

Approach: Cognitive

Aim: To assess effects of the Reading Recovery programme on literacy progress in low-achieving children

Method: Longitudinal study

Type of sample: Opportunity sample

Participants: Children with low reading attainment in one school where a multisensory Reading Recovery intervention was introduced. The lowest attaining children identified for the most scrutiny were performing well below expectations for their age (6 years) at the outset of the study in September 2005. At the start of the study the children had literacy levels below those of a 5-year-old.

Procedure: This study followed up the impact on children's literacy in London schools a year or more after intervention had been received. In the 2005–6 school year, literacy progress was compared of the lowest achieving children in 42 schools serving disadvantaged urban areas. The researcher was not involved in the interventions. It was anticipated that children would be selected for various forms of support according to assessed level of need, that some children would receive interventions early and late in the year, and some interventions would still be incomplete at end of Year 1 assessments. Progress of children on Reading Recovery was compared against progress of similar children in other schools who received other forms of intervention during the same period.

Results:

- In the year of the main study (2005–6), those children who received Reading Recovery achieved significant gains in all assessments compared with those who did not.

- At the end of the year, the literacy achievement of children who had received Reading Recovery (RR) was in line with their chronological age. The comparison group was 14 months behind with an average reading age of 5 years, 5 months.

- In July 2007 the literacy achievement was again compared of those same children remaining in the same 42 schools. At the end of Year 2, the children who had received Reading Recovery in Year 1 were achieving within or above their chronological age band on all measures and were still around a year ahead of the comparison children in schools where Reading Recovery was not available.

- The Reading Recovery children had an average word reading age of 7 years 9 months, compared to 6 years 9 months for the comparison children.

- Writing achievement showed a significant difference between Reading Recovery and comparison children. At the end of Year 2, the children who had received Reading Recovery were able to write twice as many correctly spelled words as those children who were in the comparison group.

- Over 86 per cent of those who received Reading Recovery in Year 1 went on to achieve an age-appropriate level 2+ in National Curriculum Reading assessments at end of Year 2.

- Comparison figures for the lowest achieving children in non-Reading Recovery schools were 57 per cent achieving National Curriculum Level 2+

- In writing, over 83 per cent of those who received Reading Recovery in Year 1 went on to achieve the age-related National Curriculum Level 2+, compared to 58 per cent in the comparison groups.

- At the end of Year 1, in word reading and phonic skills, children in classrooms in schools without access to Reading Recovery were 4 months behind those children in Year 1 classrooms in schools where Reading Recovery was available.

- At the end of Year 2, at average age of seven and a half, the classes of children without Reading Recovery had mean word reading and phonics skills of 7 years, while those in schools with access to Reading Recovery had mean skills for the lowest-achieving children identified in Year 1 of over 7 years, 3 months.

- More than 80 per cent of children who had Reading Recovery in Year 1 were considered by their teachers to have made average to exceptional progress in oral communication over the year.

- Almost half the children who began Year 1 as the lowest achieving in their classroom were considered by their teachers to have made average growth in self confidence, whereas a third of the children who received Reading Recovery were also thought to have made above average and exceptional growth.

- Ability to follow directions, a significant aspect of becoming an effective learner in the classroom, was reported by Year 1 classroom teachers to have grown at average to exceptional rates for more than 80 per cent of children who received Reading Recovery in the year.

Discussion: The author concluded that the Reading Recovery programme, while expensive, was a very effective intervention.

Evaluation

Method

This study was not a **controlled** intervention. The authors did not report details of the comparison interventions. Without more precise data, it is impossible to know whether it was the particulars of the Reading Recovery intervention or simply the amount of focused attention in small groups that led to the impressive gains. However, for whichever reason, the data indicate that the intervention resulted in the children who received Reading Recovery making impressive and sustained gains.

Key Study: 16.3.1 Gender differences in educational achievement

J. Mellanby, M. Martin and J. O'Doherty (2000), 'The "gender gap" in final examination results at Oxford University', *British Journal of Psychology*, 91 (3), 377–94

Approach: Individual differences

Aim: To investigate whether individual differences predict performance in final examination results at Oxford University

Method: Self-report

Type of sample: Self-selecting sample

Participants: 232 final year undergraduates (117 female, 115 male) at the University of Oxford studying a wide range of subjects, including arts and sciences

Procedure: The researchers constructed a measure containing items combined from previously validated scales and an initial pilot study was conducted on 65 students to test out validity and reliability of the measure. The items related to the following constructs:

- Verbal/non-verbal ability
- Motivation
- Mood
- Self-esteem/self-efficacy
- Interpersonal relationships
- Working habits

The measure took an hour to complete and was responded to in a classroom setting approximately 2–3 months prior to final examinations. When final results were made public, an average was obtained of the marks awarded across all papers sat by each participant. Responses to the measure for each of the six constructs were analysed for gender differences. Multiple regression analysis was performed in order to assess whether any of the variables predicted final examination marks.

Results:

- The only variable that predicted final examination marks was score on the ability/aptitude test.
- The verbal items were better predictors of final examination marks than non-verbal items.

- Female students scored slightly lower on the non-verbal items of the ability/aptitude (especially true of the science students) but overall there was no significant difference between male and female students on the test.
- The researchers found a number of gender differences in motivation.
- Female students exhibited a stronger work ethic than male students.
- There was no significant difference in motivation.
- There was no relationship between motivation scores and final examination results.
- Male students scored higher than female students on both happiness and loneliness items.
- Female students scored higher than male students on depression and anxiety.
- For males, loneliness was a weak predictor of examination success.
- For females, depression was a predictor of examination success (students who reported higher levels of depression were higher achievers in the final examinations).
- Male students scored higher on self-esteem/self-efficacy than female students but there was no relationship between scores on this construct and results in final examinations.
- There were no differences between males and females on interpersonal items.
- Female students had stronger work ethics than male students but there was no relationship between work ethic and performance in final examinations.

Discussion: The authors concluded that the only individual differences variable that predicted performance in the final examinations was the ability/aptitude test and that none of the individual differences variables explained the superior performance of males in the finals examinations, in which a higher proportion of males than females are awarded first–class marks. The authors concluded that as individual factors did not explain the 'gender gap', situational factors must explain the differential in finals performance/grades. In this case, the situational factor suggested by the authors as likely to explain this was the nature of the assessment method.

Evaluation

Method

This was a well-controlled the results study of which showed that there appear to be no individual differences that explain the 'gender gap'. Trait anxiety was measured rather than state anxiety. It is possible that had state anxiety been measured, this might have predicted final examination results. This could be one of the ways in which the examination process at Oxford might lead to differential performance.

Can you think of alternative explanations for the 'gender gap' that relate to the examination process?